Cosmopolitanism

A MILLENNIAL QUARTET BOOK

ALTERNATIVE MODERNITIES,
edited by Dilip Parameshwar Gaonkar

GLOBALIZATION, *edited by Arjun Appadurai*

MILLENNIAL CAPITALISM AND THE
CULTURE OF NEOLIBERALISM, *edited
by Jean Comaroff & John L. Comaroff*

COSMOPOLITANISM, *edited by
Carol A. Breckenridge, Sheldon Pollock,
Homi K. Bhabha, & Dipesh Chakrabarty*

PUBLIC CULTURE BOOKS

Cosmopolitanism

Edited by Carol A. Breckenridge, Sheldon Pollock,

Homi K. Bhabha, and Dipesh Chakrabarty

DUKE UNIVERSITY PRESS * DURHAM & LONDON 2002

In honor of D. R. Nagaraj

20 February 1954–12 August 1998

Scholar, Visionary, Friend

and Inspiration for this book.

Contents

Sheldon Pollock, Homi K. Bhabha, Carol A. Breckenridge, and Dipesh Chakrabarty   Cosmopolitanisms   1

Sheldon Pollock   Cosmopolitan and Vernacular in History   15

Arjun Appadurai   Spectral Housing and Urban Cleansing: Notes on Millennial Mumbai   54

Dipesh Chakrabarty   Universalism and Belonging in the Logic of Capital   82

Mamadou Diouf   The Senegalese Murid Trade Diaspora and the Making of a Vernacular Cosmopolitanism   111

T. K. Biaya   "Crushing the Pistachio": Eroticism in Senegal and the Art of Ousmane Ndiaye Dago   138

Walter D. Mignolo   The Many Faces of Cosmo-polis: Border Thinking and Critical Cosmopolitanism   157

Wu Hung   Zhang Dali's *Dialogue:* Conversation with a City   189

Ackbar Abbas   Cosmopolitan De-scriptions: Shanghai and Hong Kong   209

Contributors   229

Index   233

Cosmopolitanism

Cosmopolitanisms

Sheldon Pollock, Homi K. Bhabha,

Carol A. Breckenridge, and Dipesh Chakrabarty

There must be some way out of here.

Cosmopolitanism comprises some of today's most challenging problems of academic analysis and political practice, especially when analysis and practice are seen—as they are seen in the essays that make up this collection—as a conjoint activity. For one thing, cosmopolitanism is not some known entity existing in the world, with a clear genealogy from the Stoics to Immanuel Kant, that simply awaits more detailed description at the hands of scholarship. We are not exactly certain what it is, and figuring out why this is so and what cosmopolitanism may be raises difficult conceptual issues. As a practice, too, cosmopolitanism is yet to come, something awaiting realization. Again, this is not because we already understand and can practice it but have not—a mode of action whose rules we are familiar with and need merely to apply. Cosmopolitanism may instead be a project whose conceptual content and pragmatic character are not only as yet unspecified but also must always escape positive and definite specification, precisely because specifying cosmopolitanism positively and definitely is an uncosmopolitan thing to do.

The indeterminacy of how to achieve a cosmopolitan political practice feeds back into the problem of academic analysis. As a historical category, the cosmopolitan should be considered entirely open, and not pregiven or foreclosed by the definition of any particular society or discourse. Its various embodiments, including past embodiments, await discovery and explication. In this way, the components of the linked academic-political activity of cosmopolitanism become mutually reinforcing: new descriptions of cosmopolitanism as a historical phenomenon and theoretical object may suggest new practices, even as better practices may offer a better understanding of the theory and history of cosmopolitanism.

The foregoing assessment is not always acknowledged, let alone explicitly argued, in various recent contributions to the discussion of cosmopolitanism.[1] These texts do serve, however, to suggest that the sense of timeliness or even urgency about the question of cosmopolitanism is widely shared. And it is worth pausing a moment, before exploring further the approaches adopted in the essays that follow, to consider what accounts for this renewed concern. Three closely related forces that are powerfully at work in the contemporary world seem especially pertinent: nationalism, globalization, and multiculturalism.

The twentieth century ended much as it began, convincingly demonstrating that nationalism, whether of an ethnic or religious or other stripe, has lost little of its power for producing evil in the world. In recognizing the harm that nationalism does in promoting territorially based identities, we do not suggest that it has been always and only a negative force. It is famously Janus-faced, and nowhere more so than in the non-West. The emphasis of anticolonial nationalisms on boundaries and territories has something to do with how European colonialism was experienced by the colonized. For many, colonialism was an acute experience of displacement. Some people were literally displaced (indigenous peoples, but also the so-called nomadic in many countries). Others, in particular those excited by and open to the newly introduced European knowledges, underwent a powerful cultural experience of being dislodged from "tradition." Think only of the various culture wars, typical of many non-Western nationalisms, over the merits and demerits of Westernization.

These experiences gave meaning to nationalist emphases on a family of ideas all of which, in the end, connected identities to imaginations of place: home, boundary, territory, and roots. These imaginations were not always tied to fixed geographical places. Pakistan, for instance, while definitely imagined from as early as the 1920s as a homeland for the Muslims of the Indian subcontinent, had only the vaguest geographical referent for a long time in its career as a concept. Yet it was powerful in its capacity to address the experience of cultural and political displacement that colonialism had meant for many Muslims in South Asia. Thus, the nationalist search for home and authenticity may have been modern—

and vulnerable, therefore, to postmodern critiques of all static, reified, and bounded imaginations of place and home—but it was not, for that reason, inauthentic or illegitimate in itself.

Granting a legitimacy to nationalism does not, however, take away from the point that the modernist (and nationalist) insistence on territorialized imaginations of identity has produced horrendous conflicts in recent history. Besides, in a world increasingly deterritorialized by migration, mediatization, and capital flows, modernist nationalisms with their tendency to connect cultures and identities to specific places have become an ever more retrograde ideology, even as they retain ever greater power to produce history.

This is not, to be sure, precisely the same history over and over. The events at the end of the twentieth century that accompanied the breakup of Yugoslavia are not easily brought under the same explanatory umbrella as those at its beginning that accompanied the breakup of the Habsburg Empire. Nationalism is not just Janus-like but is also protean. Degrees of popular support, emotional cathexis, and official manipulation differ from case to case. In addition to this multiform phenomenology of nationalism, there are countless other factors that serve to differentiate the Sarajevo of 1994 from the Sarajevo of 1914. Not the least is that, the second time around, the cosmopolitan character of the city and all that it stood for were finally destroyed.

But we would have to be fussy pedants to allow finer points of historical differences to obscure the overpowering and deeply disquieting recognition of repetition and even intensification. Moreover, the morphing of empire into nation-state and nation-state into national-statelets is no longer just a Balkan game but a universal one. Some of its most deadly serious participants are the new players of the postcolonial world, those, for instance, who seek an independent Kashmir—a failed state in the making if there ever was one—in the perilous space between two brand-new nuclear powers. It is not simply that we are going forward into the past; we are going into a past that is at the same time somehow new, a grotesque caricature of the past where the propositions of Western modernity, now catastrophically universalized, are being re-enacted. We are headed toward a League of Nations with ten thousand fractious and anxious expansion teams.

This is not a good way to organize human life.

There's too much confusion,
I can't get no relief

Emergent discourses of cosmopolitanism are riven with deep historical ironies about what it means to live in our times. What defines our *times*? What times are *ours*? It is too easy to name our moment as post–Cold War or transnational. It is fundamentally facile to claim (as many do) that new media and market technologies have ushered in undreamed of possibilities of access and connectivity on a global scale, rendering the postcolonial paradigms of justice and redistribution obsolete in the face of choice, opportunity, and enterprise. Yet despite our discontents and discomfitures, we are properly resistant to a radical revanchism that seeks a return to the certainties of a world of the either/or: either First or Third World; either communism or capitalism; either planned economies or free markets; either the secular or the sacred; either class politics above all other differences or a betrayal of the spirit of History itself.

Cosmopolitanism, in its wide and wavering nets, catches something of our need to ground our sense of mutuality in conditions of mutability, and to learn to live tenaciously in terrains of historic and cultural transition. The twilight of Transition, rather than the dawn of millennial transformation, marks the questions of our times: Do we live in a post–Cold War world *tout court,* or in the long shadow of that disastrous postwar experience of superpower collusion and competition that deformed the development of the rest of the world? Is South Africa free or is its anxious emancipation still caught in the unresolved pursuit for truth and reconciliation? Is one measure of the (lack of) success of New Labor in Great Britain its inability to deal with the old colonial problem of Northern Ireland? Is the nuclear contest between India and Pakistan part of the newly found confidence of postcolonial nations or the endgame of the trials of Partition?

As we negotiate this transitional territory, we often find ourselves in the interstices of the old and the new, confronting the past as the present. Perhaps the most significant such revisionary experience for cosmopolitical thinking is the neoliberal consensus that has become so apparent in the post–Cold War period. Where once we conceived of the world order in terms of vying and competing political systems and ideological structures, today the neoliberal emphasis falls more on individualist aspirations and universalist norms. But this revenant late liberalism reveals, in a more exaggerated form, a struggle at the heart of liberal theory, where a genuine desire for equality as a universal norm is tethered to a tenacious ethnocentric provincialism in matters of cultural judgment and recognition. The discriminatory perspectives of an older form of globalization—colonization—seem to have revived themselves at the point at which we readily consider ourselves to be worldwide citizens forever "hooked up" (connected) on-line. All the derring-do between the local and the global in the dialectic of worldly thinking should not conceal the fact that neoliberal cosmopolitan thought is founded on a conformist sense of what it means to be a "person" as an abstract unit of cultural exchange.

Where once political discussion focused on the systemic nature of public cultures and the distribution of political goods, today there is a revival of the humanist discourse of rights founded on the unique and inviolable presence of "human" personhood. A rights culture is in many respects essential; it is historically appropriate in the light of decades of abuse of human and civil rights obscured by the totalitarian drawing of the iron curtain, or the neo-imperialist flourishing of the stars and stripes. None of this should hide the fact that the fetishization of liberal individualism has, in the past few years, created a cosmopolitan imaginary signified by the icons of singular personhood. What represents the spirit of world citizenship today? In recent years the answer to this question has not elicited ideas and ideals, but philanthropic individuals— Mother Theresa (for her love of the world's poor), George Soros (for his economic investment in Central Europe), Ted Turner (for his billion dollar contribution to the United Nations), the late Princess Diana (for her identification with the global issues of AIDS and land mines), and perhaps Bill Gates (for his lordly hold on the universe).

A cosmopolitanism grounded in the tenebrous moment of transition is distinct from other more triumphalist notions of cosmopolitical coexistence. Modernity has never fallen short of making universalist claims to world citizenship, based on the spectacular success of the Enlightenment as a pedagogical and political project. Capitalism envisages itself as a worldwide network of markets and profits; communism appeals to workers of the world to unite; late liberalism argues passionately against instrumentalism or determinism, and for the recognition of the human as the bearer of universal rights. But each of these worldly visions is framed by the ideal of national sovereignty; and nationhood is the social form that renders modernity self-conscious—conscious of being contemporary—so that the cosmopolitan spirit may inhabit a world that is ethically synchronous and politically symmetrical. But, sadly, we know better than to claim (in the spirit of Gertrude Stein) that a nation is a nation is a nation. Nationhood—or nation-*ness*—may be the common currency of world culture and international politics, but its varied geopolitical histories have demonstrated, more often than not, the terrible asymmetries of the idea of modernity itself.

The cosmopolitanism of our times does not spring from the capitalized "virtues" of Rationality, Universality, and Progress; nor is it embodied in the myth of the nation writ large in the figure of the citizen of the world. Cosmopolitans today are often the victims of modernity, failed by capitalism's upward mobility, and bereft of those comforts and customs of national belonging. Refugees, peoples of the diaspora, and migrants and exiles represent the spirit of the cosmopolitical community. Too often, in the West, these peoples are grouped together in a vocabulary of victimage and come to be recognized as constituting the "problem" of multiculturalism to which late liberalism extends its generous promise of a pluralist existence. Cultural pluralism recognizes difference so long as the general category of the people is still fundamentally understood within a national frame. Such benevolence is often well intentioned, but it fails to acknowledge the critique of modernity that minoritarian cosmopolitans embody in their historic witness to the twentieth century.

What we are calling a minoritarian modernity (as a source for contemporary cosmopolitical thinking) is visible in the new forms of transdisciplinary knowledges that we initiate in the "multicultural" academy. Where once we attempted to teach difference by emphasizing areal locality and specificity, today we try to struggle free from the self-fulfilling dialectic of the general and the particular. Instead we attempt to provincialize Europe and we seek cosmopolitical genealogies from the non-Christian Sanskrit world. In each of these cases we are involved, at the same time, in a vernacularization of a great tradition and the amplification of a *petit récit*. Transdisciplinary knowledge, in the cosmopolitan cause, is more readily a translational process of culture's in-betweenness than a transcendent knowledge of what lies beyond difference, in some common pursuit of the universality of the human experience.

None of them along the line
know what any of it is worth

We have suggested that the nature of late-twentieth-century nationalism, multiculturalism, and the globalization of late liberalism has created a historical context for reconsidering concepts of cosmopolitanism. These categories are by now commonplaces for debate. Many of the key terms central to these debates—"universal," "theoretical," "abstract," "conceptual"—have been characterized as implicitly masculine because of their properties of mastery, distance from experience, indifference to specifics, and concern for absolutes in human life. These are the terms of a disembodied, free-floating, or generalizing scientific or humanistic thought. To focus, therefore, on these three historical practices is to ignore another pressure and inspiration to think about the cosmopolitan, namely, feminism. Feminism has learned to wrestle with problems and attendant possibilities while struggling to keep the situated rather than the universal subject in the foreground.

Thus, for cosmopolitanism, feminism may serve a role similar to but different from the other contested "isms" of the late twentieth century—nationalism, multiculturalism, and globalism—whose critiques are grounded in other economies and ideologies of difference and similarity. U.S. mainstream feminisms have noted that the "our" of our times is a noninclusive our that consists of able-bodied, white, heterosexual men. Asian American and African American feminists have pointed out the racialized nature of U.S. mainstream feminism itself, and together they have made an argument for the constitutive nature of gender and race in relation to each other. South Asian feminism has had to probe its class and cultural moorings in the world of the Hindu upper class with its attendant erasure of the lower class woman as well as the woman marked as Muslim, Christian, or tribal. Thus, all feminisms have had to struggle with their own universalisms.

No true universalism can be constructed without recognizing that there is a diversity of universals on which analyses are based, and that these are often in fact quite particular—not universals at all, but rather interpretations devised for particular historical and conceptual situations. These are less universals, and more in the nature of arguments for the universal. Twentieth-century feminism developed concurrently in many parts of the world with an apparent promise of universality. It held out the hope that feminism would be good for all womankind and would dispel all national, racial, and cultural barriers.[2] Feminism was to be a global touchstone for all humankind. But feminism has had to critically engage historical change, as well as the tendency towards exclusion in centers of dominance, based on gender, race, class, and regional biases. Thus, recognition of the plurality of feminisms (and their own need for internal debate and differentiation) has now become a commonplace alternative to the idea that there exists a singular, universal feminism.

Just as feminist thought continues to struggle with the objections to universal discourse, so also cosmopolitanism must give way to the plurality of modes and histories—not necessarily shared in degree or in concept regionally, nationally, or internationally—that comprise cosmopolitan practice and history. We propose therefore that cosmopolitanism be considered in the plural, as cosmopolitanisms. In so doing, we leave open the question of the center and periphery in intellectual debates, and we hope to avoid the imposition of practices and histories that do not necessarily fit interpretations devised for historical situations elsewhere.

Feminisms in relation to cosmopolitanisms: this opens up two problematic issues. First, how can we think feminism to develop a cosmopolitanism that is not based on the concept of a "citizen of the world"? Who is the subject of citizenship? Is citizenship a necessary common frame to be shared universally? Is the cosmopolitan necessarily about the production of the sort of individual interest, will, and belief that most ideologies of citizenship appear to require? What would be the basis for a feminist cosmopolitanism that understands solidarities as something other than the coincidence and coordination of individual wills? The second is an issue of scale: if cosmopolitanism seeks to take the large view, how can we think the intimate under its sign without restricting intimacy to the domestic sphere? Any *cosmofeminism* would have to create a critically engaged space that is not just a screen for globalization or an antidote to nationalism but is rather a focus on projects of the intimate sphere conceived as a part of the cosmopolitan. Such a critical perspective would also open up a new understanding of the domestic, which would no longer be confined spatially or socially to the private sphere. This perspective would allow us to recognize that domesticity itself is a vital interlocutor and not just an interloper in law, politics, and public ethics. From this reconfigured understanding of the public life of domesticity and intimacy it follows that spheres of intimacy generate legitimate pressure on any understanding of cosmopolitan solidarities and networks. The cosmofeminine could thus be seen as subverting those larger networks that refuse to recognize their own nature as specific systems of relations among others. That is, we would no longer have feminism as the voice of specificity interrogating the claims of other putative universals. Instead we would have the cosmofeminine as the sign of an argument for a situated universalism that invites other universalisms into a broader debate based on a recognition of their own situatedeness. A focus on this extensional understanding of domesticity and intimacy could generate a different picture of more public universalisms, making the domestic sphere subversive of thin claims to universalism.

There are many here among us
who feel that life is but a joke.
But you and I, we've been through that

It is in the context of these powerful trends, which show every sign of intensifying, that the essays on cosmopolitanisms that follow have tried to situate themselves. They are all responding to the phenomena of nationalism, globalization (including its most violent embodiment, European colonialism), and multiculturalism. The exercise of bringing feminisms to bear on cosmopolitanism, however, remains. Cosmofeminism is a space yet to be well inhabited. Although the perspectives and analyses of the essays here are heterogeneous, this heterogeneity is not something we mean to express in a concessive clause, as if we found it a cause of concern about incoherence or of regret at failing to reach consensus. On the contrary, we intentionally sought ways to ensure precisely the kind of mix we offer here. We were interested to see what new archives might be brought to bear on the analysis of cosmopolitanism; to discover whether the historical and, what is equally important, the geocultural perspective on the problem could be extended beyond the singular, privileged location of European thought and history; and to determine whether disciplinary approaches could be varied so as to move the discussion beyond the stultifying preoccupations of Western philosophy and to allow the possibility of capturing the wider range of cosmopolitan practices that have actually existed in history. For it is only through such procedures—adducing new empirical data on the variety of cosmopolitanisms and the new problematics that accompany them, decentering the conventional locus, and investigating from a wide range of scholarly perspectives—that new and post-universalist cosmopolitanisms, of the sort variously proposed in these essays, have the potential to come into being.

Most discussions of cosmopolitanism as a historical concept and activity largely predetermine the outcome by their very choice of materials. If it is already clear that cosmopolitanism begins with the Stoics, who invented the term, or with Kant, who reinvented it, then philosophical reflection on these moments is going to enable us always to find what we are looking for. Yet what if we were to try to be archivally cosmopolitan and to say, "Let's simply look at the world across time and space and see how people have thought and acted beyond the local." We would then encounter an extravagant array of possibilities.

We would find a new significance in the Asia-wide circulation of Sanskrit poetry in the first millennium whereby participation in a translocal culture, uneven and restricted by life chances though it was, neither required enforcement at the point of a sword nor entailed the obliteration of everything already in place. We would recapture a moment before Kant of a cosmopolitan humanism in the University of Salamanca and Francisco de Vitoria, thinkers for whom European expansion meant not traveling to distant places, meeting interesting peoples, and killing them, but rather confronting head-on the challenge of enlarging the definition of humanity as they understood it. We would see, furthermore, that the category of capital itself—that most aggressively universalizing of categories—has no simple, unidirectional relationship to historical difference, even in the thought of its apparently most aggressively universalizing of theorists, Karl Marx. Altogether beyond the purview of a self-limiting Western philosophical reflection—where cosmopolitanism becomes just another chapter in a history of dead ideas—is the archive of architecture and housing in Asia. Studying the multitudes and fates of pavement dwellers in Bombay/Mumbai, a city crowded with empty buildings, would enable us to grasp a new kind of endangered cosmopolitanism already coded in the recent rectification of names signaled by that brutal forward slash; just as an analysis of the twinned or inverted histories of Shanghai and Hong Kong might complexify our categories by offering two very different yet equally cosmopolitan formations. If postcolonial Africa is off the cosmopolitan map for Kant or the Stoics, consider what could be learned (both in terms of the possibilities and tensions of cosmopolitanism) from the biography of a rural Senegalese Muslim brotherhood and its transformation into one of the most remarkable global trading networks of the contemporary world; or from the recent history of the photographed and aestheticized body in Senegal, and its negotiation with trans-African, Islamicate, and cosmopolitan norms of eros—especially eros that sells.

Two things should already be clear from the kinds of materials that make their appearance in this collection of essays and the problematics they generate. The first is how radically we can rewrite the history of cosmopolitanism and how dramatically we can redraw its map once we are prepared to think outside the box of European intellectual history. And the second is how manifold is the range of practices that might allow for new and alternative theorization. Consider again, as an instance of export cosmopolitanism, the circulatory networks of Sanskrit literature in precolonial Asia and the vast space they covered, from Central Asia to the South China Sea. Or, as cases of import cosmopolitanism, the architectural styles of pre-war Shanghai, where people tried to rebuild the whole world on their city streets (with Tudor-style villas, Spanish-style town houses, Russian-style churches, German-style mansions, Shanghai-esque lane houses, and Li long housing complexes); or the transformation of the nude in contemporary photography in Senegal into an image at once profoundly domesticated and irreducibly exoticized. All these instances are ways of living at home abroad or abroad at home—ways of inhabiting multiple places at once, of being different beings simultaneously, of seeing the larger picture stereoscopically with the smaller.

A certain kind of logic teaches us a law of the excluded middle: an object may be here or there, but not in both places at once; something may be x or not-x, but not somewhere in between; a predication can be only true or false. Whether this logic holds in all possible worlds or not is for others to say. But the application of its dualism in the realm of cultural and political action is decidedly modern. Indeed, it constitutes a core project of modernity. And here we encounter a striking paradox in the epistemological-historical trajectory of cosmopolitan practices. The more recent these practices are, the more intensely and reflexively mediated and networked they are. Yet, at the same time, the more occluded becomes the very fact of their being mediated and networked. Or rather, the mediation is not so much concealed as rendered illegitimate: cosmopolitan practices come to be seen as mixtures of things believed to have been previously unmixed and on that account, in the eyes of many (such as nationalists), all the more authentic. In fact, modernity itself is just this contradictory, even duplicitous, attempt to separate and purify realms—the natural, social, and empyrean realms, with their things and people and gods—that have never been separate and pure, and still are not. This holds true above all for supposedly individuated and unique cultures, each of which is better seen—more historically seen—as a "quasi object" located at the intersection of a range of other cultural quasi objects.[3] What the new archives, geographies, and practices of different historical cosmopolitanisms might reveal is precisely a cultural illogic for modernity that makes perfectly good nonmodern sense. They might help us see that cosmopolitanism is not a circle created by culture diffused from a center, but instead, that centers are everywhere and circumferences nowhere.

This ultimately suggests that we already are and have always been cosmopolitan, though we may not always have known it. Cosmopolitanism is not just—or perhaps not at all—an idea. Cosmopolitanism is infinite ways of being. To understand that we are already cosmopolitan, however much and often this mode of being has been threatened by the work of purification, means to understand these ways in their full breadth through a disciplinary cosmopolitanism. That is why this particular volume ranges across language and literary history, critical intellectual history, political philosophy, ethnography, urban studies, architectural history, and art history. And, had there been time and space, it could have gone on without disciplinary limit in exploring cosmopolitan practices, which are themselves without limit.

Besides attempting to expand the repertory of archives, geographies, histories, and disciplines that have bearing on the discussion of cosmopolitanisms, the essays here, each in their own way, seek to address the politics of cosmopolitanism. It is in the political sphere that our fail-

ure to realize what we have always been has had the most awful consequences, the sorts that have awakened the sense of urgency behind this
collection. All the authors are sensitive to the peculiar demands of this
object of analysis: the politics of the question of cosmopolitanism are
as irreducible as they are untotalizable. Here again, accordingly, given
that the absolute universalisms of Western cosmopolitanism must forever subvert it from within and from the start, real strength may lie
in division—at least, in a division that holds division as a value—and
true unanimity in a consensual dissensus. In one essay, accordingly, it is
shown how, from within Marx's own analysis of the categories of capital
and abstract labor that would appear to homogenize all historical difference, we may find across-the-grain thinking, ideas that suggest resistance to the sublation of difference into the logic of capital even as capital expands. In another essay, a new cosmopolitan politics is expressed
in the idiom of "arbitrage," that is, doing better in the domain of social
power, identities, and communities what multinational corporations already do well in the domain of business. In another, the formulation
offered is "critical and dialogical cosmopolitanism," wherein diversity
itself might become a universal project. In yet a fourth, a politics "both-
cosmopolitan-and-vernacular"—in short, a refusal to choose—is theorized as a possible option out of the lived experience of real people.

These may sound like ever more private academic fantasies, and perhaps they are. But the authors share deeply a sense that such questions
are important to the fate of human collectivities—a sense that comes
out of their actual engagements, whether with Bombay pavement dwellers, Murid traders, or colonial discourse and other coercive cosmopolitanisms of the past. And they know, if they know nothing else, that we
should not talk falsely now, the hour is getting late.

NOTES

All epigraphs are taken from Bob Dylan's *All Along the Watchtower*.

1. See, for instance, Martha Nussbaum with respondents, *For Love of Country: Debating the Limits of Patriotism*, ed. Joshua Cohen (Boston: Beacon Press, 1996); Vinay
Dharwadker, ed., *Cosmopolitan Geographies: New Locations in Literature and Culture* (London: Routledge, 2000); Kimberly Hutchings and Roland Dannreuther, eds.,
Cosmopolitan Citizenship (New York: St. Martin's Press, 1999); Roel Meijer, ed., *Cosmopolitanism, Identity, and Authenticity in the Middle East* (Richmond, England: Cur-
zon, 1999); and Pheng Cheah and Bruce Robbins, eds., *Cosmopolitics: Thinking and
Feeling Beyond the Nation* (Minneapolis: University of Minnesota Press, 1998). Ap-

parently unknown to the authors in *Cosmopolitics* is the remarkable series of studies by the historian of science Isabelle Stengers, which argues for a form of politics no longer contained within the separation of nature and society that characterizes Enlightenment and modernity. Stengers, *Cosmopolitiques,* 7 vols. (Paris: La Découverte, 1997).

2. Asuncion Lavrin, "International Feminisms: Latin American Alternatives," in *Feminisms and Internationalism,* ed. Mrinalini Sinha, Donna Guy, and Angela Woollacott (Oxford: Blackwell, 1999), 175.

3. See Bruno Latour, *We Have Never Been Modern,* trans. Catherine Porter (Cambridge: Harvard University Press, 1993).

Cosmopolitan and Vernacular in History

Sheldon Pollock

Few things seem to us as natural as the multiplicity of vernacular languages that different peoples use for making sense of life through texts, that is, for making literature. And few things seem as unnatural as their abandonment and gradual disappearance in the present. In fact, literary language loss is often viewed as part of a more general reduction of cultural diversity, one considered as dangerous as the reduction of biological diversity to which it is often compared. The homogenization of culture today, of which language loss is one aspect, seems without precedent in human history, at least for the scope, speed, and manner in which changes are taking place.

This commonsense view of the world needs two important qualifications. First, the vernacular ways of being that we see vanishing everywhere were themselves created over time. These are not primeval ways of autochthons, for autochthons (like the Spartoi of Thebes, "the sown people" born from the dragon teeth planted by Cadmus) do not exist outside their own mythical self-representation. Second, by the very fact of their creation, the new vernaculars replaced a range of much older cultural practices. These earlier practices, which seemed to belong to everywhere in general and nowhere in particular, affiliated their users to a larger world rather than a smaller place. They were, in a sense to be argued out in this essay, cosmopolitan practices. These great transformations in the course of the last two millennia — from the old cosmopolitan to the vernacular, and from the vernacular to the new and disquieting cosmopolitan of today — resulted from choices made by people at different times and places, for very complex reasons. Studying the history of such choices may have something important, perhaps even urgent, to tell us about choices available to us in the future.

In earlier work I have studied the period following the old cosmopolitan epoch, which I called the *vernacular millennium*.[1] This began in southern Asia and western Europe with remarkable simultaneity in the early second millennium, and it developed with equally striking parallels over the following five centuries. I say "began" emphatically: vernacular literary cultures were initiated by the conscious decisions of writers to reshape the boundaries of their cultural universe by renouncing the larger world for the smaller place, and they did so in full awareness of the significance of their decision. New, local ways of making culture — with their wholly historical and factitious local identities — and, concomitantly, new ways of ordering society and polity came into being, replacing the older translocalism. These developments in culture and power are historically linked, at the very least by the fact that using a new language for communicating literarily to a community of readers and listeners can consolidate if not create that very community, as both a sociotextual and a political formation.

While the literary-cultural processes of this reshaping are remarkably similar in southern Asia and western Europe, the political logics they followed appear to have differed fundamentally. In Europe, vernacularization accompanied and enabled the production of the nation-state; in India, it accompanied and enabled the production of a political form we may neutrally call the vernacular polity, in order to signal its difference. In both worlds, however, vernacularization helped initiate an early modern era, each again marked by its specific type of modernity. And it is only now for the first time, when this epoch seems to be drawing to a close as vernacular modes of cultural and political being are everywhere coming under powerful pressures from an altogether new universalizing order of culture-power (call it globalization, or liberalization, or Americanization), that we may begin to conceive of this past history as a whole and make some sense of it for cultural and political theory.

I would like here to elaborate on these earlier arguments by situating the vernacular millennium within a comparative-historical account of the cosmopolitanisms that preceded it. These, too, comprised forms of identity that reveal themselves as produced and entirely provisional; they are located securely in time and in the choices made by the producers of culture to participate in new frames of reference, routes of circulation, and kinds of community. And each had its own specific political logic. My concerns will be, first, with tracing the parallels between these cosmopolitan formations, as well as the dramatic differences that become perceptible when we place them side by side; and, second, with considering the ways they may have contributed to shaping the vernacular varieties that replaced them (whose histories, for their part, I can only briefly summarize here). Very different cosmopolitan and vernacular practices have existed in the past, and these may have important implications for future practices in the face of what often seems to be the single, desperate choice we are offered: between, on the one hand, a national vernacularity dressed in the frayed period costume of violent revanchism and bent on preserving difference at all costs and, on the other, a clear-cutting, strip-mining multinational cosmopolitanism that is bent, at all costs, on eliminating it.

Let me take a moment to explain how and why I proceed as I do in my historical analysis of cosmopolitan and vernacular ways of being and the kinds of cultural and political belonging to which they have related, as well as my purpose in trying to make sense of this history. First, my intention here is to think about cosmopolitanism and vernacularism as action rather than idea, as something people do rather than something they declare, as practice rather than proposition (least of all, philosophical proposition). This enables us to see that some people in the past have been able to be cosmopolitan or vernacular without directly professing either, perhaps even while finding it impossible rationally to justify either. By contrast, the attempt to vindicate cosmopolitanism or vernacularism — the production of the very discourse on the universal or the particular — seems to entail an objectification and abstraction, and their associated political practices, that have made the cosmopolitan so often take on the character of domination and the vernacular, that of inevitability.

Second, the specific practices I have in mind are those of literary culture, by which I mean most simply how people do things with texts: writing, reciting, reading, copying, printing, and circulating texts. These may be expressive, discursive, or political texts, but I am interested at present, above all, in the first kind. For purposes of our discussion here, *cosmopolitan* and *vernacular* can be taken as modes of literary (and intellectual, and political) communication directed toward two different audiences, whom lay actors know full well to be different. The one is unbounded and potentially infinite in extension; the other is practically finite and bounded by other finite audiences, with whom, through the very dynamic of vernacularization, relations of ever-increasing in-communication come into being.[2] We can think of this most readily as a distinction in communicative capacity and concerns between a language that travels far and one that travels little.

Doing things with texts, the practices of literary culture, may seem a long way from the desperate choice mentioned above. And yet the communication of literary culture importantly shapes the social and political sensibilities that make such choices possible. Literature, in particular, constitutes an especially sensitive gauge of sentiments of belonging: creating or consuming literature meant for large worlds or small places is a declaration of affiliation with that world or place. The production and circulation of literature, accordingly, are utterly unlike the production and circulation of things. The universalization of particular technologies or the particularization of universal ones that characterize a dominant form of contemporary globalization carries no hint of belonging; the practices of literary culture, by contrast, are practices of attachment.[3]

As for the "literary" in particular, let me stress that this was no open category in the worlds and places under consideration here, but something reducible and reduced to a theoretical and practical system of differences from all other kinds of texts, a system of conventionality and intentionality. Although people who think about such things now can perceive the literary in all sorts of texts and all sorts of texts in the literary, in these earlier systems not everything could be literature and literature could not be everything. At the beginning of the first millennium, Sanskrit and Latin writers had yet to read Derrida, and so they failed to grasp that there is no way to identify the literary object, that literature has no essence, that the documentary is irreducibly rhetorical. Quite the contrary, Sanskrit literary theorists were true essentialists in their search for what they called the "self" of poetry. If they failed to agree on what it was, they had no doubt it existed. Accordingly, the instability of textual types that to our eyes may be phenomenologically obvious was to theirs ethno-epistemologically impossible — and therefore historically irrelevant to us except as a second-order problem.[4]

Third, I consider the cosmopolitan and the vernacular comparatively and historically, and I axiomatically reject the narrow European analytical and temporal frameworks that are usually thought to contain them. The absence nowadays of any interest in the macrohistorical reconstruction and analysis of these matters is little short of astonishing. No doubt it is another consequence of what Norbert Elias once identified as the social science "retreat into the present"—this despite the fact that social science is premised on a narrative of the pre-present, especially the pre-modern, that is still only partially written.[5]

The practices of literary communication that actualize modes of cosmopolitan and vernacular belonging to be examined here are those of southern Asia and western Europe. And since the analytical framework is comparative and the temporal framework is vast, we need to think in terms of elementary practices and to be drastically schematic and shamelessly reductive. There exists a remarkable parallel in the historical development of literary communication in these two worlds, where a long period of cosmopolitan literary production was followed by a vernacularity whose subsequent millennium-long ascendancy now everywhere shows signs of collapse. This historical symmetry, along with a very wide range of formal congruences, distinguishes the southern Asian and western European cases sharply from others. Contrast, for example, the wide sphere of Chinese literary communication, where the vernacular transformation in places like Vietnam or Korea occurred so late as to appear to be the project of a derivative modernization.[6] That said, profound differences are to be found in the ideological forms and in the modalities of social and political action to which these communicative practices relate and which they underwrote. One world presents —and here are two sweeping generalizations for which some substantiation will be provided in what follows—what we may identify as a coercive cosmopolitanism and a vernacularism of necessity, where participation in larger or smaller worlds is compelled by the state or demanded by the blood; the other world presents a voluntaristic cosmopolitanism and a vernacularism of accommodation, where very different principles are at work inviting affiliation to these cultural-political orders.

Just as remarkable as the underdevelopment of macrohistorical comparativism is the fact that analyses of cosmopolitanism are themselves rarely cosmopolitan. The widespread ahistoricism no doubt contributes to this, as does the tendency to concentrate on pronouncements rather than practices. Discussion typically takes place on a highly localized conceptual terrain and in a very vernacular idiom constituted by European culture. But cosmopolitan is not necessarily to be equated with a cultural-political form of universal reason, let alone with a universal church or empire, any more than vernacular is to be taken to be synonymous with national. On the contrary, as I have already suggested, it has historically been possible to be the one or the other without asserting the compulsion of the national-cultural through talk of mother-tongue and mother's milk — of language and blood — or offering spurious universalizations of this or that particular rationality or deity or power.

As important as it is not to reify the cosmopolitan or the vernacular by foregrounding doctrines while ignoring actions, we must guard against filling either category in advance with any particular social or political content. My whole point here is to suggest how variable this content has been and may still be. Yet it is no easy thing to think outside the Euro-forms, for they inevitably prestructure for us the content of both the cosmopolitan and the vernacular. The very terminology we use imprisons us, assuming for the moment that we believe etymology is truth and predetermines the thought even of the etymologically ignorant. The term *cosmopolitan* presupposes a great deal, while at the same time it ironically undercuts its own logic: it assumes the universal intelligibility and applicability of a very particular and privileged mode of political identity, citizenship in the *polis* or Greek city-state. The term *vernacular,* for its part, refers to a very particular and unprivileged mode of social identity — the language of the *verna* or house-born slave of Republican Rome — and is thus hobbled by its own particularity, since there is no reason to believe that every vernacular is the idiom of the humiliated demanding vindication.

All this is reasonably well known, but the constraints remain considerable, and some scholars have tried to find ways out. The alternatives are scarcely less problematic, however. Take the binary "philologies of community" and "philologies of contact."[7] The troublesome assumptions here are not hard to identify. For one thing, community is posited as existing primevally and prior to all interaction; for another, universalizing forms of culture are implicitly supposed to affect community from the outside (through "contact"). Communities, however, are never uncreated but rather create themselves through a process of interaction — emulation, differentiation, and so on — with non-community, or, rather, with what by that very process becomes non-community. Any claim to indigenousness thus becomes simply evidence of historical ignorance of the source — or suppression of the source — from which the indigenous has been borrowed. Global cultural forms, for their part, are generated from within communities themselves, and thus only in a restricted sense stand outside some of them. Instead of cosmopolitan and vernacular, therefore, or any one of their conceptual derivatives, I would actually prefer to use terms of Indian cultures (Kannada, for example, or Telugu) that make far fewer assumptions — terms, for example, that refer simply to cultural practices of the great "Way" and those of "Place" (*marga* and *deshi,* respectively). But, in fact, as we will see, those cultures' own understanding of these terms significantly restricts their domain of reference.

Last, one needs to ask clearly and unambiguously why we should even bother to think historically about these matters. For this hardly seems meaningful any longer in a world where last week's news seems to be history enough, and where historical thinking has anyway lost its innocence to ideology critique, discourse analysis, or — perhaps the worst predator of all — boredom. The problem of why we want historical knowledge has a degree of urgency directly proportionate to our awareness of the fact that the past is always written from location in the present. In this case, however, it seems especially pressing since we are dealing with a question that, after all, we raise because it is a matter not of the past or even of the present but of the future — a matter of choices yet to be made about self and other, freedom and necessity, even war and peace. Given all this, it strikes me as unhelpful to say (as a leading intellectual historian of early modern Europe puts it in a recent analysis of the history of liberty) that our historiographical purpose should be simply to "uncover the often neglected riches of our intellectual heritage and display them once more to view," holding ourselves "aloof from enthusiasm and indignation alike."[8] The continual invocation of this sentiment of dispassion since Tacitus first gave expression to it makes it no more true or practicable, or anything more than a preemptive strike against critics. Our enthusiasm and indignation shape our argument willy-nilly. One can hardly doubt, in fact, that the neo-Roman theory of positive freedom that the historian has so valuably reconstructed for us is the theory he prefers. And it may reasonably be asked whether such passions do more to undermine historical argument the more they are suppressed.

We must come clean about our purposes, and the more modest these purposes are, the better. There is nothing very problematic or theoretically interesting about examining the past to see how people have acted and trying to understand the acts with bad consequences and the acts with good. We do this even though we know that the historical knowledge derived from such examination carries no guarantee of any kind that better practices must necessarily follow. A history of the cosmopolitan and vernacular might therefore seek—enthusiastically and indignantly—to compare past choices, when there have been choices, in order to inform future ones. Such choices will always be responses to conditions of politics and culture far more complex than any single account can hope to capture, conditions that sometimes seem to exceed the very possibility of intentional and knowledgeable action. But if intentions and knowledge count, good intentions are better than bad, and knowledge is better than ignorance. Shankara, the eighth-century Indian thinker, put it with unarguable simplicity: "Two persons may perform the same act, both the one who understands and the one who does not. But understanding and ignorance are different, and what one performs with understanding becomes far stronger than what one performs in ignorance."[9]

The pertinence of my long-term and comparative historical analysis of literary practices and the meaningfulness of past cosmopolitan and vernacular choices to future ones will become more intelligible if we reformulate them in a more familiar idiom. This I try to provide in the latter part of this essay by examining how Antonio Gramsci took up these questions in the 1930s. I then briefly consider how several recent attempts to rehabilitate vernacularism from the left may be illuminated by this long-term earlier history. To these, in conclusion, are juxtaposed the views of some postcolonial thinkers who—beneficiaries again of a historical tradition, but one very different from that of Europe—seem to me to suggest possible escape routes from the dilemma confronting us in the disparate cosmopolitan-vernacular conflicts (the case of Serbia being paradigmatic) that closed out the second millennium.

*

If we conceive of the practice of cosmopolitanism as literary communication that travels far, indeed, without obstruction from any boundaries at all, and, more important, that thinks of itself as unbounded, unobstructed, unlocated—writing of the great Way, instead of the small Place—the world of writers and readers that Sanskrit produced, on the one hand, and Latin on the other, are remarkably similar.[10] In addition to their universalist spatiality, the two languages are comparable in their temporal development as written codes for what both conceptualized as this-worldly (*laukika, saeculare*) communication after centuries of the liturgical, magical, and generally supramundane textuality (and largely oral textuality) to which they had restricted themselves.

A little before the beginning of the first millennium, after centuries of such geographical and discursive restriction, the two languages embarked on an extraordinary process of spatial dissemination and expressive elaboration. Within four or five centuries, Sanskrit would be found in use for literary and political discourse in an area that extended from today's Afghanistan to Java and from Sri Lanka to Nepal. There was nothing unusual about finding a Chinese traveler studying Sanskrit grammar in Sumatra in the seventh century, an intellectual from Sri Lanka writing Sanskrit literary theory in the northern Deccan in the tenth, or Khmer princes composing Sanskrit political poetry for the magnificent pillars of Mebon and Pre Rup in Angkor in the twelfth. Near the end of the cosmopolitan epoch, the poet Bilhana—who had himself traveled in search of patronage through the subcontinent from Kashmir to Gujarat to Banaras and south to Karnataka—could announce that "there is no village or country, no capital city or forest region, no pleasure garden or school where learned and ignorant, young and old, male and female alike do not read my poems and shake with pleasure."[11] His boast may have exaggerated the social circulation of his work, but he was describing the universe for which Sanskrit poets and intellectuals had been writing for the preceding thousand years.

Half a world away, Latin had been disseminated across an equally vast space, one that at the height of the empire extended on the west from Britannia, Hispania, and Mauretania (in north Africa) to Mesopotamia and Palestina in the east. And in places as diverse as Gallia, Lusitania, Tripolitana, Egypt, Cappodocia, and Syria, writers were producing literature destined for circulation throughout this space.[12] Horace could claim readers for his odes in Dacia and on the Black Sea, and Martial could brag that his work traveled as far as Britannia and that in towns on the Rhone in Gallia men young and old, and girls as well, were reading his epigrams.[13] Unlike Sanskrit literary competence and communication, which remained continuous throughout the first millennium, this grand model of Latinity would be disrupted (by the movements of peoples, the destruction of educational institutions, and the general erosion of linguistic competence) in the fourth, seventh, and tenth centuries, and attempts to recreate it largely by state intervention (the Carolingian and Ottonian renewals) would be made again and again. Otherwise, both the fact and the perception of universality were in the two cases remarkably analogous. This universality pertained to substance, too, as well as to space. For what people wrote was derived from similar modes of cultural discipline, care for language, and study of literary canons and masterworks of systematic thought. In a very literal sense, both Sanskrit and Latin were written to be readable across space and through time — as indeed they were.

With this pair of features, however — unbounded spatiotemporal circulation and normativity in literary and intellectual practice that sought to ensure that circulation — the parallels between the two types of cosmopolitanism end. In all other respects, they differed as radically as the historical experiences that produced them. We may begin our brief review of these divergences by restating an earlier point about terminology. It is striking to note that there is no specific Sanskrit term aside from the "Way" itself (which has narrow application to the world of literary style) for referring to what, as a result, I have named the *Sanskrit cosmopolis*.[14] Unlike the spatial category *orbis terrarum* and the literary and cultural category *Latinitas*, which both appear at the beginning of Latin's cosmopolitan career (with Cicero) and become increasingly prominent in imperial Rome, there is no self-generated descriptor for either the spatial or the cultural sphere that Sanskrit created and inhabited.[15] *Samskrti*, the classicizing term adopted for translating "culture" in many modern South Asian languages, is itself unattested in Sanskrit in this sense. The fact that Sanskrit never sought to theorize its own universality is consistent with its entire historical character as a cosmopolitan formation, an alternative form of cosmopolitanism in which "here," instead of being equated with "everywhere," is equated with "nowhere in particular."

Latin traveled where it did as the language of a conquest state, first Roman and later (through what Claude Nicolet has called the "nostalgia of ecumenism") in the imperial recreations under Charlemagne and Otto, but also as the language of a missionizing and eventually a conquest church.[16] The state for which Latin spoke was centralized and militarized; it was standardized (in terms of such things as currency and law), and rationalized, with populations enumerated for taxation and territory delimited by frontiers that could be very concrete indeed (Hadrian's wall in northern Britain, now a UNESCO World Heritage tourist site, was designed as a twelve-foot-high, ten-foot-thick, seventy-five-mile-long barrier to "separate the Romans from the barbarians").[17] To impose its will, the Roman state employed coercion, taxation, legal machinery, intimidation, and, on occasion, a policy of Romanization in cultural and political behavior, with selective award of citizenship to incorporate elites from the periphery.

As for the Latin language itself, wherever it traveled it obliterated what it found. Italic literary cultures and, later, those of the western provinces (Gallic, Celtic, Iberian) gave way before the same combination of military victory and administrative cooptation, with profound and lasting transformations of their cultural systems. By the end of the first century B.C., all languages other than Latin had disappeared from the inscriptional record of Italy; Gallic and the languages of Iberia vanished within a couple centuries of conquest; and Celtic scarcely was permitted to enter the record at all, even in areas where we know it long persisted as a medium of oral communication. In North Africa, Punic and Libyan maintained a documentary existence and oral vitality for some centuries, but their long-term trajectory conformed to that of every other language that confronted Latin: toward extinction. The Roman Near East (west of the Euphrates) was, according to Fergus Millar's recent study, the site of even more dramatic linguistic devastation: Graeco-Roman imperial culture allowed little that preexisted to outlast it; in fact, only the Jews and the Palmyrenes retained their pre-Roman script languages.[18]

In other areas of life, such as religious practices, there seems to be evidence of a general indifference to the cultural diversity of conquered peoples, perhaps even an imperial policy of toleration. But in the domains of both the literary and the political, Romanization represented what has been called "a sort of decapitation of the conquered culture."[19] Focusing on such practices of culture and power rather than on professions of moral commitment thus gives us a rather different vision of Roman cosmopolitanism from what we might infer from the writings of, say, the Stoics. These thinkers may have thought themselves to be *kosmou politeis,* citizens of the world (though they never actually said so in Latin), but this seems at least in part owing to the fact that they had been able to transform the *kosmos* into their *polis,* or, rather—as the poet Ovid put it on the eve of Augustus's eastern campaign—to transform the *orbis* into their *urbs,* the world into their own city. Here, incidentally, we find the historical correlate of the theoretical objection made to a recent account of Stoic cosmopolitanism—offered as a model for *fin-de-millénaire* Americans unsympathetic to the so-called national conversation in which they were being invited to participate—namely, that it is basically "an invitation to those who are different . . . to become like us."[20] Whoever could not be incorporated into the single Roman city, such as the Parthians (Rome's eastern enemies), became subject to an imperial political demonology that provoked no counterexpression of cosmopolitan solidarity from the Stoics. In the face of such imperial declarations as the one Augustus made in his last testament ("When foreign peoples could safely be pardoned I have preferred to preserve rather than to exterminate them"—words written to make known to foreign peoples Rome's "powers of collective life and death"), the universalism the Stoics offered was astonishingly timid indeed.[21]

The Sanskrit cosmopolis was also created by action, though not the actions of a conquest state. It was made, instead, by the circulation of traders, literati, religious professionals, and freelance adventurers. Coercion, cooptation, juridical control, and even persuasion are nowhere in evidence. Those who participated in Sanskrit cosmopolitan culture chose to do so, and could choose to do so. This was not, of course, a world of absolute free will. In addition to everyday limits on life chances, traces of archaic ritual restrictions on participation in some dimension of Sanskrit culture (especially its liturgical side) were preserved far into the cosmopolitan period. The ambivalence about demotic participation in the Sanskrit cosmopolitan order is effectively captured in a verse found in a thirteenth-century anthology. It praises the Sanskrit poetry of a simple potter, declaring that "caste is no constraint for those rendered pure by the Goddess of Speech," and in doing so affirms the old restrictions on access to Sanskrit even as it seeks to deny them.[22] Neither was it a cosmopolis entirely without otherness. According to the representation of the physical world that found its stable formulation by the fifth century and was to be transmitted more or less unchanged for a thousand years, the inhabitable sphere was a vast continent "ever beset at its borders by the uncivilized."[23] But here again, boundaries and cultural restrictions had far less salience in action than they may have had in representation. Contrast the very different practices in our two cosmopolitan worlds in the early centuries of the millennium at the point where they nearly met in western Asia. Here Rome sought to contain if not destroy the region's inhabitants — demonized by Horace as the *Parthos feroces,* the ferocious Parthians — while at the same time peoples akin to the Parthians, the Shakas and Kushanas, were migrating into the southern Asian subcontinent. The Shakas helped create the great cosmopolitan cultural order of Sanskrit by producing the first royal public inscriptions that made use of the language (and, according to some scholars, by stimulating the invention of new genres of Sanskrit literature itself); the Kushanas patronized new and highly influential forms of Sanskrit Buddhism and established a remarkable transregional political order that would link South and Central Asia.

The space of Sanskrit culture and the power that culture articulated were never demarcated in any concrete fashion; the populations that inhabited it were never enumerated; nowhere was a standardization of legal practices sought, beyond a vague conception of moral order (*dharma*) to which power was universally expected to profess its commitment. Nor was any attempt ever made to transform the world into a metropolitan center; in fact, no recognizable core-periphery conception ever prevailed in the Sanskrit cosmopolis. Every center was infinitely reproducible across cosmopolitan space, such that the golden Mount Meru and the river Ganga could be and were transported everywhere. As a result, people in tenth-century Angkor or Java could see themselves no less than people in tenth-century Karnataka as living not in some overseas extension of India but inside "an Indian world."[24] The production of this kind of feeling beyond one's immediate environment, this vast cosmopolitanization of southern Asia, has rightly been described as "one of the most impressive instances of large-scale acculturation in the history of the world."[25] It comprised the synthesis and circulation of a wide range of cultural and political practices through borrowing, lending, and perhaps even the convergent production of comparable forms across a vast space. This entire culture-power complex was invented on the fly, so to speak, which makes the very idea of "Indianization" or "Sanskritization" a crude sort of teleology, erroneously presupposing as cause what was only produced as effect. Moreover, the processes of identity formation, cultural choice, and political governance involved in the invention of the Sanskrit cosmopolitan order can be very unfamiliar to us. Power, for example, was interested in culture but not in a way that necessarily reduced culture to an instrument of legitimation, as Weberian sociology might lead us to suppose a priori. Here and elsewhere, we need to theorize Indian cosmopolitanism from its effects.

One such effect in the domain of language was that, far from proscribing local script vernaculars, Sanskrit mediated their creation everywhere it traveled and often at the very moment it arrived. To be sure, these languages would be confined to the realm of the documentary and excluded from that of the expressive for many centuries—half a millennium in the case of Javanese, Kannada, Telugu, or Marathi; a full millennium in the case of Khmer, Hindi, or Newari. This was, I believe, because the literary function was coterminous with the political function, and the sphere of the political—"extending to the horizons"— was, by definition, the exclusive preserve of a Sanskrit that knew no boundaries but the horizons themselves.[26] But for local language to be a language of record—to inscribe a temple endowment, a mortgage, a deed—was for it to be an instrument of central cultural significance; what we now call French and German were not authorized for such a function until the fourteenth or fifteenth century. An additional, small but telling sign of the difference between our two cosmopolitanisms is the graphic sign itself. Roman script was constitutive of Latin literature: *arma virumque cano* could be written in only a single alphabet. The graphic forms of Sanskrit literature, by contrast, were innumerable: *vagarthau iva samprktau* could be inscribed in Javanese script; in Thai, Sinhala, and Grantha in Tamil country; and in Sharada in Kashmir— a substitutability unique among Benedict Anderson's "immense communities" of premodernity.[27]

Contrast, moreover, the two foundational cosmopolitan fictions whose opening words have just been quoted—here I make a concession to thinking about declarations, though these remain declarations about practices. At the opening of the *Aeneid,* Virgil "sings of arms and the man," the flight from Troy to Italy, the origins of the Latin people (*genus Latinum*), the high walls of Rome, and *imperium* without end. In his fourth-century courtly epic, *Raghuvamsha,* Kalidasa bows down to the mother and father of the universe, who are "fused together like sound and sense," in order that he might more deeply understand sound and sense when he tells the story of a universalistic political power, the dynasty of the mythopoetic Raghus (who are only faintly allegorized to the imperial Guptas, unlike Aeneis to Augustus).[28] The two texts are offering us here two profoundly different visions of the "cosmos" that is meaningful for human life: in the one case, the "circle of the lands" (orbis terrarum) that have fallen under Roman power, in the other, "all that moves with life" (*jagat*). They also offer two profoundly different conceptions of how literary culture functions purposefully in the cosmos, whether as a verbal instrument for celebrating power or as a celebration of the power of the verbal instrument itself.

We have thus two cosmopolitanisms, not a European comprehensive universalism (as T. S. Eliot, for instance, in his own provincial way thought of Virgil) and a narrow Asian particularism. They were generated by a very similar set of literary practices that also underwrote, in very different ways, a new vision of power. And if the cosmopolitanisms were similar in transcending the local and stimulating feelings of living in a large world, their modalities were radically different: the one coercive, the other voluntaristic.

*

Thus a certain symmetry allows for reasonable comparison between the Sanskrit cosmopolis and Latinitas in the open-endedness of their spatializations and in the normative practices of literary communication intended to ensure that texts could circulate across a cultural space and time thought of as endless. The vernacular formations that superseded them, for their part, have a range of parallels that are even more astonishing. Like the two models of cosmopolitanism that they replaced, however, they show important and irreducible differences as well. A comparative argument about vernacularization obviously presupposes some shared understanding of the object of analysis. And it is precisely because no such understanding exists that vernacularization, despite its crucial importance, has so long been off the map of historical cultural studies.

As I noted at the start, vernacularization is a new way of doing things with texts, especially written literary texts, in a stay-at-home language. By *written,* I exclude the oral, even if the written may continue to be performed and received orally; by *literary,* I exclude the documentary. Both these latter categories, the literary and the documentary, however porous in contemporary theoretical terms, are fully distinguishable within the subjective universe of the premodern actors involved. By *stay-at-home,* I exclude the well-traveled cosmopolitan idiom, and even though stay-at-home languages may sometimes travel far and eventually become cosmopolitan themselves (as in fact happened with Latin), the moment of vernacularization is characterized by a full if sometimes anxiety-ridden awareness of affiliation to a domain of literary communication that is finite. And last, by *new,* I affirm not only that vernacularization begins but also that lay actors know it begins or, rather, know that they are beginning it. Vernacularization cannot be explained by a natural history of cultural change (the result of an erosion of competence in a cosmopolitan idiom, for example), and it does not stand outside history (despite the common view that every putatively inaugural text always presupposes lost predecessors, ad infinitum). People invent vernacular literary cultures as such, in the same way as they invent the Italian sonnet, the English epistolary novel, the Kannada *champu,* and the Marathi *abhang.*

Thus conceived, the process of vernacularization represents a profound and wholly active historical transformation in literary-cultural practices, as well as in the practices of political power that formed both the narrative substance and real-world context of so much of the literature in question. It will be helpful here to review very briefly the historical trajectory of vernacularization in western and southern Eurasia, from its restricted beginnings in the last centuries of the first millennium to its completion in most places by the sixteenth century, while at the same time noting the character of the political location in which it was fostered and its relationship toward the cosmopolitan aesthetic that it would replace. In all these features — chronology, polity, the localization of the global — the southern Asian and western European cases show quite remarkable parallels. We will then be in a position to consider the factors that make them different and give one the character of a vernacularization of necessity and the other a vernacularization of accommodation.

The vernacularization of the Sanskrit world began in the last century of the first millennium in the central Deccan plateau. Here, in the course of the ninth to eleventh centuries, Kannada and Telugu were transformed into languages for literature and political expression after four or more centuries of subliterary existence, during which Sanskrit functioned as the sole medium for the production of literary and non-documentary political texts. The constellation of political and aesthetic features visible here manifests itself in many other regions over the coming five centuries: to a large degree, literary production consisted of texts derived from cosmopolitan genres and of the appropriation of many of their formal features (in point of lexicon, metric, and the like). But a new aesthetic of Place (deshi) moderated these borrowings by balancing them with local forms, while at the same time new projects of spatiality—a kind of vernacular chronotope, in Mikhail Bakhtin's idiom, that plots out the domain of vernacular culture, that puts culture in its place for the first time—began to find expression in literary texts.[29] The primary stimulus for vernacularization in both cases was provided by the courts of the ruling dynasties in Karnataka (the Rashtrakutas and Western Chalukyas) and Andhra (the Eastern Chalukyas), who had begun likewise to turn increasingly to the vernacular as the language of chancery communication.

Around the same time, or in the next few centuries, across southern Asia vernacular cultures burst on the scene of literary history: Sinhala (ninth century), Javanese (tenth), Marathi (thirteenth), Thai (fourteenth), and Oriya (fifteenth), among many others. Again, this occurred largely at the instigation of courtly elites: in Polonnaruwa in Sri Lanka; in the emergent polities of Kadiri, Singhasari, and Majapahit of eastern Java; among the Devagiri Yadavas of Maharashtra (in this case the work was in fact lost); at the Thai courts of Sukhotai and Ayuthaya; and among the Gangas and Gajapatis of Orissa. And everywhere, again, literary idioms and models from cosmopolitan Sanskrit were assimilated for the creation of literatures in regional languages, while reordered notions of political space and aspirations of governance were coded in the new vernacular texts—texts that for the first time began to speak coherently of such places as "the cultivated-land of Kannada," "the heart of the land of Andhra," and "Beautiful Lady Lanka." Even Tamil, the one South Asian regional language with a history of literary production that long antedated the start of the vernacular millennium, and Hindi, which was almost certainly first fashioned into a vehicle for vernacular literature outside the domain of the court by Sufi poets in the fourteenth and fifteenth centuries, began to develop new modes of expression and courtly characteristics during this period. In the first case, this took place under the imperial Cholas (in the eleventh and twelfth centuries); in the second, it took place under north Indian principalities such as Orcha and Gwalior that fell within the power shadow of the Mughals (in the fifteenth and sixteenth centuries).

Individual episodes in the history of vernacularization in western Europe are better known, though it bears repeating that a synthetic account (which theorizes vernacularity, establishes its historical trajectory, and explores its linkage to the political sphere) remains to be written. Western European vernacularization begins in earnest — with the production of texts that enter into a secure tradition of reproduction and circulation — at the court of Alfred in late-ninth-century England (thus virtually contemporaneously with events in Karnataka). Here Latinate literary culture, especially in its renewed form during the Carolingian imperium, provides the model consciously followed for an intensive translation program under direction of the court intellectuals, who at the same time began to project a far more coherent vision of territoriality and the unity of Angelcynn. It was this Insular vernacular culture that Anglo-Norman elites discovered at the end of the eleventh century, and when, as one recent study puts it, they were thus "confronted . . . for the first time with the idea and the fact of an extensive and glorious vernacular literature" they developed a French analog, the "sudden issue of imaginative cultural engineering."[30] The creation of a continental French literary culture, for its part, begins soon thereafter with an unprecedented proliferation of new textualizations, above all of the *chanson de geste* and related genres. At precisely the same time (but as far as we know, without direct connection), courts in Occitania created a new genre of literature, the troubadour lyric, that would help stimulate comparable vernacular transformations at courts across the western Mediterranean to Italy and Germany.

It was the corpus of northern French chanson de geste that would provide the model for the *Poema de mio Cid* (1207), a work without historical precedent in any Iberian language and which signals the beginning of vernacular literature in Spain. In the same epoch, the court of Castile (largely in imitation of the wonder that had been Cordoba) was dramatically creating a vernacular documentary state of the sort we are soon to find elsewhere in western Europe. This attained its fullest expression at the court of Alfonso X "El Sabio" in the mid–thirteenth century, where one major court project was a new law code in the vernacular, along with a new discourse on the history of the vernacular space

(*Estoria de Espanna*).[31] In France, the process attains its most power-ful expression at the court of François I in the mid–sixteenth century. Writers of the Pléiade such as Pierre Ronsard saw themselves charged with the task of securing the triumph of the vernacular, and their works need to be understood in relation to the new forms of language govern-mentality that the French court was then instituting.

There is no need here to provide further detail or mention the other well-known developments from Dante to Luther, but it is worth noting one last example from central Europe, which presents something of a model instance of the entire process of cultural-political transformation comprised under the idea of vernacularization. (The vernacularization of eastern Europe follows an analogous pattern, though it occurs much later and within the context of a very different cosmopolitanism: Byzan-tium and Eastern Christianity.) Among Hungarian-speaking peoples, for almost half a millennium the medium of textual production was ex-clusively Latin. It is only in the sixteenth century, in a turn that may be linked as much to new political energies stimulated by the Ottoman vic-tory of 1526 as to the Reformation, that vernacular intellectuals begin to inscribe Hungarian-language literary texts, almost simultaneously pro-ducing an entire apparatus of Hungarian literary culture on the Latin model (dictionaries, grammars, and histories). Here the social location of vernacularization appears, exceptionally, to occur outside the centers of political power, though it may have been precisely the instability of the Hungarian court after 1300 that retarded the turn toward regional-language literary production.

Even this brief review should suffice to invite rethinking of a num-ber of long-held beliefs about vernacularization. Let me briefly look at three. First, we have seen repeatedly that the bearers of vernaculariza-tion in both southern Asia and western Europe were the cultural and political elites who were associated with or directly controlled the royal court. Gramsci and Bakhtin, two of the few thinkers to have understood the significance of this transformation while appreciating it as a political and social (as well as cultural) phenomenon, were thus both wrong to believe that the vernaculars in Europe were upraised against a Mandarin Latinity and came to be written down only when "the people" regained importance, or that the vernacular *tout court* represented a popular social force to be distinguished from and set against an "official" Latin.[32] Unquestionably, some altogether different cultural-political process is at work in the cases we have mentioned. To understand this process means to understand, among other things, the new and more limited vision of governance that seems to be projected through new forms of territorialization in early vernacular texts. For it was now that, thanks to the work of literary vernacularization, regions came for the first time to be coherently conceptualized as such (if not always for the first time to be actually named): Tamil akam, Kannada nadu, Lanka, Maharashtra, Yavadvipa, England, France, Hispania.

Also wrong is the historiography that (following Ernest Gellner) makes industrialization the engine for the vernacular transformation.[33] We may not be able to say with precision what changes in the material world may have contributed to the conditions of possibility for vernacularization, but it is certainly clear that monocausal explanations have to be avoided. A vast expansion of agricultural production across Eurasia; the development of a new, complex, and profitable international trading network that linked Bruges in westernmost Europe to Hangchow in eastern China through intermediary nodes in South Asia such as Cambay and Cochin, and that reached its apogee in the mid-fourteenth century; the movement of nomadic peoples across Eurasia that first made this network possible and that powerfully (if differentially) affected the social and political conditions of southern Asia and western Europe; the expansion of Islam on its eastern and western frontiers (recall that Gibraltar and Sind were both captured by Arab armies in the same year, 711) bringing new modalities of literary culture to India while disrupting older forms of cultural reproduction in Europe—all these world-historical events no doubt helped create an environment in which, for the first time, the choice to think and write locally began to make better sense than writing and thinking globally.[34] Then again, the "lonely hour of the last instance" in which the economic is determinant may never have arrived in this world—why, after all, should the social science logic of capital be generalizable beyond capitalism?—and something altogether different may be at issue in this transformation, something like peer-polity emulation or a new aesthetic value of being "in place." Although different proximate causes may thus be identified for specific developments in different regions, there seems to have been a widely shared sense that everybody was going native, as earlier they had gone global.

The third point in need of rethinking (closely related to the first) is

the standard assumption that counterdominant religious movements —
those in India grouped under the inadequate and historically vague
term devotionalism (*bhakti*), along with Buddhism in Southeast Asia,
and even the Reformation in Europe — drive forward vernacularization.
Vernacularization does not, generally speaking, have demotic spiritual
origins, but rather courtly, political-aesthetic origins. Here Buddhism,
a vehicle of widespread vernacular transformation in parts of Asia, is
typical in its social location among the mercantile, political, and cultural elite. And whereas the development of new vernacular literary
cultures might sometimes draw on the energies of religious change, as
in sixteenth-century Hungary or Sufi northern India, many historical
cases show quite clearly that religious movements often reacted against
an already existing high vernacular (what I have called the *cosmopolitan vernacular*) that attempted to replicate an imperial culture-power
formation at the regional level.[35] In this, the Kannada case is again exem-
plary. The Militant Shaiva (Virashaiva) movement that arose in Karnataka during the twelfth and thirteenth centuries advocated a relocalized
idiom, perhaps even a return to premanuscript and preliterary culture
(since the *vacanakaras* or "makers of utterances" eschewed both high-
cultural genres and inscription as such), and certainly a political order
that did not seek regional empire.

But, again, with the creation of the cosmopolitan vernacular, the new
reading communities, and new visions of vernacular political space,
comparability between the two worlds of vernacularization ends.

Recently, I have tried to sketch out some of the remarkable divergences in the conceptualization of the vernacularization process in
southern Asia and western Europe.[36] These pertain to every aspect of
language ideology, including the sources and moral status of language
diversity, the correlation between language and community, and, perhaps most important, the linkage between vernacular language and
political power. On all counts, the two cases present incommensurate
universes. While care for language was as intense in southern Asia as
anywhere in the world, no southern Asian writer before the colonial
period ever represented this care by means of an affective attachment
to language, as Dante was the first to do when in the introduction to
his *Convivio* he spoke of "the natural love for one's own language":
"Not simply love but the most perfect love is what I ought to have, and
do have, for [my vernacular]."[37] Prior to Europeanization, no southern

Asian writer ever biologized the relationship to the vernacular as one of maternal generation; the notion "mother tongue" itself, as scholars have repeatedly noted, has no conceptual status whatever in pre-European South Asia.

Furthermore, no southern Asian writer ever held the view, common at the start of the vernacular millennium in Europe, that "languages make peoples," as the epigram of a tenth-century Christian poet puts it. In fact — and here is a distinction that makes a most serious difference — there exists no explicit discourse on vernacular language origins at all that ties them with peoples, as there is no discourse on the origins of peoples themselves (dynastic lineages excepted). Origins of languages and peoples, morphing into chronicles and histories of kingdoms and peoples, can fairly be called an obsession in Europe during the first half of the vernacular millennium. These include the late-medieval speculations on the Greek sources of the Spanish language, the Celtic-Gallic or Germanic-Frankish sources of French, and the Celtic-British sources of English; the historical origins myths that trace the French to the Trojans (end of the twelfth century), the Scots to the Scythians (1320), and the Hungarians to the Huns (1283); and full-dress historical narratives such as the *Anglo-Saxon Chronicles* (1000), the Alfonsine *Estoria* (ca. 1270), and the *Grandes chroniques de France* (late fourteenth century).[38]

In southern Asia, by contrast, if we are to take seriously the term by which people referred to the vernaculars — they are, after all, first and foremost the "languages of Place" (*desha-bhasha*) — then we must conclude it is as much region as anything that makes language. Kannada, for example, is the language of "the land of black soil," Malaya[la] that of "the sandalwood mountains," Dakani that of "the south," Braj that of the place of Krishna's birth, and Gwalayeri that of "the mountain of cowherds." They are, accordingly, not facts of biology, like the language of the Franks, for example, or of the Angles, which would eventually underwrite a culture-power region of birth, the *natio*. On the contrary, in many cases they seem to be facts of ecology.[39] (How the culture of Place, deshi, which for a millennium stood in contrast to the cosmopolitan Way, marga, would be transformed into *Swadeshi* — "our own place," that is, "national" — in India's early-twentieth-century engagement with colonialism, is a story for another occasion.)

Nor did any writer in southern Asia ever directly link political power with linguistic particularism like Lorenzo de' Medici when he counseled fifteenth-century Florentines to "work for the enhancement of Florentine power by writing in Tuscan," or Wenceslas II, who a century earlier had been offered the crown of Poland on the grounds that "it is fitting that those who do not differ much in speaking the Slavic language enjoy the rule of a single prince." No language in southern Asia ever became the target of direct royal regulation; sanctions were never imposed requiring the use of one (like French for legal practices under François I) or prohibiting the use of another (like Polish under the Teutonic knights). Indeed, around the time episodes of vernacular extermination were occurring in Europe, vernacular kings in what is now Karnataka were issuing royal inscriptions in Telugu in the east and Marathi in the west, as well as in Kannada, and in their court they would be entertained with songs in these languages as well as in Avadhi, Bihari, Bengali, Oriya, and Madhyadeshiya—producing, in fact, a virtual cosmopolitanism of the vernaculars.[40]

In short, all the indices of vernacular power that the history of Europe invites us to think of as constitutive of the vernacularization process are absent in the historical experience of southern Asia. If language was of interest to courtly elites in southern Asia—and it was most certainly of the greatest interest—the logic by which they conducted their cultural politics was as unfamiliar as that of their cosmocratic predecessors, for whom Sanskrit's principal value seems to have resided in its capacity for an aestheticization of the political. Thus, despite striking parallels in the times and structures of cultural change, vernacularization in these two worlds differed as profoundly as their respective forms of cosmopolitanism. In Europe, we find everywhere a necessary correlation between people, polity, and language. In South Asia, by contrast, there appears to have been some linguistic and cultural accommodation to the conditions of a region on the part of those who entered it; and if power typically expressed itself in the language of Place, power did not make that language instrumental to its own self-conception, let alone to the being of the citizen-subject.

*

Thus, around the beginning of the first millennium, two vast, historically influential supraregional cultures and their associated conceptions of power—*imperium sine fine* (power without limit) and *diganta rajya* (power to the horizons)—came into existence at either end of Eurasia.

They were discursively embodied preeminently in a new literature that could be read everywhere because it was composed in a language that traveled everywhere. They shared a wide variety of additional concerns as well: language discipline, normativity, canonicity, rhetoric. By the arrest of change and the erasure of the local that they ensured, all these factors tended to promote the emancipation of literature from space-time — the great angst of the vernacular is its spatiotemporal entropy — precisely as political power was meant to be emancipated. The social processes by which these cultural forms were disseminated and adopted and promoted, however, had nothing whatever in common. They related to power in ways that differed as utterly as the practices of power themselves, which shared little beyond belief in the infinitude of governance. The two formations are rightly regarded as cosmopolitan, both for their conception of culture-power as unlimited and for the varied notions of belonging to — acting in, writing for, speaking to — a limitless world that, at a certain level of consciousness, they most decidedly comprised. I have characterized the radical difference in the processes by which this consciousness was generated as one between compulsion and choice.

These cosmopolitan orders were dramatically challenged by new forms of culture and power that were brought into being around the beginning of the second millennium and, within a few centuries, were transcended by these new forms almost everywhere. In neither world, it should be stressed, was success ever truly achieved in reconciling the cosmopolitan and the vernacular, albeit both Latin and Sanskrit preserved a residual force into the nineteenth century, providing a code for the display of scholarship or the cultivation of nostalgic antiquarianism by vernacular intellectuals and writers. We do not yet fully understand the precise material conditions for the great vernacular transformation, any more than we understand those for the quasi globalisms that preceded it. But even certitude of the material grounds would seem to have little bearing on our analysis. What we are able to perceive clearly is that vernacular languages or languages of Place at that moment and for the first time came to be used for producing written literary cultures and their concomitant political cultures of the emergent documentary states. They thus helped, in their different ways, to constitute the nation-states of Europe and the vernacular polities of southern Asia; helped to constitute, as well, the early modernity that these new cultural-political formations represented, and which, accordingly, arrived more or less simultaneously and wholly independently in the two regions.

Here, too, however, ideologies of language and instrumentalities of culture differed profoundly. In the one case, the relationship between different peoples and their languages was determinate, so much so that peoplehood became a function of language (a conception that, for all the relativity and contingency that we find to undermine it, continues to weaken strong minds).[41] In the other, this relationship seems almost ecological: just as places create water and soil, so they were thought virtually to create languages, which people use like water or soil. In western Europe, language was held to be subservient to power. Indeed, it became explicitly the "attendant of empire" (*compañera del imperio*) at the very moment that power was first projected in a truly global manner in Iberian colonialism (the famous phrase is Nebrija's, who used it when dedicating his Castilian grammar to Queen Isabella in 1492). In South Asia, language was a vehicle of aesthetic distinction, style, or something else that reveals no simple purpose to be explained according to the functionalist models of modern social science. These differences I have sought to order by identifying the first as a vernacularity of necessity and the second as a vernacularity of accommodation.

I am very much aware that this brief history of cosmopolitanism and vernacularism and their elementary aspects has ignored vast complexities. An especially important omission, which would have required far too much space to make good here, is discussion of the dialectic between cosmopolitan and vernacular that creates them both. (These cultural forms are not just historically constituted but mutually constitutive, for if the vernacular localizes the cosmopolitan as part of its own self-constitution, it is often unwittingly relocalizing what the cosmopolitan borrowed from it in the first place.)[42] I have had to run the risk of caricature, too, in creating a largely demonic North to juxtapose to a largely angelic South, refreshing departure though that might seem; and a complex process of change has been reduced by and large to a logic of pure idealism. But, granting all these shortcomings, the historical reconstruction offered here does make claim to a certain reality that yet further qualification should not be permitted to flatten. First, the cosmopolitan and the vernacular have been actual and profound culture-power alternatives in Asia no less than in Europe. Second, both were everywhere and always produced by deliberate choices and conscious practices. The transformations we have examined in the ways people make culture and organize power cannot be explained by the naturalization of cultural change, where mechanisms triggered by material or technological innovation are thought simply to trigger cultural evolution. By the same token, what some are inclined to characterize as vernacular primordiality is shown to be a chimera; vernacularity has always and everywhere been produced. Third, however comparable may have been the basic conditions of possibility that obtained across the Eurasian world during the fifteen-hundred-year period that helped produce cultural and political change of a very comparable sort, the differences in both the cosmopolitan and vernacular formations in the two spheres are deep and irreducible. All this prompts us to rethink the historical character of local and supralocal attachments, if only insofar as the processes of literary culture considered here—the production and circulation and consumption of expressive texts—are able to embody them.

No less complex than the problem of knowing this past, however, is the question of why we want to know it at all. Can the understanding of such historical experiences as we have reviewed here open up for us a domain of alternative possibilities at a time when the choices of culture-power before us all seem bad and the dilemmas intolerable yet unavoidable? Cosmopolitanism and vernacularism in their contemporary Western forms—American globalization and ethnonationalism—is one such domain of bad options. It is hard not to see their most deformed developments in the confrontation between NATO and Serbia that closed out a century of confrontation. No simple formula will capture the complexity of this confrontation, but it is not too far wrong to see it as pitting a dying vernacularity—or, at least, something that could be retailed as vernacularity to the people of Serbia—grown mistrustful, pathological, and ethnocidal, against a new kind of cosmopolitanism with a mission that some have characterized by the useful if worrisome oxymoron "militaristic humanism."

India, for its part, is hardly immune now to bad choices. The worst at present is that between a vernacularity mobilized along the most fragile fault lines of region, religion, and caste and the grotesque mutation of the toxins of postcolonial ressentiment and modernity known as Hindutva, or fundamentalist Hinduism. Hindutva's political organization, the Bharatiya Janata Party (BJP; Indian People's Party), took secure control of the national government in March 1998; its paramilitary wing, the

Rashtriya Swayamsevak Sangh (RSS; National Volunteers Union), and its ideological wing, the Vishwa Hindu Parishad (VHP; World Hindu Council), have now unprecedented access to central power. The very names of these groups now speak what had never been spoken before, postulating in the one case a single Indian "peoplehood" (*janata*) and in the other Hinduism as an aggressive universalism (*vishwa*). The latter is produced not by an affective attachment to the large world, but by the dislocations of diaspora, as a recent RSS tract in its own confused way makes clear:

> For a Hindu, the entire universe is his home. He considers himself as belonging to the whole world. For him, "*Swadesho bhuvanatrayam*" [The triple world—earth, sky, and heaven—is one's own Place] is not a mere slogan, but is the very spirit ingrained in his mind. As such, from time immemorial, Hindus are widely spread the world over. Hindus reside in more than 150 countries and have been at-home wherever they have reached. In fact, in a couple of countries like Mauritius, Fiji, Trinidad, etc., they form the majority and by this virtue are occupying high positions in those countries. It is no wonder that when swayamsevaks [RSS cadres], who take pride in being the harbingers of the Sangh ideology, and who for other reasons go abroad, also start Sangh Shakhas [Union branches] in countries they choose to reside in.[43]

Universalism exists for the RSS only in the network of its branch offices, in the magnitude and extent of its paramilitary network. This Hindutva complex of which the RSS is part, the so-called Sangh Parivar (Family of Organizations), as it has recently come to be known, instantiates the very type of "reactionary modernism" familiar from interwar Europe: it is committed at once to a wholesale nuclearization of India's military capabilities (as demonstrated in the BJP's May 1998 nuclear test), and to a cultural program of pseudotraditionalism that has cynically coopted and polluted the great cosmopolitan past. Thus the BJP proclaimed 1999 the "Year of Sanskrit," while the RSS now cultivates the practice at its branch meetings of issuing commands in Sanskrit. All this is carried out in the name of a new swadeshi, a new militant vernacularism. "The new watchword is 'Swadeshi,'" according to the BJP vice president: "The world has been told in unmistakable terms that India cannot be taken for granted."[44]

I want to begin thinking about the kinds of choices between the cosmopolitan and the vernacular that are now available—mostly bad and bitter and sad choices, it seems—in relation to the historical past we have just surveyed by putting them into a more familiar idiom with a discussion of two short texts from the early 1930s by Antonio Gramsci that are concerned with the vernacular-national and cosmopolitan-universalist problematics. Gramsci, it bears repeating, is virtually unique in the scholarly record for the innovative and passionate reflection he devoted to the large questions of literary culture and political power over the long history of the West, though it is not clear that he ever succeeded in developing a coherent position about the competing claims of the cosmopolitan and the vernacular as either cultural or political values. For one thing, he seems to have placed the blame for the failure of national consciousness to develop in Italy on a certain "cosmopolitan casteism" and the long-term alienation of the intellectual class from the state, something intimately connected in Gramsci's mind with the continuing use of Latin and the concomitant failure of a national language—indeed, Dante's "illustrious vernacular"—to come into being. The very development of his notion of the "national-popular," however, as a pure strategy for mass mobilization beyond the Communist Party proper suggests his regret at the unhappy kinds of compromises required at that historical juncture, to say nothing of his appreciation of the sheer factitiousness of the national sentiment itself. I doubt I am alone in often sensing here a tension in Gramsci's thought between, on the one hand, an ideal of cultural cosmopolitanism and political internationalism and, on the other, the very pragmatic pressures of national-popular action.[45] The two small texts to be considered meditate, in their own way, on these problems.

The first of these texts is actually a summary of and comment on an article published in 1929 by Julien Benda (with whose ideal of the intellectual "non-pratique" Gramsci must otherwise have had no sympathy) concerning the relationship between the particular and the universal in literature.[46] Benda notes that serious people—he mentions André Gide—believe a writer able to serve the general interest only to the degree that he or she produces work that is more particular. Gide himself had originally developed this idea within a purely aestheticist paradigm: one cannot promote the universal or any other good without the perfection of "artistic power, however defined," and the latter is something always derived from and depending on the particular. The particular for many in the 1920s, however, was, precisely, the national: the question Benda and Gramsci accordingly ask is whether being particular itself is necessarily a function of being national, as many conservative intellectuals insisted, such as those who in 1919 asked in a public manifesto, "Is it not by nationalizing itself that a literature takes on a more universal signification, a more humanly general interest? . . . Is it not a profound error to believe that one can work on behalf of European culture through a denationalized literature?"[47]

What interests me in these reflections on the literary particular, beyond the genealogy of the idea and its remarkable implications—that the particular is the real general and that nationalism may "equivocate" as the true universalism—is the response offered by Benda and endorsed by Gramsci. This takes two forms. For one, the national particular is said to be only a "first-degree" variety, rather like the species category "mammal" that characterizes all humans, whereas a "second degree" of particularization, and the more important, is a function of distinguishing oneself from one's fellow citizens.[48] For another—and this is the far more powerful insight—Benda and Gramsci differentiate between two modalities of particularity: there is a radical difference, as they emphatically put it, between *being* particular and *preaching* particularism. Expressed in the terms that have been used in the present essay, this distinction comprises the understanding that while vernacularity is essential for art and for life, we can distinguish between a vernacularity of necessity and one of accommodation and strive somehow to achieve the latter.[49]

The second text is a brief comment on the past and future of the idea of the Italian nation-state. Gramsci raises the question of the universal while pursuing the same basic problem as in the first text, wondering now whether the forces that produced the unification of Italy must also inevitably produce a militaristic nationalism.[50] His response is actually rather curious. He argues that such nationalism is antihistorical: "It is, in reality, contrary to all the Italian traditions, first Roman and then Catholic," which he tells us are cosmopolitan. But then, as if sensing how unhistorical or incomplete is the answer he has just given, he asks whether a new type of cosmopolitanism may ever be possible, beyond "nationalism and militaristic imperialism: Not the citizen of the world as *civis romanus* or as Catholic but as a producer of civilization."[51] In other words: Is it at all possible to be universal without preaching universalism?

The antinomy between the particular and the universal, the vernacular and the cosmopolitan, the national and the international—not all precisely the same phenomenon, to be sure, but now inextricably linked—has lost little of its salience since Gramsci's day. Quite the contrary, it seems to have shown itself to be ever more urgent and intractable, with new and even more complex versions of vernacularity developing in response to what is perceived as cosmopolitanism in its ugly-American embodiment. To get a sense of where we stand now, it may be helpful to look very briefly at two recent attempts made by very accomplished thinkers, inheritors of one of the historical types of vernacularism and cosmopolitanism whose genesis we have traced, to rehabilitate the national-vernacular under a liberal or progressive guise. In conclusion, we can ask whether any response to this new indigenism may be available in a postcolonialism that may be thought still to bear the impress or stored energy—or whatever may be the right metaphor—of those other, very different types of cosmopolitan and vernacular histories.

In his recent book on multicultural citizenship, Will Kymlicka introduces the idea of what he calls "societal culture." This, we are told, is "a culture which provides its members with meaningful ways of life across the full range of human activities, including social, educational, religious, recreational, and economic life, encompassing both public and private spheres." In fact, these turn out to be no different from national cultures and are said to constitute the true basis of freedom. While Kymlicka is aware that the congeries of practices he terms societal cultures "did not always exist" but derive (in accordance with Gellner's flawed theory) from the new elevation of the vernacular in the service of the educational homogenization required by industrialization, they somehow escape the historicity of the nineteenth-century moment of their genesis. Vernacular cultures are given and there; they demand unequivocally to be accommodated just as they are, unquestioned in any way about their present, let alone historical, constitution. In fact, they are portrayed as the only "meaningful context of choice for people" and worth preserving at all costs. Violations of the space of vernacular cultures, accordingly—through open borders, for example—would be a disaster since "people's own national community would be overrun by settlers from other cultures, and . . . they would be unable to ensure their survival as a distinct national culture." Most people (somehow Kymlicka knows most people) "would rather be free and equal within their own nation . . . than be free and equal citizens of the world, if this means they are less likely to be able to live and work in their own language and culture."[52] A necessary vernacularism if there ever was one.

Tom Nairn has a less openly culturological defense of vernacular nationalism; he approaches the problem through the domain of the political. Nairn argues that the events of 1989 buried the old internationalism of promoting working-class solidarity to counteract capitalism and nationalism. In its place has come "internationality," the bland but dangerous homogenization of the world whose very effect (a familiar argument here) is to produce local resistance, often violent resistance. The only way forward now, we are instructed, must be through and not outside nationalism (and of course through capitalism). All that internationalists have left to do is to "decide what sort of nationalists they will become." In other words, the only way to be universal now is to be national. As for the dangers? Well, asks Nairn, "Are the fragmentation and anarchy really so bad?" These words were written two years into the siege of Sarajevo, five years into the renewed struggle in Kashmir, ten years into the movement for Tamil Eelam — with Rwanda one year away, Chechnya two, Srebrenica three. Of course, these are not identical situations — nor have all twentieth-century horrors, many far worse than these, been wholly subsumable under the extreme vernacular mobilization of nationalism. Yet each of these recent cases seems to me to be poised in its own way on the particularistic brink, the vernacular — or what Nairn calls the "Ethnic Abyss," which seems increasingly resistant to Nairn's denial that "there is no abyss, in the hysterical liberal sense."[53]

Kymlicka and Nairn represent a wide range of thinkers for whom vernacularity stands outside history (except to the degree that history continually demonstrates its necessity) and constitutes an essential component of human existence. They therefore hold the conservation of vernacular culture and the acquisition of vernacular polity — now coterminous with nationalism — to be a categorical imperative in the face of a universalism seen only as compulsory. To such a vision of the present and future we may juxtapose the perspective of those who have inherited (if not always self-awarely) the very different traditions of the South Asian cosmopolitan and vernacular sketched out in the foregoing pages. These are legatees, in addition, of the world's longest and most fraught engagement with globalization in its harshest forms, colonialism. It is a striking fact that one finds among these intellectuals so rich an inventory of strong formulations about particulars and universals—especially Asian particulars and European universals—and related problematics of European thought. Contrast for a moment the relative indifference to these matters among, say, Chinese intellectuals, with their very different history. This is something one may account for, I think, as a kind of sedimentation of historical experience—without thereby committing oneself to an iron determinism—but its value is harder to assess. Getting beaten up all the time by the schoolyard bully has a way of focusing the mind on violence more than is the case for kids left unhurt. No doubt, such historical experience does not convert automatically into an advantage for thought or practice, as Dipesh Chakrabarty has often taken care to remind me, but it clearly converts into a propensity for thinking. We may not be wrong to suppose, therefore, that these two powerful formative experiences (a long experience with autonomously produced cosmopolitan and vernacular practices, followed by the new and heteronomous cosmopolitanism of colonialism) have inclined some thinkers to search harder—not for a unified theory of transcendence, but for what Chakrabarty has characterized for me as "cracks in the master discourses" and, more important, for practices for overcoming the dichotomous thinking that marks our current impasse.

It is from within the world of these intellectuals—I have in mind the recent work of Partha Chatterjee, but a number of others including the late D. R. Nagaraj provide good examples—that some of the more compelling suggestions are being offered on ways to address the desperate choices imposed by modernity.[54] Might it not be possible, as some of these thinkers suggest, to transcend the dichotomies of modernizing cosmopolitanism and vernacular traditionalism by understanding that the new must be made precisely through attachment to the past, and by recognizing that only such attachment enables one to grasp what can and must be changed? Take as one example the seemingly irreconcilable alternatives of the universalist discourse of the liberal state—where secularism demands the submergence of religious difference in a homogeneous juridical order—and the historical particularities of a given community's ways of life (it being understood that these are, in fact, historical). Might this irreconcilability not yield to a strategic politics that seeks to institute such a transformation from within communities themselves (whether Muslim, Vaishnav, Maratha, or other), while resisting demands for liberalization or democratization that are official, top-down, and imposed from the outside? In other words, affective attachment to old structures of belonging offered by vernacular particulars must precede any effective transformation through new cosmopolitan universals; care must be in evidence, a desire to preserve, even as the structure is to be changed. Assuredly, many of the discursive components in such arguments are available in other contemporary debates, but the mix here seems to me special. It consists of a response to a specific history of domination and enforced change, along with a critique of the oppression of tradition itself, tempered by a strategic desire to locate resources for a cosmopolitan future in vernacular ways of being themselves. Analogously, the choice between the global and the local, whether in literary culture or in the organization of power, may now find some kind of resolution in the blunt refusal to choose from among the alternatives, a refusal that can be performable in practice however difficult to articulate in theory.[55]

None of this thinking should be taken as exemplification of "hybridity" in its usual connotations of mélange or mongrelization—a banal concept and a dangerous one, implying an amalgamation of unalloyed, pure forms, whether vernacular or cosmopolitan, that have never existed. The practice I have in mind, on the contrary, is a tactical reversal of domination—a resistance-through-appropriation, as it has been described—which, in fact, approximates what I take to be the very process of vernacularization before modernity.[56] This practice derives from a realization born of accumulated historical experience of both pre- and postcoloniality that the future must somehow become one of *and* rather than *either/or*. Such a proclamation admittedly has the ring of a slogan, and a certain unpleasantly utopian ring at that. Neither does it mechanically yield policy outcomes capable of helping us directly address today's most pressing questions of the cosmopolitan and vernacular (such as the minority cultural rights that we must support or the ethnochauvinist politics that we must resist). In fact, I have borrowed this particular formulation from the German sociologist Ulrich Beck, whose argument is not a precipitate of comparable historical experience but derives instead from an abstract model of risk theory, and precisely for this reason seems all the less compelling.[57] Yet the proposal to seek *and* may derive some pragmatic sustenance from an awareness of the varied cosmopolitan and vernacular possibilities that have been available in history. To know that some people in the past have been able to be universal and particular, without making either their particularity ineluctable or their universalism compulsory, is to know that better cosmopolitan and vernacular practices are at least conceivable — and perhaps even, in a way those people themselves never fully achieved, eventually reconcilable.

NOTES

I am grateful to Benedict Anderson for his meticulous and constructively contentious reading of the essay. Homi Bhabha, Carol A. Breckenridge, Dipesh Chakrabarty, Caitrin Lynch, and Mica Pollock helped me sharpen a number of the arguments and bear no responsibility for those that have remained dull.

1. Sheldon Pollock, "India in the Vernacular Millennium: Literary Culture and Polity 1000–1500," in *Early Modernities,* ed. Shmuel Eisenstadt, Wolfgang Schluchter, and Björn Wittrock, special issue of *Daedalus* 127, no. 3 (1998): 41–74.

2. On the important idea of incommunication and its history (exemplified in the case of Bangla and Oriya), see Sudipta Kaviraj, "Writing, Speaking, Being: Language and the Historical Formation of Identities in India," in *Nationalstaat und Sprachkonflikt in Süd- und Südostasien,* ed. Dagmar Hellmann-Rajanayagam and Dietmar Rothermund (Stuttgart: Steiner, 1992), 25–65, especially 26.

3. See Roland Robertson, "The Universalism-Particularism Issue," in *Globalization: Social Theory and Global Culture* (London: Sage, 1992), 102.

4. For Derrida's unhistorical essentialization of the nonessentialized nature of literature, see his *Acts of Literature,* ed. Derek Atridge (London: Routledge, 1992), especially 40–49.

5. See Norbert Elias, "The Retreat of Sociologists into the Present," in *Modern German Sociology,* ed. Volker Meja, Dieter Misgeld, and Nico Stehr (New York: Columbia University Press, 1987), 150–72. The greater part of what is purveyed as the "premodern" in a work like Anthony Giddens's *The Consequences of Modernity* (Stanford, Calif.: Stanford University Press, 1990), finds little support, and much contradiction, in the historical record of southern Asia.

6. Sejong's demotic reforms in Korea in the mid–fifteenth century, and the development of *chu-nom* script in Vietnam around the same time, did not produce anything remotely comparable to what we find in fifteenth-century southern Asia or western Europe.

7. Ulf Hannerz, "Culture between Center and Periphery: Toward a Macroanthropology," *Ethnos* 3–4 (1989): 210–11.

8. Quentin Skinner, *Liberty before Liberalism* (Cambridge: Cambridge University Press, 1998), 118.

9. K. S. Agase, ed., *Chandogyopanisat with the Commentary of Shankara* (Poona: Anandashrama Press, 1902), 1.1.10 (my translation).

10. This and the following section draw on evidence and argument from a book I am now completing, *The Language of the Gods in the World of Men: Sanskrit and Power 300–1500*, where I acknowledge the complexity of these questions in a way that is impossible in a short essay such as this one.

11. Vishwanath Shastri Bharadvaj, ed., *Vikramankadevacarita of Bilhana*, 3 vols. (Varanasi: Samskrit Sahitya Research Committee of the Banaras Hindu University, 1964), 18.89 (my translation).

12. In the eastern part of this world, Latin had to contend with another cosmopolitan language, namely Greek, which would have its own complex interactions with the Slavic vernaculars in the later Byzantine empire. See, for example, *Byzantium and the Slavs in Letters and Culture*, ed. Ihor Sevcenke (Cambridge: Harvard Ukrainian Research Institute; Naples: Instituto Universitario Orientale, 1991).

13. For Martial, see Paul Veyne, "Humanitas," in *The Romans*, ed. Andrea Giardina (Chicago: University of Chicago Press, 1994), 365, and William Harris, *Ancient Literacy* (Cambridge: Harvard University Press, 1989), 227. Harris also cites Horace on p. 224.

14. Sheldon Pollock, "The Sanskrit Cosmopolis, A.D. 300–1300: Transculturation, Vernacularization, and the Question of Ideology," in *The Ideology and Status of Sanskrit in South and Southeast Asia*, ed. J. E. M. Houben (Leiden: E. J. Brill, 1996), 197–247.

15. On the history of the concept of *Latinitas* ("'Latinness' . . . and especially the literary style that marked the high literature of Rome and those who sought to perpetuate it"), see W. Martin Bloomer, *Latinity and Literary Society at Rome* (Philadelphia: University of Pennsylvania Press, 1997), 1–2, where the point is also made that Latinitas and orbis terrarum are probably calqued on *Hellenismos* and *oikoumene* in the Greek world. We might also compare, without speculating on their origins, such later terms as *Arabiya* and *Farsiyat*.

16. Claude Nicolet, *Space, Geography, and Politics in the Early Roman Empire* (Ann Arbor: University of Michigan Press, 1991), 33.

17. See *De Vita Hadriani* of Aelius Spartianus 11.1: *murumque per octoginta milia passuum primus duxit, qui barbaros Romanosque divideret*. Available as of July 2000 on line at http://www.gmu.edu/departments/fld/CLASSICS/sha.hadr.html.

18. Fergus Millar, *The Roman Near East, 31 B.C.–A.D. 337* (Cambridge: Harvard University Press, 1993).

19. Ramsay MacMullen, *Changes in the Roman Empire: Essays in the Ordinary* (Princeton, N.J.: Princeton University Press, 1990), 32 (see also 62).

20. In "The Occidental Tagore," *Boston Review* 19, no. 5 (1994): 22, Lloyd Rudolph's response to Martha Nussbaum's "Patriotism and Cosmopolitanism," in the same magazine. Her essay has since been reprinted as *For Love of Country: Debating the Limits of Patriotism* (Boston: Beacon Press, 1996). The prominence given to classical cosmopolitanism in contemporary discussions seems (to this lapsed classicist, at any

rate) to be much exaggerated. The word *kosmopolites*, for instance, seems to occur only in the much-cited (Greek) utterance attributed to Diogenes in Diogenes Laertius's biography, as well as in the work of Philo, the (Greek) Jewish philosopher of Alexandria. Neither the word itself nor any of its derivatives (nor even *cosmopolis*) occurs in classical Latin. On Ovid's *(ingens) orbis in urbe (fuit)*, a common trope, see Nicolet, *Space, Geography, and Politics*, 114 and cf. 33.

21. The judgment on Stoic timidity is Veyne's, "Humanitas," 348–50. He cites and discusses Augustus's *Res gestae* 3.2 on 353–54. On the Parthians, see, most recently, Philip Hardie, "Fifth-Century Athenian and Augustan Images of the Barbarian Other," *Classics Ireland* 4 (1997): 46–56; Hardie calls attention to the long afterlife of the images created here.

22. Embar Krishnamacharya, ed., *Suktimuktavali of Jalhana*, Gaekwad's Oriental Series 82 (Baroda: Oriental Institute, 1938), 45.69 (my translation). This is a good example of what Freud called *Verneinung*, or the negation whereby repression is simultaneously maintained and denied.

23. Vayupurana 45.82 (my translation); as printed in Willibald Kirfel, *Bharatavarsa (Indien): Textgeschichtliche Darstellung zweier geographischen Purana-Texte nebst Übersetzung* (Stuttgart: W. Kohlhammer, 1931), 36.

24. The phrasing is that of Oliver Wolters, "Khmer 'Hinduism' in the Seventh Century," *Early South East Asia: Essays in Archaeology, History and Historical Geography*, ed. R. B. Smith and W. Watson (New York: Oxford University Press, 1979), 438. The uncentered world of Sanskrit has quite archaic origins; on the problem in ritualism, see Charles Malamoud, "Sans lieu ni date: Note sur l'absence de fondation dans l'Inde Védique," in *Traces de fondation*, ed. Marcel Detienne (Louvain: Peeters, 1990), 183–91.

25. Paul Wheatley, "India beyond the Ganges," *Journal of Asian Studies* 42 (1982): 28.

26. What is said of the mythic emperor Raghu by the poet Kalidasa in the fourth century—"His chariot of conquest would rest only at the furthest horizon" (*Raghuvamsha* 3.5)—would be repeated in reference to other, historical kings for centuries to come.

27. Benedict Anderson, *Imagined Communities* (London: Verso, 1983), 20–25. I am not overlooking the fact that all these scripts ultimately derive from a single Indian prototype. My point is that regional graphic diversity was allowed to develop, in fact, was even sought.

28. See Virgil, *The Aeneid of Virgil*, ed. T. E. Page (London: MacMillan, 1962), 1.1–7 and H. D. Velankar, ed., *Raghuvamsha* (Bombay: Nirnaya Sagara Press, 1948), 1.1.

29. Mikhail Bakhtin, *The Dialogic Imagination: Four Essays* (Austin: University of Texas Press, 1981), 84–258.

30. David Howlett, *The English Origins of Old French Literature* (Dublin: Four Courts Press, 1996), 165–66.

31. The vernacular story for Iberia is particularly well told in the writings of the late Colin Smith, most recently "The Vernacular," in *The New Cambridge Medieval History*, vol. 5, ed. David Abulafia (Cambridge: Cambridge University Press, 1995–2000).

32. See Antonio Gramsci, *Selections from Cultural Writings* (Cambridge: Harvard

University Press, 1991), 188, 168; Mikhail Bakhtin, *Rabelais and His World* (Bloomington: Indiana University Press, 1984), 465–74.

33. See Ernest Gellner, *Nations and Nationalism* (Oxford: Blackwell, 1983), and Pollock, "Vernacular Millennium," 66–67. Gellner's thesis has been much discussed — see most recently *The State of the Nation: Ernest Gellner and the Theory of Nationalism,* ed. John Hall (Cambridge: Cambridge University Press, 1998) — but not in terms of its fundamental historiographical problems.

34. For a recent attempt to grasp these different factors as a whole — agricultural expansion, population increase, the impact of pastoral nomads, developments in state formation — in explaining new developments in territoriality in the subcontinent, see David Ludden, *An Agrarian History of South Asia* (Cambridge: Cambridge University Press, 1999), chap. 2.

35. See Sheldon Pollock, "The Cosmopolitan Vernacular," *Journal of Asian Studies* 57 (1998): 6–37.

36. Pollock, "Vernacular Millennium," 62–65.

37. Dante, *Il Convivio.* Vol. 5 of *Opere di Dante,* ed. G. Busnelli and G. Vandelli (Florence: Felice Le Monnier, 1964), 1.10.4 (*Lo naturale amore della propria loquela*) and 1.13.10 (*non solamente amore, ma perfettissimo amore sia quello ch' io a [mio Volgare] debbo avere ed ho*).

38. The Christian poet is cited by Robert Bartlett, *The Making of Europe: Conquest, Colonization and Cultural Change 950–1350* (Princeton, N.J.: Princeton University Press, 1993), 198: *gentem lingua facit.* No synthetic account exists of the cultural-political genealogies of early modern Europe. See, for now, *Nation und Literatur im Europa der frühen Neuzeit,* ed. Klaus Garber (Tübingen: Niemeyer, 1989), 36; and Susan Reynolds, *Kingdoms and Communities in Western Europe 900–1300,* 2d ed. (Oxford: Clarendon Press, 1997), 250–331.

39. Analogously, the cosmopolitan languages in southern Asia are facts of language processes themselves (*samskrta,* "refined"; *prakrta,* "unrefined"; *apabhrashta,* "corrupted"), unlike the ethnonyms of other cosmopolitan languages such as Arabiya, Farsi, English.

40. For the citation from Lorenzo's commentary on his sonnets, see Douglas M. Painter, "Humanist Insights and the Vernacular in Sixteenth-Century France," *History of European Ideas* 16 (1993): 68. On language prohibition, extermination, and politics, see Bartlett, *Making of Europe,* 202–3 (where the envoys to Wenceslas II are cited). The cultural practices of Deccani kings are described in Someshvara's twelfth-century encyclopedia, the *Manasollasa* (Baroda: Gaekwad Oriental Series, 1961), vol. 3, 1–83.

41. Charles Taylor, for example, is not alone in his conviction that language is the "essential viable and indispensable pole of identification" and that this identification stands outside history. See Pierre Birnbaum, "From Multiculturalism to Nationalism," *Political Theory* 24 (1996): 39 (where the Taylor citation is given), and compare Anthony Appiah, "Identity, Authenticity, Survival," in Charles Taylor, *Multiculturalism: Examining the Politics of Recognition,* ed. Amy Gutman (Princeton, N.J.: Princeton University Press, 1994), 156.

42. A modest example is provided in Pollock, "The Cosmopolitan Vernacular," 21–25.

43. This is cited from the RSS pamphlet "Widening Horizons," available as of December 1999 on-line at http://www.rss.org/rss/library/books/WideningHorizons/ch8.html. For a recent general critique of Hindutva culture and politics, see *The Concerned Indian's Guide to Communalism*, ed. K. N. Panikkar (New Delhi: Penguin, 1999).

44. See K. R. Malkani, "BJP History: Its Birth, Growth and Onward March," available as of December 1999 on-line at http://www.bjp.org/history.htm.

45. On the development of the national-popular, see the helpful essay of David Forgacs, "National-Popular: Genealogy of a Concept," in *The Cultural Studies Reader*, ed. Simon During (London: Routledge, 1993), 177–90. I leave it to others to determine whether Forgacs is correct to state that Gramsci believed that, in general, "the cosmopolitan traditions of the Italian intellectuals had impeded the molecular ideological activity by which [an intellectual and moral] reformation could be brought about" (186).

46. Gramsci, *Selections from Cultural Writings*, 260–61 ("Julian Benda"). Benda's article is "Comment un écrivain sert-il l'universel?" *Les nouvelles littéraires*, 2 November 1929, 1. (I make reference to material from the original article inasmuch as it was known to Gramsci, though not explicitly addressed in his note.) This largely restates ideas in Benda's *La trahison des clercs* (Paris: Grasset, 1927; cf. 97–99, 296–98), which is a still-troublesome text. See, for example, Ernest Gellner, "La trahison de la trahison des clercs," in *The Political Responsibility of Intellectuals*, ed. Ian Maclean, Alan Montefiore, and Peter Winch (Cambridge: Cambridge University Press, 1990). For the ideal that "le clerc doit se proclamer non-pratique" (except, evidently, when he demands the reform of the *cléricature*), see Benda, *La trahison des clercs*, 231–35.

47. The signatories of this hypernationalist document, "Pour un parti de l'intelligence," included Paul Bourget, Maurice Barrès, Jacques Maritain, and Francis Jammes.

48. Ernest Renan, says Benda, is not a "necessary effect" of the French consciousness, but "an arbitrary, even unforeseeable event," and his true particularity and value lie in the degree of his difference from the group of which he is part, in the way that any human being's value is what sets him or her apart from the species ("Comment un écrivain sert-il l'universel?," 1).

49. Benda himself, as we can see in hindsight, was dead wrong—or grossly premature—to infer (on the grounds that one does not pray for the healthy) that the fervor with which the "nationalization of the esprit" was being preached in 1929 signaled its imminent dissolution in a new European consciousness.

50. Gramsci, *Selections from Cultural Writings*, 246–47 ("Interpretations of the Risorgimento [ii]").

51. Gramsci, *Selections from Cultural Writings*, 246.

52. Will Kymlicka, *Multicultural Citizenship* (Oxford: Clarendon Press, 1995), 76, 80, 93. Despite his Gellnerian model, Kymlicka somehow counts Native American cultures as "genuinely distinct societal cultures," like those of the Puerto Ricans or

Québecois (79–80). A strong critique of Kymlicka is offered in Jeremy Waldron, "Minority Cultures and the Cosmopolitan Alternative," in *The Rights of Minority Communities,* ed. W. Kymlicka (Oxford: Oxford University Press, 1995), 93–119.

53. Tom Nairn, "Internationalism and the Second Coming," in *Mapping the Nation,* ed. Gopal Balakrishnan (London: Verso, 1996), 267–80; the texts quoted are on 274–76. Originally published in *Daedalus* 122, no. 3 (1993): 115–40.

54. See, for example, Partha Chatterjee, *A Possible India: Essays in Political Criticism* (Delhi: Oxford University Press, 1997); D. R. Nagaraj, *Collected Essays* (Delhi: Oxford University Press, forthcoming), and D. R. Nagaraj, "Introduction," in Ashis Nandy, *Exiled at Home* (Delhi: Oxford University Press, 1998). I forbear citing my Chicago colleagues, whose engagement with these questions is on display in this volume.

55. Chatterjee puts several of these ideas well (see *A Possible India,* especially 261–62 and 280–85). The sensitivity he evinces should not be blithely generalized, however, whether in the sphere of power or culture. Consider how, in a fit of misguided vernacularism, the Communist Party–Marxist government of West Bengal in 1981 prohibited English-medium instruction in elementary education; this law was rescinded in 1998 after heated protests by working-class people who were outraged at the opportunities for advancement being denied to them (a precedent ignored by the government of Tamil Nadu, which instituted a similar law regarding Tamil in autumn 1998). The attempt to preserve vernacularity on the backs of the poor is a familiar liberal strategy; see Gramsci, *Selections from Cultural Writings,* 166.

56. See Homi Bhabha, "Signs Taken for Wonders," in *The Location of Culture* (London: Routledge, 1996), especially 112–15.

57. Ulrich Beck, *The Reinvention of Politics: Rethinking Modernity in the Global Social Order* (Oxford: Polity Press, 1997).

Spectral Housing and Urban Cleansing:
Notes on Millennial Mumbai

Arjun Appadurai

Arjun Appadurai

A BRIEF HISTORY OF DECOSMOPOLITANIZATION

Cities like Bombay—now Mumbai—have no clear place in the stories told so far that link late capitalism, globalization, post-Fordism, and the growing dematerialization of capital. Their history is uneven—in the sense made commonsensical by a certain critical tradition in Marxism. It is also characterized by disjunct, yet adjacent, histories and temporalities. In such cities, Fordist manufacture, craft and artisanal production, service economies involving law, leisure, finance, and banking, and virtual economies involving global finance capital and local stock markets live in an uneasy mix. Certainly, these cities are the loci of the practices of predatory global capital—here Mumbai belongs with Bangkok, Hong Kong, Saõ Paulo, Los Angeles, Mexico City, London, and Singapore. But these cities also produce the social black holes of the effort to embrace and seduce global capital in their own particular ways, which are tied to varied histories (colonial and otherwise), varied political cultures of citizenship and rule, and varied ecologies of production and finance. Such particularities appear as images of globalization that are cracked and refracted. They are also instances of the elusiveness of global flows at the beginning of the new millennium.

Typically, these cities are large (10–15 million people) and are currently shifting from economies of manufacture and industry to economies of trade, tourism, and finance. They usually attract more poor people than they can handle and more capital than they can absorb. They offer the magic of wealth, celebrity, glamour, and power through their mass media. But they often contain shadow economies that are difficult to measure in traditional terms.

Such cities, too, are the site of various uncertainties about citizenship. People come to them in large numbers from impoverished rural areas. Work is often difficult to obtain and retain. The rich in these cities seek to gate as much of their lives as possible, travelling from guarded homes to darkened cars to air-conditioned offices, moving always in an envelope of privilege through the heat of public poverty and the dust of dispossession. Frequently, these are cities where crime is an integral part of municipal order and where fear of the poor is steadily increasing. And these are cities where the circulation of wealth in the form of cash is ostentatious and immense, but the sources of cash are always restricted, mysterious, or unpredictable. Put another way, even for those who have secure salaries or wages, the search for cash in order to make ends meet is endless. Thus everyday life is shot through with socially mediated chains of debt—between friends, neighbors, and coworkers—stretched across the continuum between multinational banks and other organized lenders, on the one hand, and loan sharks and thugs, on the other.

Bombay is one such city. It has an interesting history as a set of fishing villages, many named after local goddesses, linked by bridges and causeways and turned into a seat of colonial government in western India. Later, in the second half of the nineteenth century, it blossomed as a site of commercially oriented bourgeois nationalism, and, until the 1950s, it retained the ethos of a well-managed, Fordist city, dominated by commerce, trade, and manufacture, especially in the realm of textiles. Well into the 1970s, in spite of phenomenal growth in its population and increasing strain on its infrastructure, Bombay remained a civic model for India. Most people with jobs had housing; most basic services (such as gas, electricity, water, and milk) reliably reached the salaried middle classes. The laboring classes had reasonably secure occupational niches. The truly destitute were always there, but even they fit into a complex subeconomy of pavement dwelling, rag picking, petty crime, and charity.

Until about 1960, the trains bringing in white- and blue-collar workers from the outer suburbs to the commercial and political core of the city (the Fort area in South Bombay) seemed to be able to move people around with some dignity and reliability and at relatively low cost. The same was true of the city's buses, bicycles, and trams. A three-mile bus ride in 1965 Bombay cost about 15 paise (roughly the equivalent of two U.S. cents at then-current rates). People actually observed the etiquette of queuing in most public contexts, and buses always stopped at bus stops rather than fifty feet before or after them (as in most of India today).

Sometime in the 1970s all this began to change and a malignant city began to emerge from beneath the surface of the cosmopolitan ethos of the prior period. The change was not sudden, and it was not equally visible in all spheres. But it was unmistakable. Jobs became harder to get. More rural arrivals in the city found themselves economic refugees. Slums and shacks began to proliferate. The wealthy began to get nervous. The middle classes had to wrestle with overcrowded streets and buses, skyrocketing prices, and maddening traffic. The places of leisure and pleasure — the great promenades along the shore of the Arabian Sea, the wonderful parks and *maidans* (open grass fields designed for sport and pastime in the colonial era), the cinema halls and tea stalls — began to show the wear and tear of hypermodernization.

As this process began to take its toll on all but the wealthiest of the city's population, the groundwork was laid for the birth of the most markedly xenophobic regional party in India — the Shiva Sena — which formed in 1966 as a pro-native, Marathi-centered, movement for ethnic control of Bombay. Today the Shiva Sena controls the city and the state and has a significant national profile as one of the many parties that form the Sangh Parivar (or coalition of Hindu chauvinist parties). Its platform combines language chauvinism (Marathi), regional primordialism (a cult of the regional state of Maharashtra), and a commitment to a Hinduized India (Hindutva, the land of Hinduness). The Shiva Sena's appeal goes back at least to 1956, shortly before Bombay was made the capital of the new linguistic state of Maharashtra and after intense rioting in Bombay over the competing claims of Gujaratis for Bombay to be in their own new linguistic state. In retrospect, 1956 marks a moment when Bombay became Mumbai, the name now insisted on by the official machineries of the city, all of which have been influenced by the Shiva Sena. Since this period, mostly through the active and coercive tactics of the Shiva Sena and its cadres, Bombay's Marathi speakers have been urged to see the city as theirs, and every few years a new enemy is found among the city's minorities: Tamil clerks, Hindi-speaking cabdrivers, Sikh businessmen, Malayali coconut vendors — each has provided the "allogenic" flavor of the month (or year).

A high point of this ethnicization of the city was reached in late 1992 and early 1993, when riots broke out throughout India after the destruction of the Babri Masjid in Ayodhya (in the state of Uttar Pradesh in north India) by Hindu vandals on 6 December 1992. Bombay's Hindu right managed in this period to join the national frenzy of anti-Muslim violence, but this violence, too, had a Bombay flavor. In keeping with more than two decades of the Shiva Sena's peculiar mix of regional chauvinism and nationalist hysterics, Bombay's Hindus managed to violently rewrite urban space as sacred, national, and Hindu space. The decades of this gradual ethnicizing of India's most cosmopolitan city (roughly the 1970s, 1980s, and into the 1990s) were also the decades when Bombay became a site of crucial changes in trade, finance, and industrial manufacture. This essay is in part an effort to capture this more than circumstantial link. I turn now to a series of ethnographic interventions whose purpose is to think through the complex causalities that mediate between the steady dematerialization of Bombay's economy and the relentless hypermaterialization of its citizens through ethnic mobilization and public violence.

I have suggested so far that Bombay belongs to a group of cities in which global wealth and local poverty articulate a growing contradiction. But this essay is not an effort to illuminate a general class of city or a global urban dilemma. It is an effort to recognize two specificities about Bombay that mark and produce its singularity. The first is to note the peculiar ambiguities that divide and connect cash and capital (two quite distinct forms of wealth) from one another. The second is to show that this disjuncture is part of what might let us understand the peculiar ways in which cosmopolitanism in Bombay has been violently compromised in its recent history. I do this by sketching a set of circumstances to make an argument about wealth, housing, and ethnic violence, that is, at this stage, circumstantial. Future work on Mumbai may allow me to be more precise about causalities and more definite about comparisons.

CITY OF CASH

In some ways, Bombay is as familiar with the history of capital as the most important cities of Europe and the United States. Long a site of seafaring commerce, imperial trade, and colonial power, Bombay's colonial elite—Parsis, Muslims, and Hindus (as well as Baghdadi Jews, Syrian Christians, Armenians, and other exotics)—helped shape industrial capitalism in the twilight of an earlier world economy built around the Indian Ocean. That earlier world economy (made vivid in Amitav Ghosh's *In An Antique Land*) can still be glimpsed in the traffic of dhows between the west coast of India and the states of the Persian Gulf, in the escalating illegal traffic in gold along this circuit, in the movement of thousands of migrants to the Gulf states from Kerala and elsewhere on the west coast, in the post-OPEC invasion of Arab tourists into Bombay seeking the pleasures of the monsoon, cheap medical care, the flesh trade, and the cheaper-than-Harrod's prices for many delicious goods. Bombay's citizens began to complain that they could no longer afford their favorite summer fruit — the Alphonso mango — because exports to the Middle East had shrunk local supplies and pushed mango prices beyond their reach.

Partly because of its huge film industry (still among the world's largest); partly because of its powerful role in trade, banking, and commerce; and partly because of its manufacturing sector, centered on textiles but extending to metalworks, automobile factories, chemical industries, and more — for all these reasons, Bombay after World War II was quintessentially a cosmopolis of commerce. People met in and through "business" (a word taken over from English and used to indicate professions, transactions, deals, and a whole ethos of commerce), and through "business" they forged and reproduced links across neighborhoods, ethnicities, and regional origins. No ethnicity in Bombay escaped stereotyping, and all stereotyping had its portfolio of jokes. What counted was the color of money.

And money leads a complex life in today's Mumbai. It is locked, hoarded, stored, and secreted in every possible way: in jewelry, in bank accounts, in household safes and mattresses, in land and housing and dowries, in boxes and purses and coffee tins, and behind shirts and blouses. It is frequently hidden money, made visible only in the fantastic forms of cars and mansions, sharp suits and expensive restaurants, huge flats and large numbers of servants. But even more, Mumbai is a city of visible money — of *cash* — where wads, stacks, piles of rupees are openly and joyously transacted.

I remember a local street hood in my 1950s Bombay neighborhood who managed to become the local controller of the numbers racket. He wore a terylene shirt with semi-transparent pockets in which there was always the glimmer and clink of a huge number of little coins, the currency of his trade. The numbers racket then was tied to the daily close of the New York Cotton Exchange (or so I was told), and this flashy fellow never tired of strolling around with a little jingle sounding from his chest. He would laugh as he bought *pan* (betel nut rolled in betel leaf) from the local *panwalla* "on credit"; and when the panwalla would grab for his transparent pocket, he would flit away, laughing, gently guarding the coins near his heart. Coins were still tokens of wealth then. Today, he would need paper money in order not to look silly.

And it was also widely felt that cash, chance, and wealth were linked. This same numbers racketeer, who happened to come from the Tamil south of India and thus could speak to me in my native Tamil, always grabbed me on the street to ask, with a half smile, for me to give him two numbers so that he could use them to place his own bets. At issue was some notion of small children as bearers of good luck, idiot savants of probability, and I, a Brahmin child from a respectable Tamil family, probably embodied bourgeois prudence as well. This flashy hood somehow fell out with his bosses, turned into a humiliated beggar over a period of a few years, and, spurned by those very street people he had used and perhaps cheated, died broke. He surely never moved out of the magic circle of cash into the hazy world of bank accounts, insurance policies, savings, or other prudential strategies. He represented the raw end of the cash economy. Today, the numbers trade, still a major part of Bombay's street economy, has shifted away from the proto-global link to U.S. commodity markets to—so the popular narrative goes—the play of pure chance: the pulling of cards out of a pot in a rumored-to-be real location in suburban Bombay every evening, with runners fanning out in minutes to report the results. This system is simply called *matka* (pot).

Yet there is a lot of interest in today's Bombay in such things as bank accounts, shares, and insurance policies—instruments all concerned with protecting money, providing against hazard, hedging risk, and enabling enterprise. Bombay's commercial economy includes a large part of its citizenry. Even poor wage-earners strive to have small savings accounts (with passbooks) and, more fascinating, no one is immune from the seduction of "whole-life" insurance. I have sometimes suspected that all of India is divided into two groups: those who sell insurance (an extremely popular trade for the less credentialed among the literate classes) and those who buy these policies. In Bombay, the Life Insurance Corporation of India is mainly housed in a building the size of a city block—a monumental vault that contains hundreds of thousands of small policies bought and sold most often from one individual to another. Starting as early as the 1960s, ordinary middle-class housewives began to see the benefits of various forms of corporate paper, including stocks, shares, and related instruments. These were bought mostly to be held—not sold—and their circulation through various financial markets was restricted and sluggish, until the last few years, when money markets have begun to get fast, volatile, high-volume, and speculative.

But back to cash. Much of Bombay's film industry runs on cash—so-called black money. This is a huge industry that produces more than three-hundred Hindi films a year for a worldwide market and reaps huge revenues at the box office. As a shrewd local analyst said to me, there is no real film *industry* in Bombay, since there is no money that is both made and invested within the world of film. Rather, film financing is a notoriously gray area of speculation, solicitation, risk, and violence, in which the key players are men who have made killings in other markets (such as the grain trade, textiles, or other commodities). Some of them seek to keep their money out of the hands of the government, to speculate on the chance of financing a hit film and to get the bonus of hanging out with the stars as well. This sounds similar to the Hollywood pattern, but it is an entirely arbitrary cast of characters who might finance a film, so much time is spent by "producers" in trolling for businessmen with serious cash on their hands. And since these bankrolls are very large, the industry pays blockbuster prices for stars, and the entire cultural economy of the film world revolves around large cash transactions in black money. Periodically big stars or producers are raided by income tax officials, and a media bloodletting about seized assets is offered to the public, before business as usual resumes.

This sort of cash is everywhere in Bombay's "business" world, in huge rumored payments to government officials or businessmen to get things done, and equally in the daily small-scale traffic in black market film tickets, smuggled foreign goods, numbers racket payments, police protection payments, wage payments to manual labor, and so on. It has been said that the "parallel" or "black" economy in India might be half again as large as the tax-generating, official economy. In Bombay, the ratio is probably higher.

Money is still considered real — in most circles — insofar as it is readily convertible to cash. Liquidity is the dominant criterion of prosperity, for both corporations and individuals. New understandings of monetary phenomena such as credit, mortgages, and other technical or temporal "derivatives" are only now entering Bombay — and that, too, for its upper middle classes. Even the most sophisticated international and national financial strategists and czars, who are now responsible for putting Bombay permanently on the map of global investment, find it difficult to escape the sensuous appeals of cash. Wealth is understood to be an abstraction, but it is never seen as fully real in forms of paper that are not currency.

Bills and coins are not primarily what moves global wealth through Bombay's industrial houses, government offices, and corporate headquarters, but they are still the hallmarks of wealth and sociability, anchors of materiality in a world of invisible wealth. This is a shadow economy whose very shadows take on their density from the steady flow of real bills and coins through the lives of many kinds of transactors. Nor is this just money fleeing the tax collector. It is also money seeking immediate expenditure, racing from pocket to pocket without the logistical drag of conversion, storage, restriction, accounting, and dematerialization to slow the fuel of consumption. And this is true for the poor and for the rich. Whether you want 10 rupees to send to your mother in a postal money order or 4,000 rupees to have a bottle of Chivas Regal delivered to your door, cash is king. The rest is rumor.

Note that none of this has much to do with galloping inflation, any simple kind of fetishization, or the absence of immense local skills in money handling, credit, trade, and trust-based transactions that are truly global. It is entirely wrong to imagine that cash transactions imply limited trust. On the contrary, since parting with cash is decisively terminal, giving and taking cash requires larger amounts of trust than dealings in other sorts of monetary instruments. Cash handed over — even more than in other cases in the world — vanishes without a trace. The diamond industry, for example, which links cutters and polishers in coastal Surat (Gujarat) with caste-linked traders in Bombay, London, Antwerp, and beyond, is an exquisite case of global transfers that use every available form of credit (based on trust) but run on the fuel of hard cash at every critical switch point.

Nor is this corruption-at-large, where cash is best for extortion and fraud, though both exist in substantial measures. Rather, cash rules in Bombay as the mobile and material instantiation of forms of wealth that are known to be so large as to be immaterial. This is more nearly a commoditization of the fetish than a festishization of the commodity, since currency here is itself treated as powerful in the extreme. What is invisible is not the currency behind the currency at hand but the *wealth* embedded in it. So moving currency around takes materialities that are themselves deeply powerful—fetishes if you will—and puts them into generalized circulation. Cash here, to borrow Fredric Jameson's phrase from a very different context, is a central "signature of the visible."

What we know about Bombay in the nineteenth century and—more hazily—before that time, certainly suggests that cash and its circulation through various kinds of commerce was a vital ingredient of sociality. It was the guarantee of cosmopolitanism because its sources were distant and varied, its local traffic crossed ethnic and regional lines, and its presence was both entrepreneurial and civic. The vital importance of Parsi philanthropists in the civic and public life of nineteenth- and twentieth-century Bombay is one of many examples of the cosmopolitanism of its public sphere.

What then is new today about cash in the city of cash? One answer is that cash and capital have come to relate in a new and contradictory manner in Bombay since the 1970s. While cash still does its circulatory work, guaranteeing a complex web of social and economic relations and indexing the fact that the business of Bombay is "business," capital in Bombay has become more anxious. This can be seen in two areas. The first is the flight of industrial capital away from the city, which is addressed later in this essay. The second is that financial capital in Bombay operates in several disjunct registers: as the basis for multinational corporations tempted by new market seductions in India, as speculative capital operating in illegal or black markets, and as entrepreneurial energy operating in a city where it is increasingly difficult to coordinate the factors of capitalist production. Yet a large cash economy still governs Bombay. This uneasy relationship between cash and capital can be seen in a variety of arenas, but housing is perhaps the best place to follow how this disjunct relationship helps create the conditions of possibility for ethnic violence.

It is a banality to say that housing is scarce in Bombay. This is so widely known to be true that it is scarcely ever discussed abstractly. But it haunts many conversations about resources, plans, hopes, and desires among all of its citizens, ranging from those who live in multimillion-dollar penthouses to those who pay protection money for rights to six feet of sleeping space in an aqueduct. It is always at issue when jobs are mentioned (But where will you live?), when marriages are negotiated (Will you give my son part of your flat as part of his dowry?), when relatives are visited (Is cousin Ashok staying with you now?), or when neighbors speculate on the identities of people going in and out of each other's flats (Is *X* a subtenant or a relative, or both?).

To speak of spectrality in Bombay's housing scene moves us beyond the empirics of inequality into the experience of shortage, speculation, crowding, and public improvisation. It marks the space of speculation and specularities, empty scenes of dissolved industry, fantasies of urban planning, rumors of real estate transfers, consumption patterns that violate their spatial preconditions, and bodies that are their own housing. The absent, the ghostly, the speculative, the fantastic all have their part to play in the simultaneous excesses and lacks of Bombay's housing scene. It is these experienced absurdities that warrant my use of the term *spectral* in a setting where housing and its lack are grossly real. What are these swollen realities?

The social traffic on Bombay's extraordinary vital metropolitan train service is entirely premised on the fact that millions of people travel increasingly huge distances (two hours and fifty miles is not uncommon) to get from home to work and back. And many of them undergo complex transformations in transit, turning from oppressed dwellers in shantytowns, slums, and disposable housing into well-dressed clerks, nurses, postmen, bank tellers, and secretaries. Their "homes" are often unstable products—a bricolage of shoddy materials, insecure social relations, poor sanitation, and near-total lack of privacy. As they move into their places of work, this vast army of the middle and working classes usually moves into more secure spaces of recognition, comfort, and predictability than the "homes" they return to at night, even when their jobs are harsh, poorly paid, or dangerous.

And this does not speak of the truly destitute: beggars; homeless children; the maimed and the disfigured; the abandoned women with small children; and the aged who wander deaf, dumb, or blind through Bombay's streets. These are the truly "homeless," who wander like their counterparts in other world cities from Chicago and Johannesburg to Frankfurt and Bangkok. These are in some cases "street people," although this category must not be taken to be wholly generic across different cities and societies. And that is because the streets themselves constitute specific forms of public space and traffic.

Much could be said about Indian street life and the life of Bombay's streets in respect to housing. But a few observations must suffice. Bombay's "pavement dwellers" (like Calcutta's) have been made famous in both sociology and popular media. It is true that there is a vast and semiorganized part of Bombay's population that lives on pavement — or, more exactly, on particular spots, stretches, and areas that are neither building nor street. These pavement dwellers are often able to keep their personal belongings with others in shops or kiosks or even inside buildings (for some sort of price, of course). Some actually live on pavements, and others sleep in the gray spaces between buildings and streets. Yet others live on roofs and on parapets, above garages, and in a variety of interstitial spaces that are not fully controlled by either landlords or the state. As we shall see in the concluding section, "pavement dwellers" and "slum dwellers" are no longer external labels but have become self-organizing, empowering labels for large parts of the urban poor in Bombay.

The important point here is that there is a vast range of insecure housing, from a six-foot stretch of sleeping space to a poorly defined tenancy situation shared by three families "renting" one room. Pavements shade into *jopad-pattis* (complexes of shacks with few amenities), which shade into semipermanent illegal structures. Another continuum links these structures to *chawls* (tenement housing originally built for mill workers in Central Bombay) and to other forms of substandard housing. Above this tier are the owned or rented flats of the large middle class and finally the fancy flats and (in a tiny number of cases) houses owned by the rich and the super rich. These kinds of housing are not neatly segregated by neighborhood, for one simple reason: the insecurely housed poor are everywhere and are only partly concentrated in *bastis* (slums), jopad-pattis, and chawls. Almost every one of these kinds of housing for the poor, including roofs, parapets, compound walls, and overhangs, is subject to socially negotiated arrangements. Very often, control over these insecure spaces is in the hands of semi-organized crime, where rent and extortion shade into one another.

Even in the apartment buildings of the rich and upper middle class, especially in the commercial core of South Bombay and in the posh areas of Malabar Hill, Cuffe Parade, Worli, and Bandra, there is a constant pressure from the house poor. The poor set up house anywhere they can light a fire and stretch out a thin sheet to sleep on. As domestic servants, they often have small rooms in the large apartment buildings of the rich, and these servants (for whom such housing is a huge privilege) often bring friends and dependents, who spill out into the stairwells, the enclosed compounds, and the foyers. The official tenants, owners, and landlords wage a constant war against this colonization from below, but it is frequently lost because—as in all societies based on financial apartheid—one wants the poor near at hand as servants but far away as humans.

At the same time, small commercial enterprises sprout on every possible spot in every possible street, attached to buildings, to telephone poles, to electricity switching houses, or to anything else that does not move. These petty enterprises are by nature shelters, so many commercial stalls are, de facto, homes on the street for one or more people. The same is true of the kitchens of restaurants, parts of office buildings—indeed, any structure where a poor person has the smallest legitimate right to stay in or near a habitable structure, especially one that has water or a roof. Electricity and heat are rare luxuries, of course.

In this setting, for the very poor, home is anywhere you can sleep. And sleep is in fact the sole form of secure being. It is one of the few states in which—though usually entirely in public—there is respite from work, from harassment, and from eviction. Sleeping bodies are to be found everywhere in Bombay and indeed at all times. People walk over sleeping bodies as they cross streets and as they go into apartments, movie theaters, restaurants, and offices. Some of these people are sleeping in spaces to which they are legitimately connected through work or kinship. Others, as on park benches and street corners, are simply taking their housing on the hoof, renting sleep, in a manner of speaking. Public sleeping is the bottom of the hierarchy of spectral housing, housing that exists only by implication and by imputation. The sleeping body (which is almost always the laboring body or the indigent body) in its public, vulnerable, and inactive form is the most contained form of the spectral house. Public sleeping is a technique of necessity for those who can be at home only in their bodies.

Here we must resituate the sleeping, indigent, and exhausted body back in the specificities of Bombay's terrain of habitation, lest we slip into the generic sense of the urban poor as a global type. For the huge presence of the not-properly-housed is part of a bigger network of fears, pressures, and powers that surround housing for everyone in Bombay. Bombay has a shrinking but still large body of tenants, governed by an obsolete rent control act that has been the subject of enormous contention since the beginnings of economic liberalization in the early 1990s. Landlords, especially in South and Central Bombay, are at war with their "old" tenants, who pay tiny rents for real estate worth fortunes in these desirable parts of Bombay. In the mid-1990s, in spite of a dramatic drop in real estate prices across the country, prices per square foot for flats in the most desirable parts of Bombay were between 8,000 and 12,000 rupees. Thus, in U.S. dollars, a fifteen-hundred-square-foot apartment would be valued at between $300,000 and $350,000. Prices in less desirable areas were predictably lower, but consider such prices in a country where more than 40 percent of the population live below the poverty line.

Since about 1992 there have been wild swings in the real estate market, partly fuelled by financial speculators, both local and global. Since 1994 or so, when real estate prices hit their all-time high, there have been drops. There is a complex legal battle, involving the city of Bombay, the state of Maharashtra, and the union government (in Delhi) to reform the tenancy acts pertaining to urban real estate to give some semblance of market rationality to real estate prices. But the tenants are powerfully organized (though relatively small in number), and the landlords like the inflated prices when they sell but not when they have tenants who pay old rent. Homeowners, in cooperatives and condominium style arrangements, also help the upward spiral since they have to think of housing as their most precious possession, potentially convertible into all sorts of other privileges.

In this context, mythologies of housing run rife, and no one is immune from dreams and fantasies. Tenants dream of a day when they will be allowed—by state fiat—to buy their houses for, say, fifteen years' worth of the "old" rent, which, from the point of view of the market, is a pittance. Landlords dream of a free market where they can kick out their poor tenants and bring in wealthy multinationals (believed to be honest and evictable). In the meantime, they allow their buildings to decay, and the municipality has now imposed a forced program of repair and restoration since the façades of these buildings and their internal structures are falling apart, creating a few major collapses and lots of accidents. So South and Central Bombay are strewn with repair projects based on a forced levy on tenants and landlords. Meanwhile, many of these old rent buildings feel like mausoleums, as tenants die or move but hold onto their places by locking them up or having servants take care of them. The vista looking from one of these buildings to another is of ghostly spaces, shut windows, silent verandas—spaces of houses without occupants, often gazing at bodies without houses on the streets and pavements below.

The market in "rental" houses is brisk and illegal, involving vast sums of cash, transacted as so-called *pagri* (key money), which often amounts to more than the market value of the house. The pagri is paid by the new "tenant," who comes in on a much higher rent, and is shared by the landlord and the "selling" tenant who, in fact, is selling his right to stay on distorted rental terms. The landlord seeks the best black money deal, and the buyer pays whatever the market demands.

This black market in "rentals" is even more distorted because its upmarket end is occupied by the multinationals who (through their middlemen) are willing to pay huge down payments (equivalent sometimes to rent for twenty years), along with a high monthly rental. In addition, dealings with multinationals allow such transactions to be legally binding and relatively transparent, as well as, in some ways, prestigious. The growing presence of multinationals with needs for office and residential space has done much to keep real estate values very high in the best parts of Mumbai, in spite of the emergent drift to find headquarters outside the city. This upper end of the market is also the zone of indigenous speculators with large amounts of black money who wish to make big returns. Below this level is the universe of middle-class owners and renters who typically entertain dreams of the big kill when they are in a position to sell their property or their rental rights. And still further down the hierarchy are the varieties of rights in tenements, slums, pavements, and shantytowns, where the buying and selling of rights is decisively connected to local thugs, ward-level politicians, and other small-time peddlers of influence.

Knitting together this complex edifice of housing-related hysteria is a huge disorganized army of brokers and dealers, whose subculture of solidarity, networking, and jealousy is notorious and resembles that of pimp sociologies in many big cities. These are the individuals who turn up like vultures in every context of viewing or potential sale or change of tenant, ever fearful that buyer and seller will cut them out or that they will lose their share of the deal to others in their own business. These are the individuals who constitute the fiber optics of rumor, price information, news about potential legal changes, and solutions to tricky problems of money transfer, security, and value. They are the foot soldiers of the spectral housing scene, themselves fuelled not by the volume of transactions but by the ideology of the big hit, when a single big transaction will make their fortunes. They are also critical parts of the "nervous system" of spectral housing in Mumbai, in which rumors of big sales, big fees, and "good" and "bad" landlords circulate. It is also these brokers who ruthlessly boycott tenants who "show" their flats just to check the market, but always back out at the last moment, just as certain buyers always back out after everything has been settled. Given the huge cash sums, the secrecy and fear, the greed and transient trust that is required for these deals to be consummated, a reputation for being a "tease" in this market can be fatal.

Beyond all this nervous greed and fluid dealing, in which few explorations actually lead to real changes of owner or occupant, and against the steady buzz of rumors about changes in the law that governs tenancy, ownership, sales, and rights, there is a larger picture of globalization, deindustrialization, and urban planning in which the nervous system of real estate deals meets the muscularity of long-term structural developments in Mumbai's economy. This story has several interactive parts.

Over the last thirty years or so, Bombay has been steadily deindustrialized, especially in its historically most important industrial sector, the production of textiles. An industry that represented the most clear case of a workable compact between state support, entrepreneurial skill, civic amenities, and productive union organization, the mill sector of Central Bombay was for decades the heart of the modernist geography of manufacture in Bombay, with the mills and their associated tenement houses occupying an area of several square miles in Central Bombay (and smaller areas elsewhere). These were solidly working-class neighborhoods, much as in the industrial cities of Europe and the United States at the height of the industrial revolution, and, like them, tied to the imperial-global economies of the nineteenth century. Over the last two decades, several forces have played havoc with this manufacturing core of Bombay. These include the growing obsolescence of equipment, as textile industries worldwide become high tech, and the reluctance of Bombay's indigenous capitalists to negotiate with the unions, stemming from their recognition that cheaper and less militant labor was available in the smaller towns of Maharashtra state (Nasik, Pune, Aurangabad, Nagpur, and many others). This process (as in many parts of the world) has been both a cause and an effect of the move toward flexible, part-time, and insecure forms of labor, the growth in which has steadily taken the fangs out of the union movement in Bombay. In recent years, a more disturbing global pull has reinforced this local process, as major multinationals also start to flee Bombay seeking lower rents, cleaner environments, more pliant labor, and simpler logistical systems.

This trend, in which national and transnational manufacturing is steadily leaving Bombay, is counterbalanced by the continued importance of Bombay's legal, political, and fiscal infrastructure, which cannot be fully outsourced to smaller towns and industrial centers. So the new geography of post-Fordism in Bombay has a set of abandoned factories (or unprofitable ones) at its heart, a growing service economy that has locational advantages not yet matched by smaller towns, a working class that is little more than a host of fragmented unions, and a workforce that has massively shifted to the service sector — with jobs in restaurants, small offices, the film industry, domestic service, computer cafes, "consulting" outfits, street vending, and the university system. In this regard, Bombay fits the broad global profile of swollen megacities that localize national/global speculative and service-oriented interests. In a sense, these are "octroi" economies that subsist by charging fees for intermediary services in transport, licenses, and the like, as industrial work fails to sustain a substantial proletariat.

Among the families that control large parts of these manufacturing enterprises that are being moved out to smaller towns, there is an effort to repackage their motives in the idiom of real estate, arguing that, as they vacate their erstwhile mills, large spaces will be opened up for the "homeless" with appropriate compensation for themselves through the state. Here is another major spectral narrative that dominates the upper ends of the nervous system of Mumbai's housing. A new imaginary is afloat, where thousands of acres of factory space are rumored to be lying idle behind the high walls that conceal the dying factories. Workers still live in the tenements of Parel, Worli, and Nagpada, and many of them listen to the sirens of the factories as they trudge toward this dying field of industrial dreams. But many of the buildings behind these high walls are silent, and, it is rumored, deals are being brokered between these industrialists, big developers, large corporations, and criminal syndicates to harvest these imagined thousands of acres in the very industrial heart of Mumbai. Rumors abound of major presentations by big developers in corporate boardrooms, displaying these lands with aerial shots and projecting the feast of hidden real estate just beyond the famine of the streets and buildings of visible Mumbai.

Here is the great imaginary of vast lands for Mumbai's poor and homeless, which might magically yield housing for those who, for a few decades, have had to go further and further out in order to find a space to live. This is the master specter of housing in Mumbai, a fantasy of huge tracts, some with very few structures on them, ready to be transformed, at the stroke of someone's pen, into Mumbai's paradise of habitation. Thus is the logic of deindustrialization and capital flight rewritten as the story of a chimerical landscape of trees, lakes, and open air waiting to be uncovered just behind the noise of the madding crowd of Central Mumbai. Yet global finance and its indigenous counterparts — as well as a host of other enterprises that rely on trade, speculation, and investment — still find Mumbai seductive, so that the pyramid of high prices and rampant inflation is kept alive and every square foot of housing is defended as personal patrimony.

From the point of view of street life, consumption is fuelled by the explosive growth in small-scale hucksters, vendors, and retailers that have flooded Mumbai's pavements, rendering them almost impassable. Many of these vendor-dominated streets peddle items having to do with the fantasy of a global, middle-class consumer, with the truly smuggled, the imitated pirates, and the homegrown simulacrum all joyously mixed with each other: bras and juicers, lamps and window shades, underwear and cutting knives, sandwich makers and clothespins, decorative kitsch and T-shirts, women's dressing gowns and men's Levis. There seems to be no real annoyance with these vendors, despite the fact that they put pedestrians in the awkward position of either walking on the road (nudged by cars that could kill them), falling into the sewage grates just next to the curb (which are sometimes open), or picking their way through carpets of T-shirts, sneakers, and drinking glasses. In this extraordinary efflorescence of street vending, we see again that cash is king, that money moves, and that some entrepreneurial energy in the greater Mumbai area has moved massively into this retail sector, its provisioning, and its marketing. This market in petty goods, itself fuelled by Mumbai's relatively high wages, has taken the place of other forms of income (for the sellers) and of expenditure (for the buyers).

This immense landscape of street-level traffic in the petty commodities of everyday life is often physically contiguous to permanent shops and glitzy stores where the A-list versions of the street commodities are also on display. These street markets (a late industrial repetition of the sort of medieval European markets described by Fernand Braudel) allow Mumbai's poorer working people, whose money is scarce but who have bought into the object assemblages of Mumbai's cashocracy, to enter the world of consumption — a world deeply influenced by real or imagined foreign objects, their local incarnations and applications.

But there is more to this than a surfeit of cash among Bombay's middle and working classes (for the indigent can only gaze at these piles of cargo). The key elements of these street bazaars (though the full taxonomy of vendor's goods is as complex as anything Jorge Luis Borges might have imagined), are the materialities of modern domesticity: bras, children's underwear, women's dresses, men's T-shirts and jeans, perfume, cheap lipstick, talcum powder, decorative kitsch, sheets and pillows, mats and posters. The people who throng these places and succeed in negotiating their deals walk away with virtual households, or elements of the collection of goods that might constitute the bourgeois household in some abstract modernist dream. Among other things, there are hundreds of vendors in Mumbai who sell old magazines from the West, including such discrepancies as *Architectural Digest* and *Home and Garden,* ostensibly meant for the creative designer in Mumbai but actually looked at by humbler consumers living in one- or two-room shacks.

These public dramas of consumption revolving around the accoutrements of domesticity constitute an investment in the equipping of houses that may be small and overcrowded, where individual space and rights may be highly restricted, and where much in the way of modern amenities may be limited or absent. These humble objects of domestic life are thus proleptic tools of a domesticity without houses, houseless domesticity. In the purchase and assemblage of these objects, which imply a domestic plenitude that is surely exaggerated, Bombay's working poor and nonprofessional service classes produce their own spectral domesticity, which in its sensuous, cash-based, pleasurable social reality recognizes the shrinking horizon of the actual houses in which these objects might have a predictable life. Of course, all modern shopping (in Mumbai and beyond) has the anticipatory, the imagined, the auratic, and the possessive about its ethos. But street shopping in Mumbai, like public sleeping, is a form of claim to housing that no one can contest or subvert in the city of cash. This is where the specters of eviction meet the agencies of consumption.

We now turn to an explicit effort to engage the slippage between Bombay and Mumbai, in this essay and in the social usages of the city. If Bombay was a historical space of commerce and cosmopolitanism, through what project did Bombay become Mumbai, so that, today, all official dealings, from control-tower traffic at Sahar airport to addresses on letters mailed to the city, must refer to Mumbai? What killed Bombay?

In the section that follows, I try to answer this question by linking the problems of scarcity and spectrality in the housing market to another kind of shrinkage, which is produced by the repositioning of Bombay's streets, shops, and homes as a sacred national space, as an urban rendition of a Hindu national geography. As struggles over the space of housing, vending, and sleeping gradually intensified, so did the sense of Bombay as a site for traffic across ethnic boundaries become reduced. The explosive violence of 1992–93 translated the problem of scarce space into the imaginary of cleansed space, a space without Muslim bodies. In and through the violence of these riots, an urban nightmare was rescripted as a national dream.

In 1996 the Shiva Sena proclaimed that Bombay would henceforth be only known as Mumbai. Even prior to this date, Mumbai had been the name for the city preferred by many of the Marathi-speaking majority, and especially by those who identify with the Shiva Sena. In one sense, the decision to officialize the name "Mumbai" is part of a widespread Indian pattern of replacing names associated with colonial rule with names associated with local, national, and regional heroes. It is an indigenizing toponymic strategy worldwide in scope.

In the case of Bombay, the move looks backward and forward simultaneously. Looking backward, it imagines the deity Mumba Devi (a goddess of one of the shrines that was vital to the fishing islands that later became Bombay). It evokes the fishing folk of these islands, and, because it is the name that was always used by Marathi speakers, it privileges their everyday usage over those of many other vernacular renditions of the name (such as the "Bambai" favored by Hindi speakers and the "Bambaai" of Tamil speakers). Of course, it gains respectability as an erasure of the Anglophone name, Bombay, and thus carries the surface respectability of popular nationalism after 1947. But its subtext looks to the future, to a counter-Bombay or anti-Bombay, as imagined by the Shiva Sena, whose political fortunes in the city wax and wane (as of this writing) but whose hold on urban life no one has dared to write off.

This is a future in which Marathi and Maharashtrian heroes and practices dominate urban culture, and this purified regional city joins a renascent "Hindu" India; it is a future that envisions Mumbai as a point of translation and mediation between a renascent Maharashtra and a re-Hinduized India. This Mumbai of the future is sacred national space, ethnically pure but globally competitive. Balasaheb Thackeray, the vitriolic head of the Shiva Sena, was happy to welcome Michael Jackson to his home a few years ago and had no trouble facilitating a major deal for Enron, a Texas-based multinational that wanted a major set of concessions for a new energy enterprise in Maharashtra. So the transformation of Bombay into Mumbai is part of a contradictory utopia in which an ethnically cleansed city is still the gateway to the world.

When the Babri Masjid in Ayodhya was destroyed by Hindu vandals on 6 December 1992, a watershed was marked in the history of secularism in India, in the context of a big effort to Hinduize India and to link local ethnopolitics and national xenophobia. The events of December 1992 were themselves the product of an immensely complex process by which the major political parties of the Hindu right, most notably the Bharatiya Janata Party (BJP), managed to turn a series of recent political changes in the Hindi-speaking northern part of India to their advantage. These changes—most important among them the new political power of lower castes—were often results of violent confrontations between lower and upper castes over land tenure, government job quotas, and legal rights. In the late 1980s, building on a century of localized movements toward Hindu nationalism and nationalized Hinduism, the BJP and its allies had mobilized hitherto fragmented parties and movements under the single banner of Hindutva (Hinduness). Seizing on the failures of other national parties, they managed to launch a full-scale frontal attack on the ideals of secularism and interreligious harmony enshrined in the constitution and to convince Hindus of all classes that their salvation lay in Hinduizing the state.

In the process, they focused particularly on a series of neoreligious strategies and practices, drawing on existing cultural repertoires, to construct the imaginary of a Hindu soil, a Hindu history, and Hindu sacred places that had been corrupted and obscured by many outside forces, none worse than the forces of Islam. Anti-Muslim sentiments, available in various earlier discourses and movements, were transformed into what Romila Thapar called "syndicated" Hinduism, and one form of this politicized Hinduism took as its major program the liberation of Hindu temples from what were argued to be their illegitimate Muslim superstructures. The Babri Masjid became the symbolic epicenter of this more general campaign to cleanse Hindu space and nationalize the polity through a politics of archaeology, historical revisionism, and vandalism. The story of the events surrounding the destruction of the Babri Masjid have been well told elsewhere, and many scholars have placed these events in the deep history of Hindu-Muslim relations on the subcontinent.

There were riots after 6 December 1992 throughout India, substantially amounting to a national pogrom against Muslims (though there was some Muslim violence against agents and sites of state power). But this was the first time there was a massive, nationwide campaign of violence against Muslims in which soil, space, and site came together in a politics of national sovereignty and integrity. Not only were Muslims seen as traitors (Pakistanis in disguise), but also their sacred sites were portrayed as a treacherous geography of vandalism and desecration, calculated to bury Hindu national geography at both its centers and its margins. In a sense, the political geography of sovereignty, focused on border wars with Pakistan, was brought into the same emotional space as the political geography of cultural purity, focused on the deep archaeology of religious monuments.

As it was the home of the Shiva Sena, Mumbai was drawn into this argument about national geography as Hindu geography in December 1992 in a special way. The story of the growth of the Shiva Sena from the 1960s to the present has been well told and analyzed elsewhere, so just a few points need be made here. The party has succeeded in identifying with the interests of Mumbai's growing Marathi-speaking lumpen proletariat while also actively destroying its left (communist) union culture. After starting mainly as a group of urban thugs, the Shiva Sena has managed to become a regional and national political force. It has hitched its regional nationalism (with deep roots in Maharashtra's ethnohistory and vernacular self-consciousness) to a broader national politics of Hindutva. It has created a relatively seamless link between its nativist, pro-Maharashtrian message and a national politics of confrontation with Pakistan. It has sutured a specific form of regional chauvinism with a national message about Hindu power through the deployment of the figure of the Muslim as the archetype of the invader, the stranger, and the traitor. The Shiva Sena has achieved this suture by a remarkably patient and powerful media campaign of hate, rumor, and mobilization, notably in the party newspaper *Saamna*, which has been the favorite reading of Mumbai's policemen for at least two decades. The Shiva Sena has done all this by systematically gutting the apparatus of city government, by criminalizing city politics at every level, and by working hand-in-glove with organized crime in many areas, notably in real estate, which brings us back to space and its politics in Mumbai.

Here we need to note certain important facts. According to several analysts, about 50 percent of Mumbai's 12 million citizens live in slums or other degraded forms of housing. Another 10 percent are estimated to be pavement dwellers. This amounts to more than 5 million people living in degraded (and degrading) forms of housing. Yet, according to one recent estimate, slum dwellers occupy only about 8 percent of the city's land, which totals about 43,000 hectares. The rest of the city's land is either industrial land, middle- and high-income housing, or vacant land in the control of the city, the state, or private commercial interests. Bottom line: 5 million poor people live in 8 percent of the land area of a city no bigger than Manhattan and its near boroughs. As some have observed, it is amazing that in these conditions of unbelievable crowding, lack of amenities, and outright struggle for daily survival, Mumbai's poor have not exploded more often.

But they did explode in the riots of 1992–93. During the several weeks of intense rioting after 6 December, there is no doubt that the worst damage was done among those who lived in the most crowded, unredeemable slums. The worst zones of violence were among the very poorest, in areas such as Behrampada, where Hindu and Muslim "toilers," in Sandeep Pendse's powerful usage, were pitted against each other by neighborhood thugs, Shiva Sena bosses, and indifferent police. Though the Indian Army was called in to impose order, the fabric of social relations among Mumbai's poor was deeply damaged by repeated episodes of arson, rape, murder, property damage, and eviction.

In these few weeks of December 1992 and January 1993, there was also a frenzied mobilization by the Shiva Sena of its sympathizers to create public terror and to confront Muslims with the message that there was no public space for them and that they would be hunted down and killed or evicted from their homes wherever possible. There was a marked increase in ethnocidal uses of a new ritual form—the *maha arati*—which was a kind of guerrilla form of public worship organized by Hindu groups to push Muslims out of streets and public spaces in areas where the two groups lived cheek by jowl.[1] These ritual acts of ethnic warfare were mostly conducted in the middle-class rental zones of Central Mumbai; but in the slums and jopad-pattis of the north and west there was firebombing and arson, street murders and beatings, and the main victims were the poorest of the Muslim poor—rag pickers, abattoir workers, manual laborers, indigents. Across the city, the Shiva Sena mobilized a national geography, spreading the rumor that the Pakistani navy was about to attack Mumbai from its shoreline on the Arabian Sea, and anxious Hindu residents turned searchlights onto the ocean to spot Pakistani warships.

Meanwhile, inside the city, Muslims were cornered in slums and middle-class areas, in their own crowded spaces, hunted down with lists of names in the hands of organized mobs, and Muslim businesses and properties were relentlessly put to the torch. There was a strange point of conjuncture between these violent efforts to create Hindu public spheres and spaces, to depopulate Muslim flats and neighborhoods, and to destroy Muslim bodies and properties, and an ongoing form of civic violence directed against Mumbai's street dwellers, which I discuss below.

In the weeks preceding 6 December, there had been a renewed effort by the Municipal Corporation to destroy the structures built by unlicensed street vendors and to destroy unauthorized residential dwellings that had sprouted throughout Mumbai. Here, municipal zeal (personified by G. Khairnar, an overzealous city official who was strangely not a Shiva Sena client) joined with political propaganda to create a tinderbox in the heavily Muslim areas of Central Bombay from Bhendi Bazaar to Byculla, especially along Mohammed Ali Road, the great Muslim thoroughfare of contemporary Mumbai. In this neighborhood, Muslim gangsters had worked with the connivance of shady financiers and corrupt city officials to build many unauthorized residential structures (through intimidation, forgery, and other subversions of the law) while terrorizing any potential resistors with armed force.

The Bombay municipality has had a tradition of chasing after street vendors for at least three decades in a constant public battle of cat-and-mouse that the vendors usually won. There was also a long and dark history of efforts to tear down slum dwellings, as in other cities in India. But in the late 1980s, this battle was intensified, as the nexus between real estate speculators, organized crime, and corrupt officialdom reached new heights. Although this nexus involved illegal housing and unlicensed vending throughout Mumbai, Khairnar's muncipal gendarmerie just happened to focus their civic violence on an area dominated by the Muslim underworld. Thus, tragically, just before the Babri Masjid was destroyed in Ayodhya, Bombay's Muslim underworld was in a rage, and Mumbai's Muslim residents were convinced that there was, indeed, a civic effort to dismantle their dwellings and vending stalls. This is where the battle for space—a heated triangle involving organized mafias, corrupt local officials and politicians, and a completely predatory class of real estate speculators—met the radical politics of Hindutva in December 1992.

The story of this encounter is sufficiently complex as to require detailed treatment elsewhere. But the big picture is relevant here. The geography of violence in Mumbai during December 1992 and January 1993 is overwhelmingly coincidental with the geography of urban crowding, street commerce, and housing nightmares in Mumbai. In this violence, two grisly specters came to haunt and animate one another in the world of Mumbai's poorest citizens, as well as its working classes: the specter of a zero-sum battle for residential space and street commerce, figured as a struggle between civic discipline and organized crime; and the specter of Mumbai's Muslims as a fifth column from Pakistan, ready to subvert Mumbai's sacred geography.

In this macabre conjuncture, the most horrendously poor, crowded, and degraded areas of the city were turned into battlegrounds of the poor against the poor, with the figure of the Muslim providing the link between scarce housing, illegal commerce, and national geography writ urban. In 1992–93, in a word, spectral housing met ethnic fear, and the Muslim body was the site of this terrifying negotiation. Of course, the middle and upper classes suffered as well, largely through the stoppage of commerce, movement, and production. But the overwhelming burden of violence—both its perpetration and its suffering—was borne by the bodies of Mumbai's toilers, and the massive sense of having no place in Mumbai (reinscribed as India) was overwhelmingly borne by its Muslims.

Here we must return to consider the links between spectral housing, the decosmopolitanizing of Bombay, and the ethnic violence of 1992 and 1993. The deliberate effort to terrorize Bombay's Muslims, to attack their vending stalls, to burn their shops and homes, to Hinduize their public spaces through violent ritual innovations, and to burn and maim their bodies can hardly be seen as a public policy solution to Bombay's housing problems. Neither can it be laid at the door of a single agency or power, even one so powerful and central to these events as the Shiva Sena. But it does seem plausible to suggest that in a city where daily sociality involves the negotiations of immense spatial stress, the many spectralities that surround housing (from indigent bodies to fantasy housing schemes and empty flats) can create the conditions for a violent reinscription of public space as Hindu space. In a city of 12 million persons, many occupying no more space than their bodies, it is not hard to see that imagining a city without Muslims, a sacred and Hindu city, free of the traffic of cash and the promiscuity of "business" (think of all the burnt Muslim shops of 1992 and 1993), could appear –briefly— to be a bizarre utopia of urban renewal. This monstrous utopia cannot be imagined without the spectral economies of Bombay's housing. But it also needed a political vision—the Shiva Sena's vision of a Hindu Mumbai—to move it toward fire and death.

The rest was contingency—or conjuncture.

ARGUMENTS FOR THE REAL

This is a grim story about one of the world's most dramatic scenes of urban inequality and spectral citizenship. But specters and utopias— as practices of the imagination—occupy the same moral terrain. And Bombay does not lack for a complex politics of the real. Throughout the twentieth century, and even in the nineteenth century, Bombay had powerful civic traditions of philanthropy, social work, political activism, and social justice. These traditions have stayed powerful in the last three decades of the twentieth century and at the beginning of the twenty-first century, where globalization, deindustrialization, and ethno-urbanism have become linked forces. Both before and after the 1992–93 riots, there have been extraordinary displays of courage and critical imagination in Mumbai. These have come from neighborhood groups (*mohulla* committees) committed to squelching rumors and defusing Hindu-Muslim tensions; from housing activists; from lawyers and social workers; and from journalists, architects, and trade union activists. All of these individuals and groups have held up powerful images of a cosmopolitan, secular, multicultural Bombay, and a Mumbai whose 43,000 hectares could be reorganized to accommodate its 5 million poorly housed citizens.

These activist organizations—among them some of the most creative and brilliant pro-poor and housing-related nongovernmental organizations (NGOs)—are making their own arguments about the political real in Mumbai. Their story, which, among other things, has forced the publication of an extraordinary judicial report on the 1992–93 riots (which the Shiva Sena government tried mightily to bury), will be fully told elsewhere. This story is also linked to the extraordinary courage of ordinary people in Mumbai, and often among the poorest of the poor, to shelter their friends and neighbors from ethnocidal mob violence. These utopian visions and critical practices are resolutely modernist in their visions of equity, justice, and cultural cosmopolitanism. In the spectral world that I have described, they are not naive or nostalgic. They are part of the ongoing struggle for that space where Mumbai's Real meets the real Bombay.

NOTES

A large scholarly literature constitutes the foundation for this ethnographic essay. In lieu of detailed citations, I offer some indications of a few major debts and scholarly engagements. This essay would have been unthinkable without the major two-volume collection of essays on Bombay edited by Sujata Patel and Alice Thorner —*Bombay: Mosaic of Modern Culture* and *Bombay: Metaphor for Modern India* (Bombay: Oxford University Press, 1995). See also *Bombay: The Cities Within* by Sharada Dwivedi and Rahul Mehrotra (Bombay: India Book House, 1995) and *Damning Verdict: Report of the Srikrishna Commission* (Mumbai: Sabrang Communications and Publishing, n.d.). My sense of the predicament of megacities in Asia and elsewhere has been deeply informed by the work of my friend and colleague Saskia Sassen. My understanding of Bombay's special housing dilemmas has been enriched by a series of case studies and reports produced by A. Jockin, Sundar Burra, Celine D'Cruz, and Sheela Patel. My debts in regard to the analysis of Hindu nationalism in Bombay are too many to list, but special mention must be made of the ongoing work of Thomas Blom Hansen—see, for instance, *The Saffron Wave: Democracy and Hindu Nationalism in Modern India* (Princeton, N.J.: Princeton University Press, 1999)— Ranjit Hoskote, and Kalpana Sharma. See also Romila Thapar, "Syndicated Hinduism" in *Hinduism Reconsidered,* edited by Günther-Dietz Sontheimer and Hermann Kulke (New Delhi: Manohar Publications, 1989), and Sandeep Pendse, "Toil, Sweat, and the City" in Patel and Thorner's *Bombay: Metaphor for Modern India.* My recourse to the trope of the *spectral* is on an ongoing engagement with the work of Jacques Derrida, Fredric Jameson, and James Siegel, though they may well not recognize themselves in this text.

This essay is dedicated to my friends in the Housing Alliance (SPARC, NSDF, and Mahila Milan) in Mumbai who are producing their own radical projects for housing in Bombay, based on situated secularism, grassroots energy, gender equity, and deep democracy. I must also thank my hosts and audiences for helpful comments and reactions at the conference on "Cosmopolitanism," University of Chicago (May 1999), and the conference on "Urban Antagonisms" organized by the World Academy for Local Government and Democracy (WALD) and held in Istanbul (also in May 1999). At the University of Chicago, I owe special thanks to numerous friends and colleagues whose comments have helped me strengthen this essay, though not as much as they might have wished: Homi Bhabha, Carol A. Breckenridge, Dipesh Chakrabarty, Jean Comaroff, John Comaroff, Claudio Lomnitz, Sheldon Pollock, Elizabeth Povinelli, Michel-Rolph Trouillot, Katie Trumpener, and Candace Vogler all provided valuable readings in the editorial context of the special issue of *Public Culture* 12(3) from which this essay originally came.

1. The maha arati is widely conceded to be a ritual innovation by the Shiva Sena, first developed in December 1992, in which a domestic Hindu ritual, traditionally conducted indoors, was converted into a large-scale, public devotional offering to

various Hindu gods and goddesses. It is marked by the centrality of sacred fires (as in most domestic worship among Hindus), and, in this new format, was also accompanied by elaborate and incendiary anti-Muslim speeches and exhortations by pro-Hindu politicians and public figures. By various reliable estimates, it appears that several hundred of these inciting rituals were staged in the period between 6 December 1992 and 15 January 1993 in major streets, intersections, parks, and neighborhoods in Bombay. The *Report of the Srikrishna Commission* notes the high correlation between these public rituals and the frenzied destruction of Muslim lives and property when the crowds dispersed after these high-intensity politico-ritual spectacles. A full account of this major new cultural form is yet to appear in print.

Universalism and Belonging in the Logic of Capital

Dipesh Chakrabarty

The shadow of cultural diversity—the diverse ways in which we "world" this earth—now falls across all universalistic assumptions about history or human nature that often underlie propositions of modern political philosophies. Their inherent Eurocentrism is what makes these assumptions suspect in the eyes of practitioners of the human sciences today. But neither cultural nor historical relativism is seen as an answer—and rightly so, for an absolutist relativism can easily be shown to be self-contradictory. Understandably, therefore, many postcolonial debates on political philosophies such as Marxism or liberalism often try to work out a middle ground between the two options of universalism and relativism. Critical energies are focused on questions such as how and where one locates this middle ground, how one delineates its contours, ways one can get out of the universalism/relativism binary, and so on and so forth. But, as discussions of human rights increasingly make clear, universalistic assumptions are not easily given up, and the tension between universalism and historical difference is not easily dismissed. The struggle to find a middle ground remains. "Strategic essentialism" (associated with Gayatri Spivak [1988]), "hybridity" (associated with Homi Bhabha [1994]), "cosmopolitanism," and the like are expressions that remind us of particular strategies formulated in the course of this struggle.

The purpose of this essay is to explore the tension between universalism and historical difference in the logic of Marx's category "capital." I do not need to demonstrate the relevance of this category. True, it belongs to the nineteenth century, but suffice it to say that, to the extent that we think of globalization as a process of globalization of capital, the category remains of interest. However, there is a need to rethink the category, and especially so in a world where Marx's key assumption that capital, by its own logic, would call forth its own dissolution through the agency of labor, has not been borne out. How do we think about an alternative to capital in such a context? Clearly, one cannot any longer think of the "beyond of capital" as something that is totally opposed to capital (such as "socialism" or "communism"). Does it even make sense to think of such a "beyond" when everything in the world seems to be coming more and more under the sway of capital itself? I read some selected texts by Marx to revisit this question. How does capital, a universal category by definition, negotiate historical difference in Marx's exposition? Does Marx's account of this negotiation carry any hints that can help us think about the question of human belonging in a globe increasingly made one by the technologies of capital?

To answer these questions, I pursue two of Marx's ideas that are inseparable from his critique of capital: his views on abstract labor and on the relationship between capital and history. Marx's philosophical category capital is planetary (or global) in its historical aspiration and universal in its constitution. Its categorical structure, at least in Marx's own elaboration, is predicated on Enlightenment ideas of juridical equality and abstract political rights of citizenship.[1] Labor that is juridically and politically free—and yet socially unfree—is a concept embedded in Marx's category of "abstract labor." Abstract labor combines in itself Enlightenment themes of juridical freedom (rights, citizenship) and the concept of the universal and abstract human being who is the subject of this freedom. More important, it is also a concept central to Marx's explanation of why capital, in fulfilling itself in history, necessarily creates the ground for its own dissolution. Examining the idea of abstract labor then enables us to see what may be politically and intellectually at stake today—for postcolonial scholars who do not ignore Marx's legacy—in the universalist humanism of the Enlightenment.

The idea of abstract labor also leads us to the question of how the logic of capital relates to the issue of historical difference. The idea of "history," as all students of Marx would know, was central to Marx's philosophical critique of capital. Abstract labor gave Marx a way of explaining how the capitalist mode of production managed to extract, out of peoples and histories that were all different, a homogeneous and common unit for measuring human activity. Abstract labor may thus be read as an account of how the logic of capital sublates into itself the differences of history. In the concluding part of the essay, however, I try to develop a distinction Marx made between two kinds of histories, which I call History 1 and History 2, respectively: pasts "posited by capital" itself and pasts that do not belong to capital's "life-process." I explore this distinction to show how Marx's own thoughts may be made to resist an idea central to Marx's critique of capital: that the logic of capital sublates differences into itself.

CAPITAL, ABSTRACT LABOR, AND THE SUBLATION OF DIFFERENCE

Fundamental to Marx's discussion of capital is the idea of the commodity. And fundamental to the conception of the commodity is the question of difference. Commodity exchange is about exchanging things that are different in their histories, material properties, and uses. Yet the commodity form, intrinsically, is supposed to make differences — however material they may be — immaterial for the purpose of exchange. The commodity form does not as such negate difference but holds it in suspension so that we can exchange things as different from one another as beds and houses. But how could that happen? How could things that apparently had nothing in common come to form items in a series of capitalist exchanges, a series that Marx would think of as continuous and infinite?

Readers will remember Marx's argument with Aristotle on this point. Aristotle, in the course of his deliberations in *Nichomachean Ethics* on such issues as justice, equality, and proportionality, focused on the problem of exchange. Exchange, he argued, was central to the formation of a community. But a community was always made up of people who were "different and unequal." On the ground, there were only infinite incommensurabilities. Every individual was different. For exchange to act as the basis of community, there had to be a way of finding a common measure so that what was not equal could be equalized. Aristotle (1981: 125–27) underscores this imperative: "They must be equalized [with respect to a measure]; and everything that enters into an exchange must somehow be comparable." Without this measure of equivalence that allowed for comparison, there could not be any exchange and hence no community.

Aristotle, as is well known, solved this problem by bringing the idea of "convention" or law into the picture. For him, money represented such a convention: "It is for this purpose [of exchanging dissimilar goods] that money has been introduced: it becomes, as it were, a middle term . . . it tells us how many shoes are equal to a house" (1981: 125). Money, according to Aristotle, represented some kind of a general agreement, a convention. A convention was ultimately arbitrary, it was held in place by the sheer force of law that simply reflected the will of the community. Aristotle introduced into his discussion the note of a radical political will that, as Cornelius Castoriadis comments, is absent from the text of *Capital*.[2] In Aristotle's words: "Money has by general agreement come to represent need. That is why it has the name of 'currency'; it exists by current convention and not by nature, and it is in our power to change and invalidate it" (1981: 126). The translator of Aristotle points out that "the Greek word for 'money,' 'coin,' 'currency' (*nomisma*) comes from the same root as *nomos,* 'law,' 'convention' " (Aristotle 1981: 126, n. 35).

Marx begins *Capital* by critiquing Aristotle. For Aristotle, what brought shoes and houses into a relationship of exchange was a mere "convention"—"a makeshift for practical purposes," as Marx translated it. Yet it was not satisfactory for Marx to think that the term that mediated differences among commodities could be simply a convention, that is, an arbitrary expression of political will. Referring to Aristotle's argument that there could not be a "homogeneous element, i.e., the common substance" between the bed (Marx's copy of Aristotle seems to have used the example of the bed and not that of the shoe!) and the house, Marx asked: "But why not? Towards the bed the house represents something equal, in so far as it represents what is really equal, both in the bed and the house. And that is—human labour" (1990: 151).

This human labor, the "common substance" mediating differences, was Marx's concept of abstract labor, which he described as "the secret of the expression of value." It was only in a society in which bourgeois values had acquired a hegemonic status that this "secret" could be unveiled. It "could not be deciphered" wrote Marx, "until the concept of human equality had already acquired the permanence of a fixed popular opinion." This, in turn, was possible "only in a society where the commodity-form [was] the universal form of the product of labour" and where therefore "the dominant social relation [was] the relation between men as the possessors of commodities." The slave-holding nature of ancient Greek society was what, according to Marx, occluded Aristotle's analytical vision. And by the same logic, the generalization of contractual equality under bourgeois hegemony created the historical conditions for the birth of Marx's insights (Marx 1990: 152). The idea of abstract labor was thus a particular instance of the idea of the abstract human — the bearer of rights, for example — popularized by Enlightenment philosophers.

This common measure of human activity, abstract labor, is what Marx opposes to the idea of real or concrete labor (which is what any specific form of labor is). Simply put, abstract labor refers to an "indifference to any specific kind of labour." By itself, this does not make for capitalism. A "barbarian" society — Marx's expression! — may be so marked by the absence of a developed division of labor that its members "are fit by nature to do anything" (Marx 1973: 105). By Marx's argument it was perfectly conceivable that such a society would have abstract labor though its members would not be able to theorize it. Such theorizing would be possible only in the capitalist mode of production in which the very activity of abstracting became the most common strand of all or most other kinds of labor.

What indeed was abstract labor? Sometimes Marx would write as though abstract labor was pure physiological expenditure of energy. For example: "If we leave aside the determinate quality of productive activity, and therefore the useful character of the labour, what remains is its quality of being an expenditure of human labour-power. Tailoring and weaving, although they are qualitatively different productive activities, are both a productive expenditure of human brains, muscles, nerves, hands, etc." (Marx 1990: 134). Or this: "On the other hand, all labour is an expenditure of human labour-power, in the physiological sense, and it is in this quality of being equal, or abstract, human labour that it forms the value of commodities" (Marx 1990: 137). But students of Marx from different periods and as different from one another as Isaak Il'ich Rubin, Cornelius Castoriadis, Jon Elster, and Moishe Postone have shown that to conceive of abstract labor as a thing-like substance, as a Cartesian *res extensa,* to reduce it to "nervous and muscular energy," is either to misread Marx (as Rubin [1975: 131–38] and Postone [1993: 144–46] argue) or to repeat a mistake of Marx's thoughts (as Castoriadis [1984: 307–8] and Elster [1995: 68] put it). Marx does speak of abstract labor as a "social substance" possessing "objectivity," but he immediately qualifies this objectivity as spectral, "phantom-like" rather than "thing-like": "Let us now look at the products of [abstract] labour. There is nothing left of them in each case but the same *phantom-like objectivity:* they are merely congealed quantities of homogenous human labour, i.e., of human labour-power expended without regard to the form of its expenditure. . . . As crystals of this social substance, which is common to them all, they are values — commodity values" (Marx 1990: 128; emphasis added). Or as he explains elsewhere in *Capital:* "Not an atom of matter enters into the objectivity of commodity as values; in this it is the direct opposite of the coarsely sensuous objectivity of commodities as physical objects," and also, "commodities possess an objective character as values only in so far as they are all expressions of an identical social substance, human labour, . . . their objective character as value is purely social" (Marx 1990: 138–39).

How then is abstract labor to be conceptualized? If we do not share Marx's assumption that the exchange of commodities in capitalism necessarily forms a continuous and infinite series, then abstract labor is perhaps best understood as a performative, practical category. To organize life under the sign of capital is to act *as if* labor could indeed be abstracted from all the social tissues in which it is always already embedded and which make any particular labor — even the labor of abstracting — perceptibly concrete. Marx's "barbarians" had abstract labor. Anybody in that society could take up any kind of activity. But their "indifference to specific labour" would not be as visible to an analyst as in a capitalist society, because in the case of these hypothetical barbarians, this indifference itself would not be universally performed as a separate, specialized kind of labor. That is to say, the very concrete labor of abstracting would not be separately observable as a general feature of the many different kinds of specific labor that society undertook. In a capitalist society, by contrast, the particular work of abstracting would itself become an element of most or all other kinds of concrete labor and would thus be more visible to an observer. As Marx (1973: 104) put it: "As a rule, most general abstractions arise only in the midst of the richest possible concrete development, where one thing appears as common to many, to all. Then it ceases to be thinkable in a particular form alone." "Such a state of affairs," writes Marx (104–5), "is at its most developed in the most modern form of existence of bourgeois society — in the United States. Here, then, for the first time, the point of departure of modern economics, namely the abstraction of the category 'labour,' 'labour as such,' labour pure and simple, becomes true in practice." Notice Marx's expression "the abstraction . . . becomes true in practice." Marx could not have written a clearer statement indicating that abstract labor was not a thing-like entity, not physiological labor, not a calculable sum of muscular and nervous energy. It referred to a practice, an activity, a concrete performance of the work of abstraction, similar to what one does in the analytical strategies of economics when one speaks of an abstract category called "labor."

Sometimes Marx writes as if abstract labor was what one obtained after going through a conscious and intentional process—much like in certain procedures of mathematics—of mentally stripping commodities of their material properties:

> *If . . . we disregard* the use-value of commodities, only one property remains, that of products of labour. . . . *If we make abstraction* from its use-value, we also abstract from the material constituents and forms which make it a use-value. It is no longer a table, a house, a piece of yarn or any other useful thing. All its sensuous characteristics are extinguished. . . . With the disappearance of the useful character of the products of labour, the useful character of the kinds of labour embodied in them also disappears; this in turn entails the disappearance of the different concrete forms of labour. *They can no longer be distinguished,* but are all together reduced to the same kind of labour, human labour in the abstract. (Marx 1990: 128; emphasis added)

Expressions like "if we disregard," "if we abstract," and "they can no longer be distinguished" may give the impression that Marx is writing here of a human subject who disregards, abstracts, or distinguishes. But Marx's discussion of factory discipline makes it clear that he does not visualize the abstraction of labor inherent in the process of exchange of commodities as a large-scale mental operation. Abstraction happens in and through practice. It precedes one's conscious recognition of its existence. As Marx (1990: 166–67) put it: "Men do not . . . bring the products of their labour into relation with each other as values because they see these objects merely as the material integuments of homogeneous human labour. The reverse is true: by equating their different products to each other in exchange as values, they equate their different kinds of labour as human labour. They do this without being aware of it." Marx's logic here, as in many other places in his writings, is retrospective.[3]

Marx agreed more with Aristotle than he acknowledged—abstract/abstracting labor, one could indeed say, was a capitalist "convention" so that the middle term in exchange remains a matter of convention after all. But Marx's position that the convention was not the result of prior conscious decision to abstract would not have allowed Aristotle's voluntarism in regard to this convention ("it is in our power to change and invalidate").[4] Abstract labor is what Marx decodes to be a key to the hermeneutic grid through which capital requires us to read the world.

Disciplinary processes are what make the performance of abstraction—the labor of abstracting—visible (to Marx) as a constitutive feature of the capitalist mode of production. The typical division of labor in a capitalist factory, the codes of factory regulation, the relationship between the machinery and men, state legislation guiding the organization of factory lives, the foreman's work—all these make up what Marx calls discipline. The division of labor in the factory is such, he writes (1990: 465), that it "creates a continuity, a uniformity, a regularity, an order, and even an intensity of labour quite different from that found in an independent handicraft." In sentences that anticipate a basic theme of Michel Foucault's *Discipline and Punish* by about a hundred years, he describes how the "overseer's book of penalties replaces the slave-driver's lash [in capitalist management]." "All punishments," Marx writes (1990: 550), "naturally resolve themselves into fines and deductions from wages."

Factory legislation also participates in this performance of disciplinary abstraction. Marx argues (1990: 635) that such legislation "destroys both the ancient and transitional forms behind which the domination of capital is still partially hidden . . . in each individual workshop it enforces uniformity, regularity, order and economy" and thus contributes to sustaining the assumption that human activity is indeed measurable on a homogeneous scale. But it is in the way the law—and through the law, the state and the capitalist classes—imagines laborers through biological/physiological categories such as adults, adult males, women, and children that the work of the reductive abstraction of labor from all its attendant social integuments is performed. This mode of imagination, Marx further shows us, is also what structures from within the process of production. It is dyed into capital's own vision of the worker's relationship with the machine.

In the first volume of *Capital*, Marx has recourse to the rhetorical ploy of staging what he calls the "voice" of the worker in order to bring out the character of his category labor. (To forestall misunderstanding, I should reiterate that Marx is writing about the relationship between categories and not between empirical people.) This voice shows how abstracted the category "worker" or "labor" is from the social and psychic processes we commonsensically associate with "the everyday." For example, this voice reduces age, childhood, health, and strength to biological or natural physiological statements, separate from the diverse and historically specific experiences of ageing, of being a child, of being healthy, and so on. "Apart from the natural deterioration through age, etc.," Marx's category worker says to the capitalist in a voice that is introspective as well, "I must be able to work tomorrow with the same normal amount of strength, health, and freshness as today." This abstraction means that "sentiments" are no part of this imaginary dialogue between the abstracted laborer and the capitalist who is also a figure of abstraction. The voice of the worker says: "I . . . demand a working day of normal length . . . without any appeal to your heart, for in money matters sentiment is out of place. You may be a model citizen, perhaps a member of the R.S.P.C.A., and you may be in the odour of sanctity as well; but the thing you represent as you come face to face with me has no heart in its breast" (Marx 1990: 342–43). It is in this figure of a rational collective entity, the worker, that Marx grounds the question of working-class unity, either potential or realized. The question of working-class unity is not a matter of emotional or psychic solidarity of empirical workers. It is not, in other words, anything like what numerous humanist-Marxist labor historians, from E. P. Thompson on, have often imagined it to be. The "worker" is an abstract and collective subject by its very constitution.[5] It is within that collective and abstract subject that, as Spivak (1988: 277) has reminded us, the dialectic of class-in-itself and class-for-itself plays itself out.[6] The "collective worker," writes Marx (1990: 468), "formed out of the combination of a number of individual specialized workers, is the item of machinery specifically characteristic of the manufacturing period."

Marx constructs a fascinating and suggestive, though fragmentary, history of factory machinery in the early phase of industrialization in

England. This history shows two simultaneous processes at work in capitalist production, both of them critical to Marx's understanding of the category worker as an abstract, reified category. The machine produces "the technical subordination of the worker to the uniform motions of the instruments of labour" (Marx 1990: 549; see also 535).[7] It transfers the motive force of production from the human or the animal to the machine, from living to dead labor. This can only happen on two conditions: the worker is first reduced to his or her biological, and therefore, abstract body, and then movements of this abstract body are broken up and individually designed into the very shape and movement of the machine itself. "Capital absorbs labour into itself," Marx (1973: 704) would write in his notebooks, quoting Goethe, "as though its body were by love possessed." The body that the machine comes to possess is the abstract body it ascribed to the worker to begin with. Marx (1990: 504) writes: "Large-scale industry was crippled in its whole development as long as its characteristic instrument of production, the machine, owed its existence to personal strength and personal skill, [and] depended on the muscular development, the keenness of sight and the manual dexterity with which specialized workers . . . wielded their dwarf-like instruments." Once the worker's capacity for labor could be translated into a series of practices that abstracted the personal from the social, the machine could appropriate the abstract body these practices themselves posited. One tendency of the whole process was to make even the humanness of the capacity for labor redundant: "It is purely accidental that the motive power happens to be clothed in the form of human muscles; wind, water, steam could just as well take man's place" (Marx 1990: 497). At the same time, though, capital—in Marx's understanding of its logic—would not be able to do without living, human labor.

ABSTRACT LABOR AS CRITIQUE

The universal category abstract labor has a twofold function in Marx: it is both a description and a critique of capital. If capital makes abstractions real in everyday life, Marx uses these very same abstractions to give us a sense of the everyday world that capitalist production creates—witness, for example, Marx's use of such reductively biological categories as "women," "children and adult males," "childhood," "family functions," and the "expenditure of domestic labour" (1990: 517, 518 n. 39, 526, 546,

547). The idea of abstract labor reproduces the central feature of the hermeneutic of capital—how capital reads human activity.

Yet abstract labor is also a critique of the same hermeneutic because it—the labor of abstracting—defines for Marx a certain kind of unfreedom. He calls it "despotism." This despotism is structural to capital; it is not simply historical. Thus Marx (1990: 395) writes: "Capital is constantly compelled to wrestle with the insubordination of the workers." And he describes discipline as the "highly detailed specifications, which regulate, with military uniformity, the times, the limits, the pauses of work by the stroke of the clock, . . . developed out of circumstances as natural laws of the modern mode of production. Their formulation, official recognition and proclamation by the state were the result of a long class struggle." Marx (1990: 489–90) is not speaking merely of a particular historical stage, of the transition from handicrafts to manufactures in England, when "the full development of its [capital's] own peculiar tendencies comes up against obstacles from many directions . . . [including] the habits and the resistance of the male workers." He is also writing about "resistance to capital" as something internal to capital itself. As Marx writes elsewhere, the self-reproduction of capital "moves in contradictions *which are constantly overcome but just as constantly posited.*" He adds, just because capital gets ideally beyond every limit posed to it by "national barriers and prejudices," "it does not by any means follow that it has *really* overcome it" (Marx 1973: 410; emphasis added).

But from where does such resistance arise? Many labor historians think of resistance to factory work as resulting either from a clash between the requirements of industrial discipline and preindustrial habits of workers in the early phase of industrialization or from a heightened level of worker consciousness in a later phase. In other words, they see it as resulting from a particular historical stage of capitalist production. In contrast, Marx locates this resistance in the very logic of capital— that is, he locates it in the structural "being" of capital rather than in its historical "becoming." Central to this argument is what Marx sees as the "despotism of capital." This despotism has nothing to do with the historical stage of capitalism. It would not matter for Marx's argument if the capitalist country in question were a developed one. Resistance does not refer to the empirical worker's consciousness or to a historical stage of capital. It is the Other of the despotism inherent in capital's logic. This argument is integral to Marx's larger point that if capitalism were ever to realize itself fully, it would also posit the conditions for its own dissolution.

Capital's power is autocratic, writes Marx. Resistance is rooted in a process through which capital appropriates the will of the worker. Marx (1990: 549–50) writes: "In the factory code, the capitalist formulates his autocratic power over his workers like a private legislator, and purely as an emanation of his own will." This will, embodied in capitalist discipline, Marx describes as "purely despotic," and he uses the analogy of the army to describe the coercion at its heart: "An industrial army of workers under the command of capital requires, like a real army, officers (managers) and N.C.O.s [noncommissioned officers] (foremen, overseers), who command during the labour process in the name of capital. The work of supervision becomes their exclusive function" (Marx 1990: 450).[8]

Why call capitalist discipline "despotic" if all it does is to act as though labor could be abstracted and homogenized? Marx is clear that this has nothing to do with the onerousness of work under capitalism. He would even use the term *torture* to describe "the lightening of labor." Marx's writings on this point underscore the importance of the concept of abstract labor—a version of the Enlightenment figure of the abstract human—as an instrument of critique. He thought of abstract labor as a compound category, spectrally objective and yet made up of human physiology and human consciousness, both abstracted from any empirical history. The consciousness in question was pure will. Marx writes: "Factory work exhausts the nervous system to the uttermost; at the same time, [through specialization and the consequent privileging of the machine,] it does away with the many-sided play of the muscles, and *confiscates every atom of freedom,* both in bodily and intellectual activity. Even the lightening of labour becomes a torture" (Marx 1973: 548; emphasis added).

Why would freedom have anything to do with something as reductively physiological as "the nervous system . . . [and] the many-sided play of the muscles"? Because, Marx (1973: 296) explains, the labor that capital presupposes "as its contradiction and its contradictory being" and which in turn "presupposes capital" is a special kind of labor—"labour not as an object, but as activity, . . . as the living source of value."[9] Marx continues, "As against capital, labour is the merely abstract form, the mere possibility of value-positing activity, which exists only as a capacity, as a resource in the bodiliness of the worker" (Marx 1973: 298). Science aids in this abstraction of living labor by capital: "In machinery, the appropriation of living labour by capital achieves a direct reality. . . . It is, firstly, the analysis and application of mechanical and chemical laws, arising directly out of science, which enables the machine to perform the same labour as that previously performed by the worker. However, the development of machinery along this path occurs only after . . . all the sciences have been pressed into the service of capital" (Marx 1973: 703–4).

The critical point is that the labor that is abstracted in the capitalist's search for a common measure of human activity is "living." Marx would ground resistance to capital in this apparently mysterious factor called "life." The connections between the language of classical political economy and the traditions of European thought that one could call "vitalist" are an underexplored area of research, particularly so in the case of Marx. Marx's language (such as his use of the words *life* and *living*) and his biological metaphors, however, often reveal a deep influence of nineteenth-century vitalism: "Labour is the yeast thrown into it [capital], which starts it fermenting." And furthermore, for Marx labor-power "as commodity exists in his [the labourer's] vitality. . . . In order to maintain this from one day to the next . . . he has to consume a certain quantity of food, to replace his used-up blood, etc. . . . Capital has paid him the amount of objectified labour contained in his vital forces" (1973: 298, 323). These vital forces are the ground of constant resistance to capital, the abstract living labor—a sum of muscles, nerves, and consciousness/will—that, according to Marx, capital posits as its contradictory starting point all the time. In this vitalist understanding, life, in all its biological and conscious capacity for wilful activity (the "many-sided play of the muscles") is the excess that capital, for all its disciplinary procedures, always needs but can never quite control or domesticate.

One is reminded here of G. W. F. Hegel's discussion, in his *Logic*, of the Aristotelian category "life." Hegel accepted Aristotle's argument that life was expressive of a totality or unity in a living individual. "The single members of the body," Hegel writes, "are what they are only by and in relation to their unity. A hand, e.g., when hewn off from the body is, as Aristotle has observed, a hand in name only, not in fact" (1975:

280; see also article 216 Additions). It is only with death that this unity is dismembered and the body falls prey to the objective forces of nature. With death, as Charles Taylor (1978: 332) puts it in explaining this section of Hegel's *Logic,* "mechanism and chemism" break out of the "subordination" in which they are held "as long as life continues." Life, to use Hegel's expression, "is a standing fight" against the possibility of the dismemberment with which death threatens the unity of the living body (Hegel 1975: 281).[10] Life, in Marx's analysis of capital, is similarly a "standing fight" against the process of abstraction that is constitutive of the category labor. It was as if the process of abstraction and ongoing appropriation of the worker's body in the capitalist mode of production perpetually threatened to effect a dismemberment of the unity that the "living body" itself was.

This unity of the body that life expressed, however, was something more than the sheer physical unity of the limbs. "Life" implies a consciousness that is purely human in its abstract and innate capacity for willing. This embodied and peculiarly human "will" — reflected in "the many-sided play of the muscles" — refuses to bend to the "technical subordination" under which capital constantly seeks to place the worker. Marx writes: "The presupposition of the master-servant relation is the appropriation of an alien will." This will could not belong to animals, for animals could not be part of the politics of recognition that the Hegelian master-slave relation assumed. A dog might obey a man, but the man would never know for certain if the dog did not simply look on him as another bigger and more powerful dog. As Marx (1973: 500–501) writes: "The animal may well provide a service but does not thereby make its owner a master." The dialectic of mutual recognition on which the master-servant relationship turned could only take place between humans: "The master-servant relation likewise belongs in this formula of the appropriation of the instruments of production. . . . It is reproduced — in mediated form — in capital, and thus . . . forms a ferment of its dissolution and is an emblem of its limitation."

Marx's immanent critique of capital begins at the same point where capital begins its own life-process: with abstraction of labor. Yet this labor, while abstract, is always living labor to begin with. The "living" quality of the labor ensures that the capitalist has not bought a fixed quantum of labor but, rather, a variable "capacity for labor." Still, being "living" is what makes this labor a source of resistance to capitalist abstraction. The tendency on the part of capital would therefore be to replace, as much as possible, living labor with objectified, dead labor. Capital is thus faced with its own contradiction: it needs abstract and living labor as the starting point in its cycle of self-reproduction, but it also wants to reduce to a minimum the quantum of living labor it needs. Capital will therefore tend to develop technology in order to reduce this need to a minimum. This is exactly what will create the conditions necessary for the emancipation of labor and for the eventual abolition of the category labor altogether. But that would also be the condition for the dissolution of capital: "Capital . . . — quite unintentionally — reduces human labour, expenditure of energy, to a minimum. This will redound to the benefit of emancipated labour, and is the condition of its emancipation" (Marx 1973: 701).

The subsequent part of Marx's argument would run as follows. It is capital's tendency to replace living labor by science and technology — that is, by the shared results of man's "understanding of nature and his mastery over it by virtue of his presence as a social body" — that will give rise to the development of the "social individual" whose greatest need would be that of the "free development of invidualities." For the "reduction of the necessary labour of society to a minimum" would then correspond to "the artistic, scientific, etc. development of the individuals in the time set free, and with the means created, for all of them." Capital would then reveal itself as the "moving contradiction" it was: it both presses "to reduce labour time to a minimum" and posits labor time "as the sole measure and source of wealth." It would therefore work "towards its own dissolution as the form dominating production" (Marx 1973: 700, 705, 706).

Thus would Marx complete the loop of his critique of capital. His critique, by definition, looks to a future beyond capital. But it does so by attending closely to the contradictions in capital's own logic. He powerfully uses the vision of the abstract human embedded in the capitalist practice of abstract labor to generate a radical critique of capital itself. He recognizes that bourgeois societies in which the idea of "human equality" had acquired the fixity of popular prejudice allowed him to use the same idea to critique them. But historical difference would remain sublated and suspended in this particular form of the critique.

Yet Marx was always at pains to underline the importance of history to his critique of capital: "Our method indicates the point where historical investigation must enter in" (Marx 1973: 460; see also 471–72, 488–89, 505). Or elsewhere: "Bourgeois economy [always] point[s] towards a past lying beyond this system" (Marx 1973: 460–61). Marx writes of the past of capital in terms of a distinction between its being and becoming. "Being" refers to the structural logic of capital—that is, the state when capital has fully come into its own. Marx would sometimes call it (using Hegel's vocabulary) real capital, capital as such, or capital's being-for-itself. "Becoming" refers to the historical process in and through which the logical presuppositions of capital being are realized. Becoming is not simply the calendrical or chronological past that precedes capital but the past that the category retrospectively posits. Without the connection between land/tool and laborers being somehow severed, for example, there would never be any workers available to capital. This severing would have to happen wherever there was capitalist production—this is the sense in which a historical process of this kind is indeed a process in the course of which the logical presuppositions of capital are worked out. A past of this kind is posited logically by the category capital. While this past is still being acted out, capitalists and workers do not belong to the being of capital. In Marx's language, they would be called *not-capitalist* (Marx's term [1973: 495]) or, one could say, *not-worker*.[11] These "conditions and presuppositions of the *becoming*, of the *arising*, of capital," writes Marx, "presuppose precisely that it is not yet in being but merely in becoming; they therefore disappear as real capital arises, capital which itself, on the basis of its own reality, posits the condition for its realization" (Marx 1973: 459; Marx's emphasis).

It goes without saying that it is not the actual process of history that does the "presupposing"; the logical presuppositions of capital can only be worked out by someone with a grasp of the logic of capital. In that sense, an intellectual comprehension of the structure of capital is the precondition of this historical knowledge. For history then exemplifies only for us—the investigators—the logical presuppositions of capital even though, Marx would argue, capital needs this real history to happen and even if the reading of this history is only retrospective. This is the sense of a retrospective reading of the past that Marx inscribed in his famous aphorism: "Human anatomy contains a key to the anatomy of the ape." His own gloss went as follows: "The intimations of higher development among the subordinate species . . . can be understood only after the higher development is already known. The bourgeois economy thus supplies the key to the ancient" (Marx 1973: 105). He made a very similar point elsewhere: "Man comes into existence only when a certain point is reached. But once man has emerged, he becomes the permanent pre-condition of human history, likewise its permanent product and result" (Marx 1978: 491). Marx therefore does not provide us so much with a teleology of history as with a perspectival point from which to read the archives.

In his notes on "revenue and its sources" in the posthumously collected and published volumes entitled *Theories of Surplus Value*, Marx gave this history a name: he called it capital's antecedent "posited by itself." Here free labor is both a precondition of capitalist production as well as "its invariable result" (Marx 1978: 491). This is the universal and necessary history we associate with capital. It forms the backbone of the usual narratives of transition to the capitalist mode of production. Let us call this history—a past posited by capital itself as its precondition— History 1.

Marx opposes to History 1 another kind of past that we will call History 2. Elements of History 2, Marx argues, are also "antecedents" to capital—in that capital "encounters them as antecedents," but—and here follows the critical distinction I want to highlight—"not as antecedents established by itself, not as forms of its own life-process" (Marx 1978: 468). To say that something does not belong to capital's "life-process" is to claim that it does not contribute to the self-reproduction of capital. I therefore understand Marx to be saying that antecedents to capital are not only the relationships that constitute History 1 but also other relationships that do not lend themselves to the reproduction of the logic of capital. Only History 1 is the past "established" by capital because History 1 lends itself to the reproduction of capitalist relationships. In other words, Marx accepts that the total universe of pasts that capital encounters is larger than the sum of those elements in which the logical presuppositions of capital are worked out.

Marx's own examples of History 2 take the reader by surprise. They are money and commodity, two elements without which capital cannot even be conceptualized. Marx once described the "commodity-form" as something belonging to the "cellular" structure of capital. And without money, there would be no generalized exchange of commodities.[12] Yet entities as close and as necessary to the functioning of capital as money and commodity do not necessarily belong by any natural connection to either capital's "own life-process" or to the past "posited by capital." Marx recognizes the possibility that money and commodity, as relations, could have existed in history without necessarily giving rise to capital. They did not look forward to capital as such. Relations, whose reproduction does not contribute to the reproduction of the logic of capital, make up the kind of past I have called History 2. This very example of the heterogeneity Marx reads into the history of money and commodity shows that the relations that do not contribute to the reproduction of the logic of capital can actually be intimately intertwined with the relations that do. Capital, maintains Marx, has to destroy this first set of relationships as independent forms and subjugate them to itself (using, if need be, violence—that is, the power of the state): "[Capital] originally finds the commodity already in existence, but not as its own product, and likewise finds money in circulation, but not as an element in its own reproduction. . . . But both of them must first be destroyed as independent forms and subordinated to industrial capital. Violence (the State) is used against interest-bearing capital by means of compulsory reduction of interest rates" (Marx 1978: 468).

Marx thus writes into the intimate space of capital an element of deep uncertainty. In the reproduction of its own life-process, capital encounters relationships that present it with double possibilities. These relations could be central to capital's self-reproduction, and yet it is also possible for them to be oriented to structures that do not contribute to such reproduction. History 2's are thus not pasts separate from capital; they are pasts that inhere in capital and yet interrupt and punctuate the run of capital's own logic.

History 1, argues Marx, has to subjugate or destroy the multiple possibilities that belong to History 2. There is nothing, however, to guarantee that the subordination of History 2's to the logic of capital could ever be necessarily complete or total. True, Marx wrote about bourgeois society as a "contradictory development"—"relations derived from earlier forms will often be found within it only in an entirely stunted form, or even travestied." But he also at the same time described some of these "remnants" of "vanished social formations" as "partly still unconquered," signalling by his metaphor of conquest that the site of a "survival" of that which seemed pre- or noncapitalist could very well be the site of an ongoing battle (Marx 1973: 105–6). There remains, of course, a degree of ambiguity of meaning and an equivocality about time in this fragment of a sentence from Marx. Does "partly *still* unconquered" refer to something that is "not yet conquered" or something that is in principle "unconquerable"?

We have to remain alert to—or even make good use of—certain ambiguities in Marx's prose. At first sight, Marx may appear to be offering a historicist reading. Marx's categories "not-capitalist" or "not-worker," for example, could appear to belong squarely to the process of becoming of capital, a phase in which capital "is not yet in being but merely in becoming" (Marx 1973: 459). But notice the ambiguity in this phrase: What kind of a temporal space is signalled by "not yet"? If one reads the expression "not yet" as belonging to the historian's lexicon, a historicism follows. It refers us back to the idea of history as a waiting room, a period that is needed for the transition to capitalism at any particular time and place. This is the period to which the Third World is often consigned.

Marx himself warns us against understandings of capital that emphasize the historical at the expense of the structural or the philosophical. The limits to capital, he reminds us, are "constantly overcome but just as constantly posited" (Marx 1973: 410). It is as though the "not yet" is what keeps capital going. Marx allows us to read the expression "not yet" deconstructively as referring to a process of deferral internal to the very being (that is, logic) of capital. "Becoming," the question of the past of capital, does not have to be thought of as a process outside of and prior to its "being." If we describe becoming as the past posited by the category capital itself, then we make being logically prior to becoming. Difference-with-capital (Marx's figure of the *not-[yet]-capitalist*) would then also be a figure of difference-in-capital—that is, an outside that is inside as well. In other words, History 1 and History 2 considered together precisely destroy the usual topological distinction between outside and inside that marks debates about whether the whole world can be properly said to have fallen under the sway of capital. Difference, in this account, is not something external to capital. Neither is it something subsumed into capital. It lives in intimate and plural relationships to capital, relationships that range from opposition to indifference.

This is the possibility that, I suggest, Marx's underdeveloped ideas about History 2 invite us to consider. History 2 does not spell out a positive program of writing histories that are alternatives to the narratives of capital. History 2's do not constitute a dialectical Other of the necessary logic of History 1. To think thus would be to subsume History 2 to History 1. History 2 is better thought of as a category charged with the negative function of constantly interrupting the totalizing thrusts of History 1.

Let me illustrate this point further with the help of a logical fable about labor power. Let us imagine the embodiment of labor power, the laborer, entering the factory gate every morning at 8 A.M. and departing in the evening at 5 P.M., having put in his/her usual eight-hour day in the service of the capitalist (allowing for an hour's lunch break). The contract of law—the wage contract—guides and defines these hours. Now, following my preceding explanation of Histories 1 and 2, one may say that this laborer carries with himself or herself, every morning, practices that embody these two kinds of pasts. History 1 is the past that is internal to the structure of being of capital. The very fact that the worker at the factory represents a historical separation between his/her capacity to labor and the necessary tools of production (which now belong to the capitalist) shows that he or she embodies a history that has realized this logical precondition of capital. *This worker does not therefore represent any denial of the universal history of capital.* Everything I have said about abstract labor will apply to him or her.

While walking through the factory gate, however, my fictional person also embodies other kinds of pasts. These pasts, grouped together here in my analysis as History 2, may be under the institutional domination of the logic of capital and exist in proximate relationship to it, but they also do not belong to the life-process of capital. They enable the human bearer of labor power to enact other ways of being in the world, other than, that is, being the bearer of labor power. We cannot ever hope to write a complete or full account of these pasts. They are partly embodied in the person-cum-laborer's bodily habits, in unselfconscious collective practices, in his or her reflexes about what it means to relate—as a human being and together with other human beings in the given environment—to objects in the world. Nothing in it is automatically aligned with the logic of capital.

The subjugation/destruction of History 2 is what the disciplinary process in the factory is in part meant to accomplish. In effect, capital says to the laborer: I want you to be reduced to sheer living labor—muscular energy plus consciousness—for the eight hours for which I have bought your capacity to labor. I want to effect a separation between your personality (that is, the personal and collective histories you embody) and your will (which is a characteristic of sheer consciousness). My machinery and the system of discipline are there to ensure that this happens. When you work with the machinery that represents objectified labor, I want you to be living labor, a bundle of muscles and nerves and consciousness but devoid of any memory except the memory of the skills the work needs. "Machinery requires," as Max Horkheimer (1994: 22) put it in his famous critique of instrumental reason, "the kind of mentality that concentrates on the present and can dispense with memory and straying imagination." To the extent that both the distant and the immediate pasts of the worker—including the work of unionization and citizenship—prepare him or her to be the figure posited by capital as its own condition and contradiction, those pasts do indeed constitute History 1. But the idea of History 2 suggests that even in the very abstract and abstracting space of the factory that capital creates, ways of being human will be acted out in manners that do not lend themselves to the reproduction of the logic of capital.

It would be wrong to think of History 2 (or History 2's) as necessarily precapitalist or feudal, or even as something inherently incompatible with capital. If any of these were the case, there would be no way humans could be at home—dwell—in the rule of capital: no room for enjoyment, no play of desires, no seduction of the commodity.[13] Capital, in that case, would truly be unrelieved and absolute unfreedom. The idea of History 2 allows us to make room, in Marx's own analytic of capital, for the politics of human belonging and diversity. It gives us a ground on which to situate our thoughts about multiple ways of being human and their relationship to the global logic of capital. But Marx does not himself think through this problem while his method, if my argument is right, allows us to acknowledge it. There is a blind spot, it seems to me, built into his method—this is the problem of the status of the category "use value" in Marx's thoughts on value.[14] Let me explain.

Consider, for instance, the passage in the *Grundrisse* where Marx discusses, albeit briefly, the difference between making a piano and playing it. Because of his commitment to the idea of "productive labor," Marx finds it necessary to theorize the piano maker's labor in terms of its contribution to the creation of value. But what about the piano player's labor? For Marx, that will belong to the category of "unproductive labor" which he took over (and developed) from his predecessors in political economy.[15] Let us read closely the relevant passage:

> What is *productive labour* and what is not, a point very much disputed back and forth since Adam Smith made this distinction, has to emerge from the direction of the various aspects of capital itself. *Productive labour* is only that which produces capital. Is it not crazy, asks e.g. . . . Mr Senior, that the piano maker is a *productive worker,* but not the piano player, although obviously the piano would be absurd without the piano player? But this is exactly the case. The piano maker reproduces capital, the pianist only exchanges his labour for revenue. But doesn't the pianist produce music and satisfy our musical ear, does he not even to a certain extent produce the latter? He does indeed: his labour produces something; but that does not make it *productive labour* in the *economic sense;* no more than the labour of the mad man who produces delusions is productive. (Marx 1973: 305; Marx's emphasis)

This is the closest that Marx ever would come to showing a Heideggerian intuition about human beings and their relation to tools. He acknowledges that our musical ear is satisfied by the music that the pianist produces. He even goes a step further in saying that the pianist's music actually—and "to a certain extent"—"produces" that ear as well. In other words, in the intimate and mutually productive relationship between one's very particular musical ear and particular forms of music is captured the issue of historical difference, of the ways in which History 1 is always already modified by History 2's. We do not all have the same musical ear. This ear, in addition, often develops unbeknownst to ourselves. This historical but unintended relation between a music and the ear it has helped "produce"—I do not like the assumed priority of the music over the ear but let that be—is like the relationship between humans and tools that Heidegger calls "the ready to hand": the everyday, preanalytical, unobjectifying relationships we have to tools, relationships critical to the process of making a world out of this earth. This relationship would belong to History 2. Heidegger does not minimize the importance of objectifying relationships (History 1 would belong here)—in his translator's prose, they are called "present at hand"—but in a properly Heideggerian framework of understanding, both the present-at-hand and the ready-to-hand retain their importance: one does not gain epistemological primacy over the other.[16] History 2 cannot sublate itself into History 1.

See what happens in the passage quoted: Marx both acknowledges and in the same breath casts aside as irrelevant the activity that produces music. For his purpose, it is "no more than the labour of the mad man who produces delusions." This equation between music and a mad man's delusion is baleful, however. It is what hides from view what Marx himself has helped us see: histories that capital anywhere—even in the West—encounters as its antecedents but which do not belong to its life-process. Music could be a part of such histories in spite of its later commodification because it is part of the means by which we make our "worlds" out of this earth. The "mad" man, one may say in contrast, is world-poor. He powerfully brings to view the problem of human belonging. Do not the sad figures of the often mentally ill, homeless people on the streets of the cities of the United States, unkempt and lonely people pushing to nowhere shopping trolleys filled with random assortments of broken unusable objects—do not they and their supposed possessions dramatically portray this crisis of ontic belonging to which the "mad" person of late capitalism is condemned? Marx's equation of the labor of the piano player with that of the production of a mad man's delusions shows how the question of History 2 comes as but a fleeting glimpse in his analysis of capital. It withdraws from his thoughts almost as soon as it reveals itself.

If my argument is right, then it is important to acknowledge a certain indeterminacy that we can now read back into many historical—and I may say, historicist—explanations of capitalist discipline. Recall, for example, E. P. Thompson's (1974: 66) classic statement in this regard: "Without time-discipline we could not have the insistent energies of the industrial man; and whether this discipline comes in the form of Methodism, or of Stalinism, or of nationalism, it will come to the developing world." If any empirical history of the capitalist mode of production is History 1 already modified — in numerous and not necessarily documentable ways — by History 2's, then a major question about capital will remain historically undecidable. Even if Thompson's prediction were to come true and a place like India suddenly and unexpectedly boasted human beings as averse to "laziness" as the bearers of the Protestant ethic are supposed to be, we would still not be able to settle one question beyond all doubt. We would never know for sure whether this condition had come about because the time discipline that Thompson documented was a genuinely universal, functional characteristic of capital, or whether world capitalism represented a forced globalization of a particular fragment of European history in which the Protestant ethic became a value. A victory for the Protestant ethic, however global, would surely be no victory for any universal. The question of whether the seemingly general and functional requirements of capital represent very specific compromises in Europe between History 1 and History 2's, remains, beyond a point, an undecidable question. The topic of "efficiency" and "laziness" is a good case in point. We know, for instance, that even after years of Stalinist, nationalist, and free market coercion, we have not been able to rid the capitalist world of the ever-present theme of laziness. Laziness has remained a charge that has always been levelled at some group or other ever since the beginnings of the particular shape that capital took in Western Europe.[17]

No historical form of capital, however global its reach, can ever be a universal. No global (or even local, for that matter) capital can ever represent the universal logic of capital, for any historically available form of capital is always already a provisional compromise made up of History 1 modified by somebody's History 2's. The universal, in that case, can only exist as a placeholder, its place always usurped by a historical particular seeking to present itself as the universal. This does not mean that one gives away the universals enshrined in post-Enlightenment rationalism or humanism. Marx's immanent critique of capital was enabled precisely by the universal characteristics he read into the category capital itself. Without that reading, there can only be particular critiques of capital. But a particular critique cannot by definition be a critique of capital, for such a critique could not take capital as its object. Grasping the category capital entails grasping its universal constitution. My reading of Marx does not in any way obviate that need for engagement with the universal. What I have attempted to do is to produce a reading in which "capital"—the very category itself—becomes a site where both the universal history of capital and the politics of human belonging are allowed to interrupt each other's narrative.

Capital is a philosophical-historical category—historical difference is not external to it but is constitutive of it. Its histories are History 1 constitutively but unevenly modified by more and less powerful History 2's. Histories of capital, in that sense, cannot escape the politics of the diverse ways of being human. An engagement with capital therefore becomes a double-sided engagement. Possessing in its constitution the necessary ideas of juridical equality and citizenly rights, capital brings into every history some of the universal themes of the European Enlightenment. Yet, on inspection, the universal turns out to be an empty placeholder whose unstable outlines become barely visible only when a proxy, a particular, usurps its position in a gesture of pretension and domination. And that, it seems to me, is the restless and inescapable politics of historical difference to which global capital consigns us. In turn, the struggle to put in the ever empty place of History 1 other histories with which we attempt to modify and domesticate that empty, universal history posited by the logic of capital brings intimations of that universal history into our diverse life practices.

The resulting process is what historians usually describe as the "transition to capitalism." This transition is also a process of translation of diverse life worlds and conceptual horizons about being human into the categories of Enlightenment thought that inhere in the logic of capital. For instance, to think Indian history in terms of Marxian categories is to translate into such categories the existing archives of thought and practices about human relations in the subcontinent. At the same time, it is to modify these thoughts and practices with the help of these categories. The politics of translation involved in this process work both ways. Translation makes possible the emergence of the universal language of the social sciences. It must also, by the same token, destabilize these universals. This translation constitutes the condition of possibility for the globalization of capital across diverse, porous, and conflicting histories of human belonging. At the same time, it ensures that this process of globalization of capital is not the same as the universal realization of what Marx regarded as its logic. And yet, for the reasons I have explained here, we cannot dismiss the universals inherent in this logic. If my argument is right, then there is no "beyond of capital" that would also be its absolute Other. Capital's Other constantly comes into being— and constantly dissolves—in the unstable space of unremitting tension that is created as History 1 perennially negotiates our numerous and different History 2's. It is only sometimes given to us to act as self-conscious agents in this process.

NOTES

This essay was first delivered as one of the two annual lectures of the Critical Theory Institute of the University of California, Irvine, and will be published in a somewhat different form in a forthcoming publication of the institute. A slightly different version of this essay, entitled "The Two Histories of Capital," constitutes a chapter in my book *Provincializing Europe: Postcolonial Thought and Historical Difference* (Princeton, N.J.: Princeton University Press, 2000). For their many helpful critical comments on earlier drafts, I am grateful to my colleagues on the editorial committee of *Public Culture,* to my three coeditors of the special issue of *Public Culture* 12(3) (Homi K. Bhabha, Carol A. Breckenridge, and Sheldon Pollock), and to my audiences at the University of California at Irvine and at San Diego, the University of Chicago, and Columbia University in the United States; the Australian National University, the University of Wollongong, and the University of Melbourne in Australia; and the Centre for Studies in Social Sciences, Calcutta, in India. Thanks are also due to Arjun Appadurai, Gautam Bhadra, David Lloyd, Lisa Lowe, George Lipsitz, Ben Madison, Mark Poster, Sanjay Seth, and Andrew Wells for encouragement and comradely criticism.

1. This proposition is discussed in and taken as the founding premise of Chakrabarty 1989.

2. See also Castoriadis 1984: 260–339, in particular, 282–311.

3. Cf. Meek 1979: 168: "The 'averaging' process, Marx's argument implies, takes place in history before it takes place in the minds of economists."

4. Castoriadis (1984: 328–29) erects a possible picture of voluntarist revolutionary politics by adopting this Aristotelian position into his Marxism: "To propose another institution of society is a matter of a political project and political aim, which are certainly subject to discussion and argument, but cannot be 'founded' in any kind of Nature or Reason. . . . Men are born neither free nor unfree, neither equal nor unequal. *We will them to be* (we will ourselves to be) free and equal" (Castoriadis's emphasis).

5. This is reminiscent of Georg Lukács's (1971: 51, 197) contention that "class consciousness" was not a category that referred to what actually went on inside the heads of individual, empirical workers. David Harvey (1984: 114) writes: "The duality of worker as 'object for capital' and as 'living creative subject' has never been adequately resolved in Marxist theory." I have criticisms of Harvey's reading of Marx on this point—one could argue, for instance, that, for Marx, the worker could never be a

thing-like "object for capital" (see later in this essay)—but Harvey's statement has the merit of recognizing a real problem in Marxist histories of "consciousness."

6. The opposition of class-in-itself and class-for-itself, Spivak (1988: 277) clarifies, does not define a program of "an ideological transformation of consciousness on the ground level."

7. Marx (1990: 505 n.18) discusses how the modern machine, in its early history, incorporated into its design the motions of the live, physical, and animate body.

8. Foucault (1979: 163) comments on these military analogies in Marx. But whereas, for Foucault, disciplinary power creates "the docile body," Marx posits the living body as a source of resistance to discipline.

9. This is why Harvey's contention (1984: 113) that Marx's "theory shows that, from the standpoint of capital, workers are indeed objects, a mere 'factor' of production . . . for the creation of surplus value" seems mistaken to me. The worker is a reified category, but the reification includes an irreducible element of life and (human) consciousness.

10. I have preferred Taylor's translation of this passage to that of William Wallace.

11. Nothing in this sense is inherently "precapitalist." Precapitalist could only ever be a designation used from the perspective of capital.

12. Cf. Marx 1990: 90: "For bourgeois society, the commodity-form of the product of labour, or the value-form of the commodity, is the economic cell-form."

13. Marxist arguments have often in the past looked on advertising as merely an instance of the "irrationality" and "waste" inherent in the capitalist mode of production. See Williams 1993: 320–26.

14. The excellent discussion of "use value" in Rosdolsky 1977: 73–95 helps us appreciate how, as a category, "use value" moves in and out of Marx's political-economic analysis. Spivak puts it even more strongly by saying that, as a category of political economy, use value can appear "only *after* the appearance of the exchange relation" (1993: 106; Spivak's emphasis). Spivak categorically states, rightly I think, that "Marx left the slippery concept of 'use value' untheorized" (1993: 97). My point is that Marx's thoughts on use value do not turn toward the question of human belonging or "worlding." For Marx retains a subject-object relationship between man and nature. Nature never escapes its "thingly" character in Marx's analysis.

15. As Marx defines it in the course of discussing Adam Smith's use of the category "productive labor": "only labour which produces capital is productive labour." Unproductive labor is that "which is not exchanged with capital but *directly* with revenue." He further explains: "An actor, for example, or even a clown, . . . is a productive labourer if he works in the service of a capitalist" (Marx 1969: 156–57; Marx's emphasis).

16. Heidegger (1985: division I, chapter 3) explains these terms in the section entitled "The Worldhood of the World." The more recent translation of *Being and Time* by Joan Stambaugh (Heidegger 1996: 64, 69) replaces "ready-to-hand" with "handiness" and "present-at-hand" with the expression "objectively present."

17. A classic study on this theme remains that by Syed Hussein Alatas (1977). The theme of laziness, however, is a permanent theme within any capitalist structure,

national or global. What would repay examination is the business school literature on "motivation" in showing how much and how incessantly the organic intellectuals of capitalism wrestle with an unsolvable question: What motivates humans to "work"?

WORKS CITED

Alatas, Syed Hussein. 1977. *The Myth of the Lazy Native: A Study of the Image of Malays, Filipinos, and Javanese from the Sixteenth to the Twentieth Centuries and Its Functions in the Ideology of Colonial Capitalism.* London: Frank Cass.

Aristotle. 1981. *Nichomachean Ethics,* translated by Martin Oswald. Indianapolis, Ind.: Liberal Arts Press.

Bhabha, Homi K. 1994. *The Location of Culture.* London: Routledge.

Castoriadis, Cornelius. 1984. "Value, Equality, Justice, and Politics: From Marx to Aristotle and from Aristotle to Ourselves. In *Crossroads in the Labyrinth,* trans. Kate Soper and Martin H. Ryle. Cambridge, Mass.: MIT Press.

Chakrabarty, Dipesh. 1989. *Rethinking working-class history: Bengal 1890–1940.* Princeton, N.J.: Princeton University Press.

Elster, Jon. 1995. *An Introduction to Karl Marx.* Cambridge: Cambridge University Press.

Foucault, Michel. 1979. *Discipline and Punish: The Birth of the Prison,* trans. Alan Sheridan. Harmondsworth, U.K.: Penguin.

Harvey, David. 1984. *The Limits of Capital.* Oxford: Basil Blackwell.

Hegel, G. W. F. 1975. *Hegel's Logic,* trans. William Wallace. Oxford: Clarendon Press.

Heidegger, Martin. 1985. *Being and Time,* trans. John Macquarrie and Edward Robinson. Oxford: Basil Blackwell.

———. 1996. *Being and Time,* trans. Joan Stambaugh. Albany: State University of New York Press.

Horkheimer, Max. 1994. *Critique of Instrumental Reason,* trans. Matthew J. O'Connell et al. New York: Continuum.

Lukács, Georg. 1971. *History and Class Consciousness,* trans. Rodney Livingstone. London: Merlin Press.

Marx, Karl. 1969. *Theories of Surplus Value,* vol. 1. Moscow: Progress Publishers.

———. 1973. *Grundrisse: Foundations of the Critique of Political Economy,* translated by Martin Nicolaus. Harmondsworth, U.K.: Penguin.

———. 1978. *Theories of Surplus Value,* vol. 3. Moscow: Progress Publishers.

———. 1990. *Capital: A Critique of Political Economy,* vol. 1, trans. Ben Fowkes. Harmondsworth, U.K.: Penguin.

Meek, Ronald L. 1979. *Studies in the Labour Theory of Value.* London: Lawrence and Wishart.

Postone, Moishe. 1993. *Time, Labor, and Social Dominion: A Reinterpretation of Marx's Social Theory.* Cambridge: Cambridge University Press.

Rosdolsky, Roman. 1977. *The Making of Marx's Capital,* trans. Pete Burgess. London: Pluto Press.

Rubin, Isaak Il'ich. 1975. *Essays on Marx's Theory of Value,* trans. Milos Samardzija and Fredy Perlman. Montreal: Black Rose Books.

Spivak, Gayatri Chakravorty. 1988. "Can the Subaltern Speak?" In *Marxism and the Interpretation of Culture,* ed. Cary Nelson and Lawrence Grossberg. Urbana: University of Illinois Press.

———. 1993. "Limits and openings of Marx in Derrida." In *Outside in the Teaching Machine.* London: Routledge.

Taylor, Charles. 1978. *Hegel.* Cambridge: Cambridge University Press.

Thompson, E. P. 1974. Time, Work-Discipline, and Industrial Capitalism. In *Essays in Social History,* ed. M. W. Flinn and T. C. Smout. Oxford: Clarendon Press.

Williams, Raymond. 1993. "Advertising: The Magic System." In *The Cultural Studies Reader,* ed. Simon During. London: Routledge.

The Senegalese Murid Trade Diaspora and the Making of a Vernacular Cosmopolitanism

Mamadou Diouf

Translated by Steven Rendall

Modernity, globalization, and cosmopolitanism are concepts whose meanings and projects (as manifest in social science literature, as well as in everyday and journalistic communication), largely overlap and co-incide at the level of procedures and operational modes. African dis-cussions of these concepts tend to privilege unilateral assimilation of the civilizing mission of colonialism and the modernization necessarily defined by the West. For some time, the latter has been supplemented by Islamic modernity, which is both modern and cosmopolitan. And while Islamic fundamentalist movements have attacked, sometimes in a violent manner, these local and unique forms of Muslim appropria-tion, postcolonial subjects continue to pursue their ambivalent and am-biguous projects of constructing autonomous or subordinate identi-ties while also struggling to reconcile native temporalities and forms of spirituality with the temporality of the world at large.

There are clearly disappointing outcomes produced by the paradigm that opposes the traditional character of African forms of spirituality to the modernity of world time (*le temps du monde*), whether it cele-brates resistance to assimilation or condemns the alienation in which the latter results.[1] The issue that continues to defy analysis is how to elabo-rate a single explanation of both the process of globalization and the multiplicity of individual temporalities and local rationalities that are inserted into it. Can we fully account for the overlapping of local systems of mercantile, cultural, and religious values with the capitalist system — which is Western and universal, at least in its claims and practices — by reference to the concepts of hybridization, postcoloniality, and cosmo-politanism? By contrast, there is the crucial question raised by Arjun Ap-padurai's work: How can something local be produced within a process of globalization so solidly committed to the celebration of cosmopolitanism? Is it a matter of appropriating this process by "annexing" it or, rather, of exploiting this process to lend new strength to local idioms, so as to impose on the global scene the original version in place of its translation and adaptation?[2]

The complexity of these situations is the source of Stuart Hall's bafflement when confronted by "the discourse of globalization" and the "discourses of hyper-globalization." He explains that in these discourses, "*everything* is transformed; *everything* is an outcast in the same way by the global processes. There isn't any local that isn't written through and through by the global. That just doesn't seem to me to be true. It doesn't ring true; I think it's a myth." Reviewing some of the questions that have been raised regarding globalization, Hall emphasizes "the intensification of the commitment to the local."[3]

This essay examines and tests two issues raised by Hall. The first issue is the role of capitalist modernity in the process of globalization, and I focus on the possibility of the emergence of modernities that are not, properly speaking, capitalist but are, at the most, non-Western versions or modalities of dealing with acquisition of wealth.[4] The second issue concerns what Hall calls "vernacular modernity," which is, as we interpret it here, the totality of the possibilities and powers of making transactions implemented through both the geography of globalization (the world as a space in which people are able to trade) and the discourses and practices of globalization (the actual operations to make ends meet—that is, to accumulate wealth).[5] I am concerned here with the various forms and expressions of incorporation and inscription into the process of globalization on the basis of a significant locality. From this point of view, we must inquire into the modes on the basis of which native modernity relies on, confronts, and/or compromises with global modernity and with cosmopolitanism, the latter considered an instrument and a modality of the incorporation of the local into the global.

The "locality" in question here is that of the Murid brotherhood, a Senegalese religious group founded in the nineteenth century by a Senegalese marabout named Amadou Bamba Mbacké. The literature on this brotherhood is more extensive than that on other Senegalese brotherhoods and Islamic movements in black Africa.[6] One can distinguish three generations of scholars of the Murid brotherhood. The first generation was concerned primarily with the theological aspects of the group and with gauging the differences and/or the conformity between Murid practices and "Muslim orthodoxy."[7] The second generation attempted to develop an anthropological, political, economic, and sociological analysis of the brotherhood.[8] The third, most recent, generation of scholars has traced Murid urban migrations in Senegal, the rest of Africa, and the countries of Europe, Asia, and the Americas, their inscription in new geographies, and the invention of specific circuits of accumulation, as well as new images and representations of their community.[9] This privileged place in ethnological, anthropological, and historical studies reflects the remarkable Murid presence in the world. Should this presence be interpreted as indicating cosmopolitanism?

In its desire to appropriate possibilities offered by globalization, the Murid locality does not seek to annex the global but, rather, to take advantage of it and to be borne by it in every sense of the word. Consequently, the approach adopted here differs in one respect from Hall's analysis, since I do not share his view that localism "is the only point of intervention against the hegemonic, universalizing thrust of globalization."[10] Most members of the Murid brotherhood come from the central part of the Wolof homeland. (The Wolofs are the largest ethnic group in Senegal.) When it first emerged, the brotherhood was favored by a twofold dynamic. On one hand, by destroying the traditional aristocracies, colonial conquest opened opportunities for Muslim religious proselytizing. The Murid Islamic brotherhood established a large clientele by offering a new religious form, a new memory, and new images to peasant communities that had been disrupted and severely disturbed by colonial military campaigns and by the bloody struggles for power in the Wolof homeland that followed raiding and a series of epidemics connected with the Atlantic slave trade. On the other hand, the brotherhood compromised with the colonial order and adopted its hierarchy and structures of command, while at the same time it evaded the colonial policy of assimilation.

Within the colony, Muridism elaborated a formula of development based on growing peanuts (the quintessential product of French colonial agriculture in Senegal) that was strongly rooted in local values. In this way, it was able to support forms of dissidence and autonomy with regard to the French imperial model — a model whose point of reference, the "four communes" of Senegal (Saint-Louis, Dakar, Rufisque, and Gorée) contrasted strongly with Murid colonial modernity.[11] Murids thus first incorporated themselves into the colonial agricultural economy, and, at the same time, they preserved, in a displaced manner, Wolof values that had been renegotiated and reinvested in the authoritarian architecture of the colonial administration of management and labor. Today Murids, dressed in their traditional *bubus* (robes) and wearing their tasseled hats, "clutter" the sidewalks of urban centers in the developed world, the commercial centers of international business, financial institutions, and construction sites and factories in the Americas, Europe, and Asia.

The precedent of the four communes helps us understand what is at stake in the debates regarding modernity and cosmopolitanism, ways of being that are too often perceived as incorporation into Western universality and the abandonment of one's own traditions in order to slip into new configurations uninfluenced by custom and religion. The privileged locus of these arabesques — free compositions if ever there were any — is the city, and the natural actors of these operations are the intellectuals, especially the artists. In his most recent work, *In Search of Africa,* Manthia Diawara addresses the question of African modernity in the context of globalization, adding politicians to the actors just mentioned.[12] If only indirectly, this essay responds to Diawara's views regarding African ways of being modern in relation to the bearers of Western modernity who are the object of his book. Diawara adopts the perspectives of assimilation/alienation and mimesis/resistance that were brilliantly dramatized in Cheikh Hamidou Kane's *L'aventure ambiguë.* This dramatization was already perceptible in C. H. Kane's reflections as a member of the planning commission for the new independent Senegalese state in the early 1960s.[13] In fact, it seems certain that the temporalities mentioned — namely, the nationalist period of decolonization and the beginning of the construction of African nation-states — and the "libraries" selected (to adopt V. Y. Mudimbe's terms) are not the only phases or the only bodies of knowledge and practices that Africans are using to incorporate themselves into the global process.[14]

This essay contends that the context has changed. At the heart of globalization, new actors, bearing a new memory that differs from that of Western modernity, are putting together their own economic scenario, buttressed by constantly remodeled traditions. These traditions anticipate a future saturated with projects of an indisputable modernity. This is the case for the Murid community in Senegal, all through its history.

The construction of the Murid community has passed through three phases, each corresponding to specific modes of inscription in space, relations with the outside world, and formulas of financial accumulation and economic production. The first phase is that of the beginning and formulation of the Murid *tariqa* (way) at the end of the nineteenth century. France had just completed the conquest of Senegambia and found peanuts to be a product suitable for agricultural exploitation and for French industry's need for vegetable oils. Thus the peanut was adopted as the chief product for developing the colony of Senegal, and peanut monoculture was even continued throughout the first three decades of the postcolonial period. After having almost entirely destroyed the hegemony of the traditional leading classes, French colonialism opened up a space for Muslim religious proselytizing. However, the French continued to mistrust the marabouts, who were suspected of wanting to wage a holy war. Nonetheless, despite the opposition and hostility of the French colonial administration to the marabout Amadou Bamba, the formation of the Murid brotherhood relied heavily on peanut growing, at which it was phenomenally successful in the first half of the twentieth century. Murids became the largest producers of peanuts in their region, the peanut-growing basin. By joining in colonial production, Murids also participated in the distribution of manufactured products in the rural areas. They thus carved out, in a contradictory way, a space for themselves within the colonial system and its economy.

From the start, Muridism attracted people from every level of society, but particularly freed slaves and people belonging to castes such as jewelers, cobblers, itinerant minstrels, coopers, and weavers.[15] As it de veloped, Muridism maintained a constant tension—on the brink of rupture—between Muslim universalism and the local version of Islam whose images and grammar it expressed. Thus in African, European, American, and Asian commercial centers, the Murids participated in Islam's cosmopolitanism on the world stage. Rather than adopting the technology or operational procedures of the West, Murids made a conscious effort to incorporate their unique temporality and rationality into world time by using their own vocabulary, grammar, and worldview to understand the world and operate within it. Adopting Jean Copans's perspective, we see that it was precisely in the initial period that Islam enabled the Murids to incorporate colonial modernity by engaging in peanut growing, thereby ensuring the success of the peanut crop at the beginning of the twentieth century.[16] The peanut played a crucial role in defining the colonial governance of the Wolof region and the whole of the colony of Senegal: it ensured peaceful relations between the colonial administration and the marabouts, and it sketched out a geography of maraboutic villages and *dahras*—Koranic schools that combine teaching with agricultural work and whose center is the village and the sanctuary in Touba.[17] Furthermore, as Vincent Monteil argues, the adoption of the universalist religion of Islam by incorporating "traditional ideologies," as well as some key aspects of the colonial project, makes the Murid Islam a specifically "black Islam."[18]

Incorporation into colonial modernity was accompanied by a strengthening of the Murid community's organization that occurred only after conflicts over succession following the death of its founder in 1927.[19] To guarantee its discipline and cohesion, the group appropriated the colonial administration's structures and logic of command, which required total submission to an unchallengeable authority. The Murid hierarchical system, with the caliph general at its head, adopted the same rules of the *talib*'s (disciple's) absolute submission to his marabout. The native translation of the logic of command and obedience is neatly summed up by a formula attributed to the founder of the brotherhood: "The talib must be like a corpse in the hands of the mortician." A categorical imperative, prescription (*ndigel*) is thus inscribed at the heart of the relation between marabout and talib. The brotherhood's modes of administration and governance, combined with the formulas for mobilizing labor, particularly in the dahras, gave it a privileged place in the colonial apparatus. The Brotherhood established itself as the chief source of peanut production, and its leaders became the main intermediaries between the colonial administration and the Wolof peasants, who it succeeded in incorporating into the brotherhood. Paradoxically, this position enabled the community to maintain its ideological autonomy and avoid colonial assimilation—particularly assimilation in terms of Islamic practices. The Murid's Islam was and is less universalist and scriptural than the Islam of the inhabitants of the four communes. For the rural Murid disciples, reading the holy words is less important than working for the marabout. This contrasts with residents of the four communes for whom the confrontation with the French over the civil code resulted in their valuation of literacy in Arabic.[20] The economic and financial accumulation produced by growing and commercializing peanuts became the instrument that made it possible to constitute "Murid objects." In this register, as in that of Islam, Muridism established itself in its uniqueness and provided itself with the signs of an identity that allowed it to maintain its distance from other identities, signs, and temporalities. In this way, it organized a unique cosmopolitanism consisting in participation but not assimilation, thus organizing the local not only to strengthen its position but also to establish the rules governing dialogue with the universal.

The material power gradually acquired by the brotherhood was to open more ample opportunities for producing a unique trajectory whose dominant figure is Cheikh Amadou Bamba. The latter's saga is the text that foreshadows the brotherhood's future power, and particularly its economic success.

Amadou Bamba, the founder of the Murid brotherhood, was the chief victim of anti-Muslim and anti-marabout colonial policies. Because of the influence acquired by his message and the strong attraction he exercised on the peasant masses that joined his movement, he was considered a marabout who might raise troops for a holy war. He was arrested by the French colonial authorities and deported to the Mayombé region of Gabon from 1895 to 1902 and to Mauritania from 1907 to 1912, before returning to Diourbel, where he lived under surveillance until his death in 1927. He was buried in Touba, the village he founded and where he lived only from 1887 to 1895. His burial there led to the founding of the Touba sanctuary, "a city on the hill." Concerning the foundation of the village, Cheikh Abdoulaye Dièye writes:

> Tradition reports that one day in 1888, as the Prophet's servant (RA) was leaving Darou Salam, he felt himself impelled by a divine force that only saints who have attained the final stage of devotion can feel.[21] It was then that the signs that were to guide him to the location of this secret place were revealed to him! He was led to the light, then flames appeared over a bush in this desert country inhabited by cactuses and wild beasts. Cheikh Amadou Bamba (RA) was transported under a tree called *Mbeep:* he trod for the first time the sanctified earth on which Touba was to be born.[22]

The holy character of the place was increased by the construction of the Touba mosque, which contains the founder's mausoleum. Begun in 1931, construction of the mosque was interrupted for financial and managerial reasons, and it did not begin again until 1945. The mosque was completed in 1963 and inaugurated by the caliph general and the president of the Republic of Senegal, Léopold Sédar Senghor. At the same time, the project of restructuring the village was launched. According to Cheikh Gueye, this marked

> the starting point for the operation that produced the current arrangement of the great mosque's esplanade and the neighborhoods . . . each one has an opening on the mosque. . . . Serigne Cheikh and his technical team, aided by the *baye fall,* laid out straight streets 20 to 25 meters wide leading to the mosque, as well as perpendicular streets 15 meters wide that defined the islands of construction.[23] Reconstruction began on the great central *pentch* [esplanade]; each concession facing the mosque was required to respect a distance of 120 meters from the latter, in order to facilitate the organization of large demonstrations and to enlarge the great mosque's esplanade, which is considered sacred. It was also decided to confirm the granting of concessions around the mosque to Cheikh A. Bamba's surviving sons.[24]

The inauguration of the mosque did not mark the end of its construction—as a Murid sign and symbol its construction is an ongoing project. Thus Touba became the place where the Murid memory and *imaginaire* were elaborated, the place where their economic, social, architectural, and cultural successes were inscribed. Occupying the center of this space, the mosque is also at the center of the Murid community's imaginaire and symbolism. It is the point of reference, the monument in which the identity of the brotherhood is concentrated. It produced both texts and images that were organized in the second phase of Muridism's development in order to make sense of the journeys of a community that had become an extensive commercial diaspora. The absolute symbols of this production are the minaret of the mosque, known as *Lamp Fall,* and the cemetery where every Murid disciple wants to be buried.[25] Places carried along to signify identity and to actualize memory, they complete the circular trajectory of the Murid disciple's life.

This center was the starting point for various efforts to colonize new

land for growing peanuts and, in the later phases of Murid development, for activities related to recycling urban waste and investing in the
informal and commercial sectors in the world's business centers. Thus
Touba was gradually invested, not only with the quality of the Murid
sacred city but also with the attributes of a significant place reevaluated
by a postcolonial liturgy that emphasizes resistance, autonomy, and the
creative cultural and economic capacities of a society freeing itself from
the grip of colonialism and from the bearers of imperial modernity.

In perfect harmony with the construction of the brotherhood's material base through peanut growing and commerce in manufactured
products, we witness Amadou Bamba's "Wolofization" of Islam. After
being initiated into the ways of *Qaddiryya* and *Tijaanyya* that were
present in West Africa, Amadou Bamba developed his own mystical
way "by abandoning all ways and all masters. He went beyond them
toward the fundamental light, the divine sun, and achieved his pact with
Muhammad (SAWS), the master of masters."[26] The properly native and
black character of Amadou Bamba's way is strongly affirmed by Cheikh
Abdoulaye Dièye, who writes: "The Cheikh thus inaugurates a new era
in the history of Islam and the black man. In fact, the black peoples of
Senegal were accustomed to go to Mauritania in search of spiritual masters. But Cheikh Bamba (RA) inverted the roles by becoming the first
black spiritual guide followed on a large scale by people of the white
race, thus showing that all men come from the same soul, and transcend
themselves only through their reverential fear of their creator."[27] During
the period of upheavals and social crises following the abolition of the
Atlantic slave trade (1815) and slavery (from 1848 on), this fear was accompanied by a major ethnic and social reorganization. It was probably
during this turbulent period that the Wolof ethnic group, which had
early developed an ability to integrate and assimilate members of other
ethnic groups, reinforced this cosmopolitan tendency. To a certain extent, by its more democratic character Muridism gave greater scope to
these operations, exploiting the twofold cosmopolitanism of Islam and
the Wolofs.

The Murid's unique cosmopolitanism is particularly evident in the
second phase of the community's development, when the first adven-
turous Murid merchants established themselves in the colonial ports of
call. In fact, long before large numbers of Murids moved to the cities in
the 1970s, and contrary to their common image as an exclusively rural

brotherhood, some Murid merchants were already involved in peanut trading in cities such as Rufisque and Kaolack. In addition, confronted by the cosmopolitanism of the ports of call, particularly in the four communes, they had already produced forms of identification by drawing on idioms borrowed from the rural repertoire of the brotherhood and combining them with urban trading procedures to make sense of urban situations. By re-creating in the city Murid religious associations (*dahiras*), they established the solid armature of a genuine "ritual community."[28] The rule of the talib's submission to the marabout and the restrictive character of the religious rules kept the Murid community on the margins of urban civility. In the city, Murids appropriated glass painting, the religious lithography introduced by the Lebanese, to narrate their own stories, alongside and/or against this colonial civility.[29] They thus constituted another library that does not draw on either the colonial imaginaire or that of natives of the four communes.

Glass painting usually recounts the prophetic saga and the battles of Islam when the prophet Mohammed was constructing the Muslim empire. Murids turned it to another purpose, using it to tell the saga of Amadou Bamba and emphasize the travails imposed on him by the colonial administration. At the same time, these repressive acts produced his holiness and his election, the stages of his deportation, and the sanctification of the journey as the perfect way of realizing oneself. In this way, the Murid merchant created a Murid enclave within the city that grounded the transitory character of his presence there. Mistreatment by the colonial administration and the miracles it produced became the founding texts of a community that defined itself and distinguished itself in a movement that requires a process of congregation taking the forms of exclusivity and closure: This is a black history and mythology in the making.[30] By hanging such pictures in their houses and shops in the markets and commercial streets, Murid merchants displayed in urban centers the marks of their appurtenance, images that referred to texts brought back from their travels and from Touba. And by securing this communitarian autonomy in the city, they guaranteed the groups' discipline under the vigilant supervision of their respective marabouts and of the caliph general.

To a large extent, the desire for an autonomous and distinctive community explains the fact—which we will return to at the end of this essay—that Murid intellectuals on one hand and commercial travelers and laborers on the other differ in their interpretation of the Murid presence in the world. This desire, interpreted as native, legitimizes the preeminence of the Baol region, the Murid homeland, at the expense of Senegal as a nation-state. The sanctification of the region of origin that confers on Murids incomparable abilities in labor and commerce is constituted precisely as the place from which the conquest of the world is to be achieved, at the same time as it ensures the salvation of Senegal as a whole in the near future. In this respect, the development of the nation can be realized only by adopting modes of economic, social, and political organization that are firmly rooted in Muridism. It is supposed to come to pass in a future whose forms are inscribed in the founder's prophecy.[31]

Two major events brought to an end these first two phases, during which the Murid Muslim community was essentially rural. The first of these relates to the death in 1968 of the second caliph general, El Hadj Falilou Mbacké. His successor, Abdou Lahat Mbacké, distanced himself from the government and sided with the peasants from whom the Senegalese government was demanding, sometimes by violent means, the repayment of debts owed to public institutions that financed agricultural activities. The third phase of Murid development began with the cycle of drought during the 1970s, which, combined with debt and impoverished soils, launched a wave of peasant movement to Senegalese cities. This subsequently inaugurated a second episode of Murid emigration out of Senegal to the great global metropolises (second, that is, to the emigration of Murid merchants to colonial ports). In this phase, the mobility organized by travel for business or labor established itself as an expressive element of the imaginaire of travel and of economic success as it was constituted in the interpretation of the founder's deportations.

"LIKE THE SAND, WE ARE BLOWN *EVERYWHERE*":
THE GEOGRAPHY OF DISPERSION

The Murids' movement toward the cities took place in three successive waves.[32] The first occurred during the period between the two world wars. The second, more extensive in scope, began at the end of the Second World War and created the first neighborhoods that called themselves by the names Touba, Colobane, and Gouye Mouride.[33] The third wave followed the worsening of the drought in the 1970s. It went beyond the boundaries of Senegal to include Africa, Europe, the Americas, and, more recently, Asia and Australia.

We have already indicated that when a Murid left his[34] homeland his first stop was usually a Senegalese city. He became involved in either commerce or informal economic activities. In every case, he kept busy and tried to build up a nest egg to establish himself or to be able to seek his fortune outside Senegal. The emblem of success was the acquisition of a tin trunk in the Sandaga market, the economic counterpart of the religious sanctuary in Touba. The extraordinary growth of the market seems to have been strongly stimulated by the activities of Murid migrants. Initially a market in foodstuffs and textiles, Sandaga has become a center for the sale of electronic devices coming from Asia (Hong Kong), the Middle East (Djedda), and America (New York).[35]

The transformation of the Sandaga market and the intensification of commercial activities were promoted by the Senegalese government's abandonment in 1986 of the policy of protecting products manufactured in Senegal. By authorizing the emergence of activities of recycling and recuperation, this decision led to the rapid development of two extremely dynamic sectors, the import-export sector and the service sector.[36] Murids quickly seized a monopoly on these activities and made them part of their identity in Senegalese urban society. The new situation favoring informal activities benefited from the gradual suppression of quotas and monopolies on certain products, such as rice, in the 1990s. In fact, the radical reorientation of economic policies from public decision-making to the laws of the market, opened, in a time of crisis, an extraordinary opportunity for Murids to invent new traditions and a new mission. As D. M. Carter suggests, "The brotherhoods have presented themselves as one of the features of a post-modern world in the streets of New York, Paris, Rome and Tokyo, as traders and in the small businesses of these and other centers as workers and trade persons," thus becoming active and inventive participants in economic globalization.[37]

From Senegalese cities and sometimes directly from their villages, Murids headed for African, European, American, and Asian cities. They wove an immense network with two poles, the spiritual (Touba) and the economic (Sandaga). During the 1970s, these Senegalese poles were complemented by network centers set up in France—at Strasbourg in the east, in contact with Germany and the wealthiest European tourists; at Marseilles in the south, near the French and Italian beaches crowded during the summer; and at Paris, at every season.[38] In Strasbourg, they were involved in violent polemics and were the object of a number of attacks. And as a merchant interviewed by Gérard Salem bitterly points out, "they speak German, too."[39] This remark not only indicates the Murids' linguistic adaptation but also the position they have acquired in the Strasbourg tourist sector. They compete aggressively with Strasbourg merchants whose most lucrative activity is selling plastic or plaster storks to tourists, especially German tourists, during the summer season. Using their global connections, the Murids are able to obtain these same products in the Chinese neighborhoods of New York at prices their Strasbourg competitors cannot match.[40]

During the 1980s, these networks grew larger as Murids established communities in Belgium, consolidated their positions in New York, and established themselves in Italy, from north to south.[41] Carter describes the contours of the Murid community in Turin: "The world of Mouridism in immigration is vast and extends from the holy city of Touba in Senegal to the major cities of Africa, Europe, the United States, Italy, Spain, France, Germany, Japan, Canada, and Australia: New York, Atlanta, Los Angeles, Turin, Livorno, Milan, Rome, Paris, Toulon, Lyon, Hong Kong, Berlin, London, Yaounde, and Madrid."[42] Victoria Ebin sketches edifying portraits of Murids who frequent this terrain, such as the five Fall brothers, based in Sandaga. They began as peddlers and salesmen in the streets of Dakar and now hold a monopoly on "cosmetic products from the United Kingdom and the United States and shoes from Taiwan"; with Korean partners, they have built a factory in Dakar for producing hairpieces.[43] The Fall brothers' business trips connect cities as different as New York, Djedda, and Dubai for jewels; New York, Rome, and Milan, for cosmetics; Djedda for perfumes and television sets; and Hong Kong for radios and costume jewelry.[44] In each city they have one correspondent and many salesmen from the Murid community who have established privileged relations with local intermediaries.[45] The center of the Fall brothers' vast web is their store in Sandaga. According to Victoria Ebin: "Known by the nickname of 'the United Nations,' it is one of the most cosmopolitan places in the city. Murid merchants, who are all connected in some way with the Falls, flock there from all over the world. They come to buy new products and to deliver others for sale. They listen to news about other people, exchange information, and discuss the possibility of obtaining a visa."[46]

The efficacy of the Murids' commercial networks and their work can be attributed to several factors. The first factor relates to the structures and ideology of the brotherhood, in particular to the talib's total submission to the marabout, which has become the strongest pillar of a brotherhood that controls a vast, dynamic network of disciples and economic activities. The second factor is the establishment of connections between the distribution points in Dakar and the Murid emigrant communities living in the international centers of wholesale commerce.[47] The third factor is participation in complex circuits of buying and selling that allow Paris or Strasbourg street merchants to sell merchandise bought in New York's Chinese neighborhoods or in Hong Kong, and merchants in Brussels to sell copper articles from Morocco to the city's Muslims.[48]

The intensity of the connections that give material form to the Murid diaspora in the world draws simultaneously on family relationships, appurtenance to the same village, the difficulty of the talibs' lives in village dahras, and allegiance to the same marabout. Inside and outside Senegal, Murids maintain the ritual community as soon as they take up residence in a new locale. They reproduce Touba by renaming the neighborhoods and cities where they live and work: Touba Sandaga and Touba Ouakam in Senegal, but also Touba in Turin. Precisely because of their logics of accumulation and their forms of organization, Murids occupy special neighborhoods in the cities where they are present in large numbers. Their overriding concern is to preserve their identity and the "rites of social exclusiveness" that are displayed and experienced in ideological, symbolic, and mythical intensification — that is, the affirmation of loyalties, the conscription of a local space at the heart of the megalopolis, the daily celebration of religiously inspired ritual ceremonies such as the reading of the *xasaïds* (the founder's poems), and the collective participation in meals and leisure activities.[49]

The communitarian reflexes thus described are strengthened by the fact that the Murids of the diaspora live, for example, in crowded apartments in dangerous neighborhoods of Marseilles and New York. Murids are often cloistered in their neighborhoods, and they are marginalized or marginalize themselves because of the incredible number of people packed into their apartments. Thus the logic of ideological enclosure is accompanied by a territorial enclosure. In a territory thus delimited, Murid diasporic culture is homogenized in a way that excludes foreign values by dramatizing and acting out Murid rituals in a systematic and exclusive manner. And by carrying out these daily acts, the diasporic culture produces intense feelings of solidarity, affection, cooperation, and mutual support. The community imposes on itself norms, values, and regimentation that outline the indisputable contours of the group's discipline. This discipline grounds the organization of financial relationships among members of the community and the establishment of a trust that is never broken. Social and ritual interaction — the recourse to mystical practices ensuring wealth, health, and success — circumscribe rules of economic exchange that conceal the community from its environment, except in business relationships.

It is in this wandering life full of privations that the *modu-modu* (as the non-Western-educated group of Murid migrants are nicknamed) is constructed.[50] He is an Italian, a New Yorker, a Marseillais, a Spaniard. He is constantly in movement. His stopover points are hotel rooms or overcrowded apartments in the main cities of the world where merchandise is piled up. He is always just stopping off, always in transit, thus erasing the notion of a fixed residence. But a center nonetheless remains: Touba — the place of spiritual and economic investment and the desired last resting place for eternity.[51] Touba is the sanctuary to which everyone must annually make a pilgrimage on the occasion of the *magal,* a two-day commemoration marking the return of Amadou Bamba from his exile in Gabon. Attracting more than a million believers in recent years, the magal repeats the community's memory and actualizes its mission, rejecting permanent establishment elsewhere as improbable. (And in so doing recalling the importance, noted earlier, of mobility as an expressive element of the Murid imaginaire.)

The modu-modu's mobility is solely geographical. He travels with his objects — his bubu cut from dark, heavy fabric; his tasseled hat; his big plastic sacks with white stripes; his enormous trunks and suitcases. And increasingly, among young people who wear jeans and sweaters to work, there is the necklace on which hangs a photo medallion of the marabout. The photo indicates that after adopting (during the colonial period) the glass painting inspired by Shiite lithography, the Murids now borrow some of their signs from the new technologies of information and communication. They display their memory with these photo medallions, as well as with posters depicting marabouts and the Touba mosque and decals of extracts from the founder's poems. As much by their attire as by their mobilization of Touba, its symbols, and its saints, and by adding the name of the holy city to that of the place where they reside, Murids escape the Westernized attire of the bearers of colonial and postcolonial modernity, as well as that of the Islamic-Arabic fashion that accompanies the trajectory of Islam as a modern, global religion.[52]

Mobility supports the Murid economic project that is realized in commercial relationships. Modu-modu is a synonym for merchant, even if, in all the cities where they are found, some Murids are also salaried workers (as in Turin), or jewelry makers or tailors (as in several African cities), or illegal street vendors or taxi drivers (not to mention intellectuals, discussed later in this essay, who are not considered "modu-modu"). Territorial mobility is combined with a considerable professional mobility.[53] Nonetheless, self-identification with the community through commerce is now the central element in the new Murid trajectory. And in this domain Murids are showing an extraordinary flexibility, not only in the registers of commercial practices, choice of products, definitions of markets, and modes of financing but also with regard to profit margins. They have thus appropriated the most important reflex of contemporary liberal cosmopolitanism, taking advantage of economic opportunity: sell whatever is in demand at a lower price, always respond to demand, and acquire captive markets. Through their networks and modes of operation, and by basing themselves solidly on their ritual community, with its structures, liturgy, texts, and images, in their own way they impose an order on the chaos of the market. They are globalizing themselves.

The objects and liturgies they produce in everyday life and their dramatizations and acts of ritual community are not forged with a view to resisting the movement of globalization. These objects and liturgies are the chief idioms Murids use to compete in the world market. Their recourse to a native grammar probably explains their ability to refuse to appropriate or assimilate, in the course of their many journeys, the language and habits of modernity as conceived by the West and world Islam. Is this because the rhythm of the brotherhood, its messages and texts, its (fictive or real) point of departure and return (after the accumulation of capital or at the time of death) are an insurmountable barrier to the assimilation of transnational Islamic or Western culture? Or is it because Touba is always there to sift, select, and propose a way of interpreting events in the world? Murid grammar does not limit itself to these operations alone. It makes openings for itself in the transnational culture, slips into them, and negotiates their share, in accord with secret rules and commercial practices. But for all that it does not subvert the world economic system, it allows itself to be borne by the system, impressing new points of inflection on it by demanding that it deal with new actors, new operations, and unprecedented and flexible forms of accumulation.

The triumph of the modu-modu as representative of the Murid community took place in the second half of the 1980s at the expense of another group much more active in the 1970s, the Murid intellectuals — students and Senegalese professionals living in Western countries, particularly in France. While there has never been any direct confrontation between the two groups, a competition between them is at the heart of tensions and conflicts that afflict the Murid brotherhood. The stakes are the management and supervision of Touba, on one hand, and questions of how to interpret, dramatize, and act out the Murid heritage and the founder's message, on the other.

"WE ARE LIKE BIRDS, WHO THINK OF HOME WHEN FLYING HIGH ABOVE THE EARTH"

Both the formation of the ritual community in a group in constant movement and the emergence of the modu-modu as exclusive identity have not only required a powerful standardization of practices, rites, and modes of socialization but have also provided a foundation for submission to strong moral obligations.[54] As Abner Cohen has observed with regard to the Hausa living in the Yoruba homeland, the ritual community presents itself as "the institution of stability-in-mobility."[55]

The logic governing Murid mobility requires the constant presence of the Touba sanctuary, along with the places constituting Murid identity: the mosque, the cemetery, and its extensions, on one hand, and the Sandaga and Okass markets, on the other.[56] The acts of re-creation implied by the existence of a sanctuary elicit new traditions and references. The construction of Murid identification was not easy to achieve, because of tensions between different groups within the brotherhood and between the brotherhood and other actors in Senegalese political, religious, and economic life. Internally, the intellectuals and the modu-modu fought for control of the brotherhood, especially of its outward signs and modes of inscription in the world.

The image of Touba as absolute reference point and sanctuary seems to have accompanied the Murid diaspora and bound it firmly to Baol, the Murid homeland. These new procedures, whether imaginary or real, are strongly connected with the growth of Murid migration. There is an undeniable concomitance between the construction of the point of reference and mobility, as if to create a fixed site, a single and unique residence. This double process of reference to construction and migra-tion is manifested in three domains: the spectacular development of the city, the creation of Murid objects, and financial investment in Touba as symbolized in the construction of the Touba city library.

The first domain, the city's development, has been studied from a geographical point of view by Eric Ross and Cheikh Gueye. In 1913, Touba was a village of slightly more than 500 inhabitants; by 1976 its population had grown to 29,634; in 1988 it was 138,896; in 2000 it is slightly more than 300,000, making it the second largest city in Senegal, after Dakar.[57] Touba is expected to have a population of about 500,000 in the course of the first decade of the twenty-first century. The Murids' holy city continues to be dynamic, and its strong attraction, which began with the first phase of the construction of the mosque, persisted and even accelerated under the caliphate of Abdou Lahat Mbacké (1968–1989). Given the sobriquet of "the builder," Abdou Lahat enlarged the mosque, began the creation of huge subdivisions for new construction, and called Murids to come and live in the holy city. With the help of financial success, his call was heard, as the increasing population figures show. In 1991, the current caliph adhered to the same course by creating a new, large-scale subdivision with 100,000 lots.

The second domain of construction and migration concerns the cre-ation of Murid objects. The background to these objects is the construc-tion of a memory whose armatures are the exiles and travails of Ama-dou Bamba, as well as the triumph displayed in the city of Touba and in the symbolism of the mosque and its minaret. The miracles that ac-companied the exiles, in particular the exile in Gabon and the sojourn in Mayombé, constitute the library on which Murids draw in order to make sense of their project of accumulation, the difficulties involved in their travel through the world, and their promised success. The miracles are the motor and the signs of the reconstruction of Touba wherever disciples reside. The attire, the trunks, and the big plastic bags identify a trajectory that reproduces—like the posters of the mosque and marabouts in hotel rooms and apartments—a history, an ambition, and a philosophy of work and community that Murids consider to be unique.

The final domain, which gives meaning to the first two, is the creation of the Touba city library. It is the work of the third caliph of the Murids, Abdou Lahat, "who undertook, following the example of Uthman (RA), to collect all the writings of Cheikh Amadou Bamba (RA) in order to make them available to the public. Then, in order to safeguard the Cheikh's works, he established a press and built the rich and sumptuous library in Touba."[58] The main consequences of these achievements were the extraordinary diffusion of the founder's xasaïds and easier access to his thoughts, in the form of pamphlets and books. Accompanying the Murid merchant in his travels through the world, these texts recount the Murid saga and express its principles, its norms, and its discipline. They have become the backbone of the ritual community, and they speak to the Murid's everyday experience. Texts adapted to mobility, they continue to bind the disciple even more strongly to a shared history—that of the success of the cheikh, of the brotherhood, and, collectively, of the disciples. They organize other borrowed objects—posters, medallions of the marabouts, and pictures accompanied by extracts from Amadou Bamba's poems.

These are three domains and three ways of domesticating the foreign and the global by recourse to native idioms that constantly seek to assert themselves in the world and to profit from it, concretely through economic activities, and symbolically by borrowing its modes and techniques of diffusing information. However, this information is not only native but disdains Islamic and Western texts with global pretensions. In contrast to the Sudanese village studied by Victoria Bernal, where local, Sufi Islam is succumbing to the restrictions of modern, cosmopolitan Islam, whose strength is "among other things, a movement from local, particularized Islams to Islam as a world religion," Murids resist with their texts, their objects, and Touba, the point of reference.[59] All these resources allow Murids to establish their uniqueness and their presence in the world. In particular, the reading of the xasaïds firmly anchors them in the space where cosmopolitan and modern Islam is deployed—the space of writing and the book.[60]

The Murids' inscription as a community in the world was not easily achieved. In their shifting and erratic trajectories, the modu-modu produce a ritual community constantly realized in the reference (Touba) and in the texts and images that constitute the memory of Muridism. This community is manifested in the acts of the founder and of his first disciples and children. In this sense, the mercantile component of the Murid community pursues, in its economic, political, cultural, and religious expressions, a peculiarly native project within a global environment. It refuses to universalize its message, even if it adopts — for example, in the attachment to Touba — strategies and modes of organization and financing associated with pentecostal and other religious movements currently experiencing phenomenal growth in Africa.

By contrast, in opposition to the native approach, since the 1970s Murid intellectuals have attempted to carry out a modernization of the brotherhood's presence and acts on both the national and the international scene. They were the first to put Muridism on the world map, first in France with their socio-professional and student organizations, and then in Senegal with the creation of the Dahira des Étudiants Mourides à l'Université de Dakar (the Murid students' association of the University of Dakar) in 1975. These organizations aimed to free the brotherhood from its strong Wolof coloring and to reorganize its apparatuses with a view to globalizing Muridism and ridding it of its images and texts that focus on miracles accomplished by Amadou Bamba. For them, it was a question of drawing support from the new library in Touba and the founder's work in order to incorporate the Murid trajectory and its scriptural grammar into the dynamics of global re-Islamization. The search for this much more individual and much less familial religious identity was expressed in the form of allegiance not to a marabout, but to the point of reference, Touba. It emerged very early among university alumni whose movement is called the Hizbut Tarkya (soldiers of the brotherhood). They have established themselves in the holy city by creating their own domain, their own commercial structures, and their own networks of membership based on the "principle of personal commitment" (for instance, by giving part of one's wealth for the exclusive use of the caliph general, who guaranteed a certain legitimacy to the *daara* — as the members of the movement like to be called).[61] This legitimacy has been deployed to challenge the genealogical principle of succession that has governed the brotherhood's life since the founder's death. In opposition to the founder's grandsons, members of Hizbut Tarkya call for an end to genealogical rule by asserting the importance of the mastery, through reading and commentary, of Amadou Bamba's message.[62] Through its organization, rule of communitarian life, and modes of financing, the Hizbut Tarkya movement participates in an effort to break with the native project of the community. A violent conflict in 1997 and 1998 between this movement and Amadou Bamba's grandsons shows the depth of the crisis and the latent tensions within the brotherhood.

According to Murid intellectuals, the search for a modern interpretation of the founder's message is voicing an urgent need not only to emphasize the Islamic orthodoxy of the Murid message but also to propose a theological and philosophical version of it that is accessible and acceptable to both the West and the East. This need implies, as the editor of the newspaper *Ndigël* wrote more than a decade ago, the "de-Senegalization of Amadou Bamba's thought by restoring its splendor as the Cheikh drew it from the Koran and from the Prophet's Sunnah. When this is done, Muridism will have access to the world at large."[63]

The future of an African commercial diaspora, always in transit, will be played out in this tension between a presence manifested in the display of a native cosmopolitanism and an acceptance in the world. And within this framework, it must be understood that the order and temporality of the world are not univocal, and they do not necessarily require imprisoning the immemorial and undisciplined temporalities of the new actors on the modern scene. Therefore, we must conclude that the alternative modernities that are emerging in the disparate processes of globalization are not situated in a synthetic perspective whose backbone is Western modernity and its injunctions. As the foregoing remarks show, it is not a matter of trying to demonstrate these modernities by the synthesis or the hybridization of the autochthonous and the global that current discourses on globalization seek to achieve, usually in an inept way, without accounting for the creativity involved in the slow and shrewd deployment of the local in global space and time. In the Murid case, there is neither a dissolution of the local in the global nor an annexation of the latter by the former. Rather, the Murid experience involves constructing original texts and images that establish themselves at the heart of the world, and by so doing create new forms of cosmopolitanism whose manifestations no longer refer necessarily and obligatorily to the acquisition of an identity through assimilation but, rather, to the display of a unique identity added to global temporality and not simply informed by the Western trajectory of modernity alone. The Murid diaspora in the world, precisely because it presents itself in the mode of a ritual community, participates in this plural representation of the world on the basis of unique achievements. Its modes of operation make its vernacular contribution to cosmopolitanism by exhibiting it at the heart of the procedures of globalization, thus promoting pluralization of cosmopolitan forms and of local variations of world time. Such pluralization of cosmopolitan forms are illustrated by the introduction of products, actors, and relational systems that have long been excluded from the Senegalese market because of the colonial pact that established a privileged and exclusive relationship with France. Actors in an international geography completely foreign to the intellectual and political elite, Murids are pursuing the enterprise of modernization through practices sanctioned by an economic success that is not only compatible with globalization but also an integral part of the process.

NOTES

1. "Le temps du monde" refers to the development process as exclusively liberal and Western driven. As a result, for non-Western cultures, it refers to a process of Westernization.

2. Arjun Appadurai, *Modernity at Large: Cultural Dimensions of Globalization* (Minneapolis: University of Minnesota Press, 1996); see especially p. 4.

3. Stuart Hall, "A Conversation with Stuart Hall," *Journal of the International Institute* 7, no. 1 (fall 1999): 15 (Hall's emphasis).

4. Hall, "Conversation," 15. Jean-François Bayart, ed., *La réinvention du capitalisme* (Paris: Karthala, 1994).

5. Hall, "Conversation," 15.

6. See Jean Copans, "Jean Copans répond. Les chercheurs de la confrérie et la confrérie des chercheurs: À chacun son Khalife et Marx pour tous?" *Politique Africaine* 1, no. 4 (November 1981): 111–21.

7. This first generation is exemplified by Paul Marty, *Etudes sur l'Islam au Sénégal,* 2 vols. (Paris: Leroux, 1917).

8. Donal Cruise O'Brien, *The Mourid of Senegal: The Political and Economic Organization of an Islamic Brotherhood* (Oxford: Clarendon Press, 1971); O'Brien, *Saints and Clerics: Essays in the Organization of a Senegalese Peasant Society* (Cambridge: Cambridge University Press, 1975); Jean Copans, *Les marabouts de l'arachide* (Paris: Le Sycomore, 1980); J. Copans, J. Couty, J. Roch, and G. Rocheteau, *Maintenance économique et changement sociale au Sénégal,* vol. 1: *Doctrine et pratique du travail chez les*

mourides (Paris: ORSTOM, 1972); Christian Coulon, *Le marabout et le prince: Islam et pouvoir au Sénégal* (Paris: Pédone, 1981); and Momar Coumba Diop, "La confrérie mouride: Organisation économique et mode d'implantation urbaine" (Ph.D. diss., Université de Lyon, 1980).

9. M. C. Diop, "Les affaires mourides à Dakar," *Politique Africaine* 1, no. 4 (November 1981): 90–100; M. C. Diop, "Fonctions et activités des dahiras mourides urbains (Sénégal)," *Cahiers d'Etudes Africaines* 11 (1982): 81–83; Gérard Salem, "De Dakar à Paris, des diasporas d'artisans et de commerçants: Etude socio-géographique du commerce sénégalais en France" (Ph.D. diss., Paris, Ecole des Hautes Etudes en Sciences Sociales, 1981); Salem, "De la brousse sénégalaise au Boul'Mich: Le système commercial mouride en France," *Cahiers d'Etudes Africaines* 21 (1981): 81–93; D. Cruise O'Brien, "Charisma Comes to Town: Mouride Urbanization, 1945–1986," in D. Cruise O'Brien and C. Coulon, eds., *Charisma and Brotherhood in African Islam* (Oxford: Clarendon Press, 1988), 135–55; A. Moustapha Diop, "Les associations Murid en France," *Esprit* no. 102 (June 1985): 197–206; A. M. Diop, "Un aperçu de l'Islam négro-africain en France," *Migrants Formation,* no. 82 (1990): 77–81; A. M. Diop, "Le mouvement associatif islamique en Ile-de-France," *Revue Européenne des Migrations Internationales* 7 (1991): 91–117; Victoria Ebin, "Mourides Traders on the Road: The Transition of a Senegalese Brotherhood from Agriculture to International Trade," unpublished manuscript, Social Science Research Council, n.d.; Ebin, "Commerçants et missionnaires: Une confrérie sénégalaise à New York," *Hommes et Migrations,* no. 1132 (May 1990); Ebin, "A la recherche de nouveaux poissons: Stratégies commerciales mourides en temps de crise," *Politique Africaine* 45 (1992): 86–99; Ebin, "Making Room versus Creating Space: The Construction of Special Categories by Itinerant Mourid Traders," in *Making Muslim Space in North America and Europe,* ed. Barbara D. Metcalf (Berkeley: University of California Press, 1996); D. M. Carter, *States of Grace: Senegalese in Italy and the New Europe Immigration* (Minneapolis: University of Minnesota Press, 1997); and Cheikh Gueye, "L'organisation de l'espace dans une ville religieuse: Touba (Sénégal)" (Ph.D. diss., Université de Strasbourg, 1999).

10. Hall, "Conversation," 15.

11. In a sense, the first process of globalization took place in Senegal under the four communes system. From the time of the French Revolution through the nineteenth century, inhabitants of these four Senegalese cities were granted French citizenship by French policy of assimilation. Their legal status as French citizens was confirmed by the law passed at the French National Assembly on 29 September 1916, stating that "the natives of the *communes de plein exercice* of Senegal are and remain French citizens as provided by the law of 15 October 1915." Consequently, they upheld their political rights while also asserting a distinct cultural identity as Muslims who need not abide by French civil code. See Mamadou Diouf, "The French Colonial Policy of Assimilation and the Civility of the Originaires of the Four Communes (Senegal): A Nineteenth-Century Globalization Project," in *Globalization and Identity: Dialectics of Flows and Closure,* ed. Birgit Meyer and Peter Geschiere (Oxford: Blackwell Publishers, 1999), 71–96.

12. Manthia Diawara, *In Search of Africa* (Cambridge: Harvard University Press, 1998).

13. Before publishing his book, C. H. Kane presented this tension in his talk at a colloquium organized by the review *Esprit* in October 1961: "A culture of orality cannot be taken serious in a world in which time and distance have ceased to be obstacles to communication. The orality of our cultures limits their range of diffusion, and thus their competitive power; as a result, we are put in a position of inferiority in our relationships with the rest of the world. This also constitutes a serious handicap in coming to terms with the world at large. Our inner feeling about our cultures will not survive our entry into the cycle of technological progress; *we will be obliged to put our soul in some secure place before donning the mechanic's blue overalls.*" C. H. Kane, "Comme si nous nous étions donnés rendez-vous," *Unité Africaine* 4 (1961) (emphasis added).

14. V. Y. Mudimbe, *The Invention of Africa: Gnosis, Philosophy, and the Order of Knowledge* (Bloomington: Indiana University Press, 1988).

15. See Martin Klein, "The Muslim Revolution in Nineteenth-Century Senegambia," in *Western African History,* ed. Daniel F. McCall, Norman R. Bennett, and Jeffrey Butler (New York: Praeger, 1969).

16. Copans, "Jean Copans répond."

17. Copans, "Jean Copans répond." Dahras are rural schools in which children live in the marabout's compound (far from their parents), learn the Koran, and cultivate the marabout's field. As adults, they are released and settle nearby the marabout or migrate—either way, they remain disciples.

18. Vincent Monteil, "Une confrérie musulmane: Les Mourides du Sénégal," *Archives de Sociologie des Religions* 14 (1962): 77–101.

19. See Christopher Harrison, *France and Islam in West Africa, 1860–1960* (Cambridge: Cambridge University Press, 1988).

20. See Diouf, "The French Colonial Policy of Assimilation."

21. *RA* is a prayer meaning "peace and reward upon him" that Muslims use when referring to the prophet and some leading Islamic figures.

22. Cheikh Abdoulaye Dièye, *Touba: Signes et symboles* (Paris: Editions Deggel, 1997), 48.

23. Baye fall is a branch of the Murid brotherhood that emphasizes labor rather than prayer.

24. Gueye, "Les marabouts urbanisants," unpublished manuscript, n.d., 6–8. Gueye (12, n. 34) explains that pentch "designates the central square of a locality where councils and markets are held. In Touba, the different pentch, where mosques and mausoleums have been built, constitute sacred spaces and are the most important structural elements of the town."

25. *Lamp* means "light," and *Fall* is a patronym; *Lamp Fall* is the sobriquet given to Cheikh Ibra Fall, one of Amadou Bamba's first disciples. He preferred to devote himself to his master's service more than to prayer and observation of Islamic rules from which he and his disciples were exempted by the marabout. He symbolizes the Murid conception of the equivalence of labor and prayer. Eric Ross offers a rather convinc-

ing interpretation of the meaning of the minaret's nickname: "Rising eighty-seven meters above Touba is the mosque's central minaret, known popularly as Lamp Fall, after Cheikh Ibra Fall, Ahmadou Bamba's most fiercely devoted mûrid. Lamp Fall is one of the tallest structures in the country, its height far in excess of the needs for call to prayer, and there can be no doubt that its main function is representational. It is a visible concrete manifestation of the Tree of Paradise, and it figures prominently in popular Mouride iconography: on tombstones, on pamphlets and calendars, and on the sides of buses." "Touba, A Spiritual Metropolis in the Modern World," *Canadian Journal of African Studies / Revue Canadienne des Etudes Africaines* 29 (1995): 227.

26. SAWS has the same meaning as RA (see n. 22). Dièye, *Touba: Signes et symboles,* 17–18.

27. Dièye, *Touba: Signes et symboles,* 30–31.

28. See Diop, "Les affaires mourides à Dakar," 79–91. Also see Abner Cohen, *Custom and Politics in Urban Africa: A Study of Hausa Migrants in Yoruba Towns* (Berkeley: University of California Press, 1969), 141.

29. Glass painting (sometimes called "reverse-glass painting") is painting done directly on the inside of glass but to be viewed from the outside. Murid glass painting depicts life stories of the founder and his most important disciples.

30. See M. Stroobel, "La peinture sous verre du Sénégal: Etude anthropologique" (Ph.D. diss., Université de Strasbourg, 1982), and M. Diouf, "Islam: Peinture sous verre et idéologic populaire," in *Art pictural zaïrois,* ed. B. Jewsiewicki (Quebec: Editions du Septentrion, 1992), 29–40.

31. Vis-à-vis the construction of the Senegalese nation-state, it should be noted that, on one hand, Murids dismiss the nation-state as a political and cultural unit irrelevant to their economic project, for their success is rooted in the brotherhood. On the other hand, Murids believe that their economic success makes them the one group able to revitalize the nation-state by injecting their ideology and practice through a Murid-inspired government.

32. The first part of the heading for this section (with emphasis added) is borrowed from an interview conducted by Ebin with a Murid merchant in New York: "Our homeland [in Western Senegal] is built on sand, and like the sand, we are blown everywhere. . . . Nowadays, you can go to the ends of the earth and see a Mouride wearing a wool cap with a pom-pom selling something to somebody." Ebin, "Making Room versus Creating Space," 93.

33. The first two names are names of the villages of Murid dignitaries, and the third means simply the "Murids' Baobab." They are found in all the Senegalese cities where Murids live.

34. As this essay is a discussion of the construction and experiences of Murid males, the use of the pronoun *he* is deliberate.

35. Ebin, "A la recherche de nouveaux poissons," 86.

36. Ebin, "A la recherche de nouveaux poissons," 86; Diop, "Les affaires mourides à Dakar."

37. Carter, *States of Grace,* 47.

38. Salem, "De Dakar à Paris."

39. Salem, "De Dakar à Paris," 37.

40. Salem, "De Dakar à Paris," 42.

41. On the Murids in New York, see Ebin, "Making Room versus Creating Space."

42. Carter, *States of Grace,* 73.

43. The quotation comes from Ebin, "A la recherche de nouveaux poissons," 87–88.

44. Ebin, "A la recherche de nouveaux poissons," 88.

45. Ebin ("A la recherche de nouveaux poissons," 95) gives the example of a Pakistani-American in New York who has become the chief supplier of electronic products for the Sandaga market.

46. Ebin, "A la recherche de nouveaux poissons," 89.

47. Ebin, "A la recherche de nouveaux poissons," 87.

48. Ebin, "A la recherche de nouveaux poissons," 87.

49. Cohen, *Custom and Politics in Urban Africa,* 156.

50. Modu-modu refers to Mamadou Moustapha Mbacké, the oldest son of the founder Amadou Bamba, who became the first caliph (1927–1945). Modu is a common nickname for Mamadou.

51. Ross ("Touba, A Spiritual Metropolis," 227) describes this desire: "The cemetery is the next most important element of the city's spiritual topography, and its location in the very heart of the sanctuary confirms its elevated status in Mouride cosmology. It is the prevailing view among the Mourides that burial in the earthly Touba virtually guarantees access to the heavenly one. The cemetery is the Gate to Paradise; physical burial amounts to passage through the Gate."

52. Bernal, "Islam, Transnational Culture, and Modernity in Rural Sudan," 132.

53. See, for example, the account of the life of Amadou Dieng collected and analyzed by Ebin, "Making Room versus Creating Space," 97.

54. The heading for this section is borrowed from an interview conducted and discussed by Ebin, "Making Room versus Creating Space," 98.

55. Cohen, *Custom and Politics in Urban Africa,* 159.

56. According to Ross ("Touba, A Spiritual Metropolis," 240), "Okass acquired national renown as a center for contraband merchandise — acting as a wholesale purveyor for markets in Senegal's other cities. . . . Today Okass remains Touba's economic heart. Despite the fact that the city's thoroughfares converge on the Mosque, its public transit network (minibuses, buggies, and carts) converges on Okass. The market occupies several city blocks." On the development and management of this market, see Diop, "Les affaires mourides à Dakar," 91–93.

57. Marty, *Etudes sur l'Islam au Sénégal,* cited by Ross, "Touba, A Spiritual Metropolis," 252. Gueye, "Les marabouts urbanisants," 1. Gueye estimates the average annual rate of Touba's demographic growth between 1976 and 1995 to be 13 percent.

58. Dièye, *Touba: Signes et symboles,* 64.

59. Bernal, "Islam, Transnational Culture, and Modernity in Rural Sudan," 131–32.

60. Bernal ("Islam, Transnational Culture, and Modernity in Rural Sudan," 133) emphasizes this issue: "At both the local and the national levels, the move toward a more scripturalist Islam is a move away from local parochial identities toward perceived conformity with a more universal set of beliefs and practices."

61. Gueye, "Les marabouts urbanisants," 19–20.

62. This concern is also found in the Paris Murid association known as Khitmal Khadim (saint, chosen by God), whose scholarly committee not only provided the preface for the book by Cheikh Abdoulaye Dièye but also financed its production and publication.

63. El Hadj Fallou Ndiaye, *Ndigël* (Paris), no. 21, second semester 1990, 1.

"Crushing the Pistachio":

Eroticism in Senegal and the Art of Ousmane Ndiaye Dago

T. K. Biaya

Translated by Steven Rendall

M. Dimé's sculpture *Serer Woman,* a work structured by a piece of Senegalese erotic symbolism, puzzled art critics at the Biennial Exposition in Venice (1993) and at the Museum for African Art in New York (1994) (figure 1). An overturned mortar forms the convex base of the sculpture; atop the mortar stands an erect pestle, the hammer end of which is decorated with bits of wood that suggest the head and braided hair of a woman. To Western eyes it might suggest the modern tradition of abstractly sculpted nudes, after the manner of Brancusi. To the African *imaginaire,* however, *Serer Woman* continues the tradition of erotic storytelling practiced by the Lawbé *griots,* presenting as it does, in allegory fashion, the anatomy of copulation. In this case, copulation is frustrated. The genital forms, despite their excitement, face away from each other: the penile pestle points upward, and the mouth of the vaginal mortar faces downward. The coitus implied by "crushing the pistachio"—that is, the penetration of the penis that causes the clitoris to be pushed inward—is impossible; just as, allegorically, no pistachio nut could be ground with a mortar and pestle so arranged. The work expresses a foiled desire, similar to the work of Ousmane Sow (Pivin and Saint Martin 1995). Genital sex itself is thwarted by means of the arrangement, and the sculpture would suggest to a Senegalese the public censorship of eroticism in Senegal.

What is perhaps paradoxical about the censorship of eroticism in Senegal is that the body is erotically valued in African societies on the condition that it is not naked but accessorized, properly prepared. The body's beauty and erotic value are achieved not when it is stripped bare but when it is worked or denatured—for example, by excision, scarification, elongation of the clitoris, and so on. Such a body modified in accord with African canons invites the tactile and olfactory sensuality of an eroticism of the skin, of the senses of touch and smell (Biaya 1999: 19). Eroticism is the body's embellishment by methods that blend its accessories with its attributes, as flesh itself is worked in such a way that blurs the distinction of the cosmetic and the organic.

A logic similar to this formalism of the body has begun to structure a relationship of eroticism to the photography of the nude in Senegal. It would be fair to say that to this point Western photographers such as U. Ommer (1986, 1997) have pursued the art of photographing the nude in West Africa most successfully. African contributions, by contrast, have tellingly included postcard reproductions drawn from Ommer's books and sold in the streets and in the major hotels in Dakar.[1] In consequence, the existing body of work, assembled mostly by international artists who travel to Africa in search of "subject matter," has largely excluded the sources of sensuality and eroticism that decide the shape of the nude locally. The raiment, jewelry, and techniques with which the naked body is made erotic are absent from the work of Ommer, who instead continues the nineteenth-century pursuit of premodern exoticism on Senegal's beaches. A similar claim might be made about figurative work in other media as well. The work of the painter Yacouba, for example, which is exhibited in Senegal's large, international hotels, serves tourists an exotic primitivism that bears the familiar influence of Matisse. In a very real sense, the African body—and, indeed, the idea of what it means for it to be naked or sensual—has been ignored by this body of work.

A recent break with this trend was made by Ousmane Ndiaye Dago, who has produced some of the most noteworthy and deeply erotic photography to be shot in Africa. While in the West the form of the nude may have made the transition from classical figure to everyday commercial product, the global circuits traveled by the nude's modern facsimiles are simultaneously very close and distant for the average African. One of the strengths of Dago's work is his sensitivity to these conditions of time and space. He has not voyaged into primitivism to make himself cosmopolitan, as Gauguin voyaged to the South Pacific and Matisse to Algeria, each to make himself modern. Dago has instead privileged the culturally hybrid to produce a rooted work that is simultaneously a document and the achievement of Senegalese erotic culture. And despite his shy protests, he has indeed produced an erotic corpus.[2] Composed of about a hundred photographs, the project's originality emerges from the creative space that Dago has opened by a mixture of three arts: painting, sculpture, and photography. The ingenious combination of these forms magnifies the attachment of Dago's interpretations of the Western-classical form of the nude to various dimensions of Senegalese culture, an attachment that is further reinforced by the documentary sequencing in which the photographs are arranged. But to understand Dago's accomplishment more fully, it will be necessary at least partly to retrace the development of eroticism in modern Senegal.

*

Since colonization, a Western-styled eroticism has increasingly set the ambience of urban public spaces in Africa (Coppiert's Wallant 1993). Visible in the arts, advertising, and leisure venues of African cities, Western erotics have assisted the achievement of modernity in the African postcolony, where sex, belly, mouth, and violence remain the ingredients of the *episteme* of command (Mbembe 1992; Bayart 1989, 1993).

Given the legitimacy with which eroticism is imbued by the centrality of leisure to capital, the circulation of Western eroticism has brought a compelling authority to bear on the practices by which modern African urban subjects are crafted from the material of "village" identity (La Fontaine 1970; Martin 1996). In these urban spaces where Western eroticism is most conspicuous, however, it has encountered a field of objects that have shaped the course of its circulation. The largest of these include the traditions of African eroticisms, the predecessor cosmopolitanism of Islamization, and robustly persistent hybrid practices.

Eroticism in contemporary urban Africa has developed on, at minimum, two registers: that on which Christianity has encountered African cultures and religions, and that on which colonial modernity has encountered an African, and largely secularized, Islam. Both registers have in common an erotic philosophy that issues from African religions. Consider Senegal: On one hand, processes and structures of global exchange in Senegal have been brokered by the cosmopolitanism of Islamic urban culture. On the other hand, metropolitan Judeo-Christian values have been inscribed into Senegalese modernity by French colonization and the Senghorian postcolonial state. The milieu of indigenous traditions and practices, however, has provided more than a backdrop for these social metamorphoses. Adherents of Islam and Christianity may comprise 90 and 10 percent of Senegal's popula-

Figure 1. Femme sérère
(Serer Woman) *by*
M. Dimé, reprinted from
Thomas McEvilley, Fusion:
West African Artists at the
Venice Biennale *(New York:*
Museum for African Art, 1993).

Sequence 1: *Djanke yu nekh*

Young women in plastic attitudes, nude and veiled.

Sequence 2: *Goor-djigen yi*, lesbian desire

Women interlaced in amatory postures, wrapped in transparent cloth.

tion, respectively; yet, despite the massive conversions and active prose-lytizing of these revealed religions, Senegalese society remains fervently animist. For example, a Senegalese would likely tell you that Senegal is a country in which the population is 90 percent Muslim, 10 percent Christian, and 100 percent animist. Indeed, no undertaking in Senegal is begun without resort to talismans, spells, and rituals, in addition to a visit to the church or the marabout. As will be seen, multiple allegiances like these have significant consequences for the forms and meanings of social practices, eroticism included.

Islam has developed in Senegal as a series of mediations between local and cosmopolitan systems. In consequence, Senegal has produced a coincidence of three forms of Islam that operate in complementary relation to each other. The first of such relations is that between ortho-dox Islam and the Islam of the maraboutic orders rooted in Sufism. The maraboutic is the more energetic and less conservative of these two strains and, as the second form, participates in the mediation between Islamic practices and the local traditions in which they are rooted. The endurance of these autochthonous traditions points to the third form of Islam in Senegal, a popular Islam, which may be said to dominate the symbolic field of objects and their cultural operation.[3]

Such is the case, at least in part, because throughout the process of Islamization, the castes of pre-Islamic social structure have not been banished but adjusted to reflect the Senegalization of Sufism.[4] As such, Senegal has witnessed the survival of the caste of the Lawbés, which wields a monopoly over erotic speech and performance, and that of the traveling musicians, the griots or *gewel* (as they are called in Wolof). Numerous ancient social structures and hierarchies have equally with-stood colonization and the Senghorian project to build a secular state.[5] Yet eroticism, theoretically an area slow to evolve because of conserva-tive religious control, has nevertheless been one in which innovation and change have advanced rapidly. The maraboutic elite, respectful of a domain of the private that it remains reluctant to trespass, has focused its censorial authority instead on public forms of speech that exceed its established proscriptions. For example, Murid marabouts invoking the teachings of the prophet Cheikh Amadou Bamba succeeded in cancel-ing the television series *Dallas* at the same time that, as polygamists, they permitted trade in the *bethio*, an erotic accessory that captures some of the social contradictions of Senegalese culture. A short skirt perfumed and decorated with erotic motifs and worn as underclothing, the bethio is said to come from Diourbel, an administrative center and holy place for Murid Muslims in Senegal.

Before the arrival of Islam in the eleventh century, eroticism in Senegal was freighted with African social and religious codes. Young men and women, even where initiation rituals were carried out, received a sexual education that began with conversations with their grandparents and continued as the children matured and exchanged information with their peers. Families were stewards to an age-old canon that included erotic games and literature, aphrodisiacs, and arts of the body. Within this tradition, hairstyle, body ornaments, and mutilations transformed the unmarked body of the neophyte into a locus of pleasures, appropriately prepared for touching, penetration, copulation, and orgasm. This was a tactile eroticism more connected with the senses of touch and smell than with the sense of sight. Its symbolic register was a space in which the ephemeral opened to the eternal, and the transitory met with perpetuity. Public erotic performances (storytelling and dance), for instance, were confined to festivals whose finite and transitory form emphasized the fleeting nature of the erotic. Simultaneously, sex organs were the procreative gateway through which returning ancestors reincarnated themselves in newborn children and achieved perpetuity through propagation (Biaya 1999).

During the religious ceremonies that punctuate everyday life today (baptism, communion, marriage, the return from a pilgrimage to Mecca), a host will still invite Lawbé griots to perform the dances and songs whose bold lyrics narrate the erotic discovery of the body. Should this entertainment be omitted, the ceremony will be said to be flat, a failure. Such performances are supposed to carry a cathartic value; at minimum their robust sexuality contrasts with the everyday repression imposed by Islam and by the state. While the professional performance of this entertainment is restricted to low-caste women, female guests to the ceremony, if with less visible enthusiasm than the Lawbés, typically join in the illicit dancing, and thus the ephemeral quality of the erotic is still reflected in the momentary suspension of social convention.

The body practices at the core of Senegal's erotic heritage were infused with fresh material by the arrival of Islam. With Islam came trade in perfumes, as well as new styles and habits of clothing; indeed, the idea of the fully clothed body was itself introduced by Islam. As they swept through Senegalese society, Islamic practices and objects that were not explicitly sexual but nonetheless sensual yielded readily to incorporation into the traditional repertory of erotic equipment. Incense, for example, whose use in Islamic practices of healing (exorcism) derives from verses in the Koran, stimulated creativity in the erotic imagination. Imported perfumes presented new olfactory facets to the erotic sensorium, as the amative woman took to wearing scented undergarments (such as the bethio) and girdles of fragrant pearls (the *fer*), which she would reveal only to her lover or husband. Known as *thiuraye*, these practices became central to the erotic arts of West Africa.

Perhaps the foremost symbol of erotic mastery to emerge in West Africa is the Senegalese figure of the *drianké*, a titillating, plump, and mature woman expert at thiuraye. Today in Senegal, a second figure exports thiuraye over the subregion, and this circulation has fostered the myth and fantasy of a Senegalese eroticism superior to other local forms. In this mythology, the Senegalese woman is identified as a predatory figure, a cunning and sexually insatiable husband-stealer. The second figure participating in this circulation is the *diskette*. Derived from *disco*, the *diskette* is a young Senegalese woman with the slender body of a fashion model, who frequents the nightlife of urban discotheques and bars. Less expert than the mature, full-figured drianké, the *diskette* nonetheless carries a double erotic charge: a body type with global erotic purchase, stamped with the thiuraye seal of erotic sophistication and craft. Dancing at Dakar's Jet 7 Club or African Star Club, with her hair and clothes in the unisex style, she is a copy of the international fashion models circulated locally by magazines (*Ebony, Amina*) and television (MTV, TV5). The *diskette* who desires the gaze of an African man (as opposed to that of the tourist, a distinct potential target) will include in her attire a double girdle of shimmering, multicolored pearls (*bine bine*), which evoke local forms of erotic play, such as the ventilator dance.[6] This is the same type of pearls that is worn hidden under the drianké's loose-fitting *bubu*, from where it emanates intoxicating perfumes. Between these two figures, the *diskette* and the drianké, one can see the basis of Dago's inflections of the nude.

But the drianké and the *diskette* are not the only new figures that sociopolitical change has produced in West Africa. Another figure is the *thierno* or Koranic master, an intellectual versed in Arabic who provides instruction in the Koran and, along with the Imam, oversees social

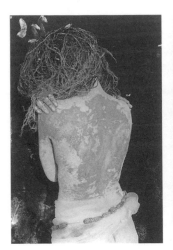

Sequence 3: *Diskette*

A young woman, photographed from behind
and naked to her thighs, wrapped with a transparent
loincloth and colored pearls, undresses to pose nude.

conduct. Since the end of the 1980s, Dakar and Saint Louis, cities in which Sufis are dominant, have experienced a resurgence of fundamentalism. In this atmosphere, many women and girls have taken again to wearing the headscarf, the *hijab*, which hides the hair. Ostensibly a symbol of orthodox conformity, the signification of the headscarf is ambiguous in Senegal. If the hijab appears to signal allegiance to Islam, it hardly accomplishes a rapprochement between more orthodox Islam and Senegalese Sufism. To the contrary, the rift between the two traditions is maintained through the symbolic association by which the headscarf acquires a second meaning: public eroticism and its negation. While T. Gerholm claims (1997: 158–59) that in Egypt the repetition of the symbols of Islam (hijab, chador, beads, prayer) make of the practice an expression of authentic piety, such a logic is inoperative in Senegal. In fact, wearing the headscarf is neither a way of rooting women in the Great Tradition nor of bringing the two Islamic traditions together, even if the hijab is usually worn during the period of the great Muslim holy days.[7]

Since its introduction to Senegal, the hijab has been incorporated into the logic of Senegalese eroticism. In marabuutic practices, wearing the headscarf used to be a way of keeping away *suli*, the power of seduction said to emanate from certain light-colored female faces (Nicolas 1985). Reinterpreted in this way by African Islam, suli expresses the power of the body's attraction and of sexual fantasy, both of which are kindled by the illicit carnal power known as *bu khess bu diek*, "the sorcery of the beautiful light-colored face." The headscarf, because it had been prayed over by the marabout, was believed to safeguard men and women against carnal temptations.

However, the hijab's recent return to the public space is in part based on a strategic choice made by Senegalese women. In the space of the secular modern state, these women, often less formally educated than men, are recasting and deploying the power of suli to reinvent themselves as erotic agents. Depending on how it is worn, the headscarf may be understood to enhance the seductive power of the face, by which suli is not diminished but magnified. Consider also what has happened in the city of Touba. Due to its erotic significance, the practice of *khessal* (depigmentation) was prohibited in this holy place by Murid authorities; women visitors to the city now frequently evade the prohibition by wearing the headscarf! A third function of the hijab is to express a

Sequence 4: *Dial dialy*

A woman undoes her loincloth to reveal a body nude but
for the *dial dialy*, a type of *fer* or erotic girdle of pearls.

woman's reaction against her dominated situation in the private sphere. When the hijab is worn at home when visitors are present, it suggests less piety than the wife's sexual self-censorship and the embrace of her role as an educator. In such a context, it articulates the four characteristics of the colonial urban woman: submission, good housekeeping, acceptance of the husband's polygamy or infidelity, and motherhood (Biaya 1996: 345–70).

Thus, the headscarf concludes with a deeply equivocal stroke the construction of the aesthetics of feminine African eroticism begun by Islamization and suggests the variety of ways in which women are beginning to reinterpret themselves socially and sexually in Senegal (Biaya 1998: 75–101). It is in such a context that one must consider the rich, if ambiguous, meaning of the symbolic veiling suggested by the curtains of braids that unfailingly conceal the faces of Dago's subjects.

A final area in which women are reworking their erotic selves is indicated by a phenomenon that Dago has deftly signaled in his corpus (sequence 2). The phenomenon known as *goor-djigen* differs importantly from lesbianism as it is understood in the West and deserves a future, more detailed analysis than this commentary permits.

Close friendships among women are very common in Senegal and frequently develop within the organization of informal social clubs. Meetings of a social circle reserved exclusively for women take place each weekend, hosted alternately by members of the group. These meetings do not necessarily concern sexuality but may commonly include discussion of the erotic strategies called *tour*. While these discussions focus on conjugal sexuality, the fact of close partnerships between the women themselves has roots in ancient African religions, where the behavior often reflected a belief in the idea of twin souls. When such twins discover each other, their kinship can be sealed by the fusion of bodies and identities. Two such people would walk hand-in-hand, bathe and massage each other's bodies, and dress and adorn each other, sharing clothing and undergarments. The degree to which Dago has pushed the form of goor-djigen toward lesbianism as it is understood in the West suggests a more cosmopolitan interpretation of this form of female partnership, as well as a willingness to push, if ever so gently, the bounds of what is socially sanctioned toward what remains taboo.

*

Sequence 5: *Thiuraye*
the preparation for an erotic night

The *drianké*, generally a middle-aged woman, undresses
to apply perfumes to her underclothing and body.

To turn now more directly to Dago's work, one could divide these sequences into two groups based on the discrepancy between European and African concepts of the "beautiful female body" — two divergent notions that could be said to be locally manifest in the figures of the *diskette* and the drianké. As such, the first group would comprise sequences 1, 2, and 3 and would be distinguishable from a second group comprising sequences 4 and 5. The subjects in the first group certainly evoke the European classical forms, in which the nude female body executes movements characterized by an obvious Greco-Roman aesthetics, recalling ancient rituals and processions depicted in painting, sculpture, and frieze. Throughout these sequences, the subject's body is that of the lithe diskette, an evocation of the models of fashion photography and mainstream Western eroticism. Sequences 4 and 5, however, may be situated along the axis of African female beauty: In them, a young, firm, plump body suggesting adolescence holds out the promise of the future "heavy woman," the beautiful African woman whose specific form will depend on the local erotic fashion. This feminine body already projects future erotic proclivities and the fantasies associated with them: Its blossoming and the eroticism it promises announce the birth of the drianké.

Dago's sequences rely on the rounded forms and arabesque lines typical of classical portrayals of the nude, but by a series of manipulations he has inserted these conventions into a Senegalese erotic trajectory. Each feature of each subject's dress and posture has a specific erotic reference: the careless way the loincloth is worn (a tightly fitted one would have suggested an uncultured eroticism), the motifs sculpted in clay and applied to the body (evoking the traditional practices of self-mutilation), and the girdles of pearls about the hips. These elements signal an African eroticism that achieves its clearest statement in the thiuraye sequence (sequence 5). Indeed, considered as a group, the collection suggests that Dago succeeds with this project in portraying the sexual education of the contemporary Senegalese woman.

In the case not only of Dago's art but of Senegalese men and women as sexual actors, the eroticized body is a place where the spirit of Islam and the spirit of classical modernity challenge each other, enter into competition, and express the inclusion of the Senegalese subject, male and female, in the contemporary world. Conversely, the ultimate foundation of eroticism seems to have remained under the control of African tradition and moral values — a living and active partner to the discourses of Islamization and the secular state which reflects by its changing shape the political and social complexity of cultural innovation in Senegal.

NOTES

I thank Robert McCarthy for his assistance in clarifying the issues in this essay and Achille Mbembe for comments on earlier drafts. I express my gratitude to Jacques Edjangue and Emmanuel Nwukor for editing the first version of this essay.

1. Photography has been practiced in Senegal for more than a century. The great masters of the art are M. Casset, N. M. Cxasset, M. Guèye, et al. (Thiobane and Wade 1999).

2. Interviews conducted with the artist on the occasion of the Inaugural Exposition of Nudes in Dakar (May 1997), in my office at CODESRIA in Dakar (March 1999), and at the Photography Month exhibit in Dakar (October–November 1999).

3. The history of Senegalese eroticism that remains to be written will necessarily follow the three cultural axes constituted by (a) this popular Islam strongly marked by local tradition, (b) the maraboutic Islam marked by the Sufi elite, and the (c) universal Islam that is marked by the Umma, Arab cooperation, and the Senegalese state (see Diop 1994; Dieng 1998).

4. Senegalese Islam never rejected traditional practices of sexuality. On the contrary, beginning in the nineteenth century during the Hegira and the Jihad of moral and religious purification, the maraboutic elite endorsed it and set up a framework within which eroticism might be exercised (Ngaide 1998; Dieng 1998).

5. Recent studies on sexuality and its practices in Senegal (Delaunay 1994: 184; Ly 1999: 46–48) have shown how, under cover of the dominant Islam, traditional sexual

and erotic practices have remained very much alive—despite L. S. Senghor's efforts to lead his compatriots to civilization by means of decrees regulating the expensive urban festivals in which the *arwatam,* an erotic dance of the Lawbés, always delights the audience.

6. This erotic dance is performed to music: the woman bends over, and with her hands on the floor, shakes her buttocks, while her partners—bold men—mime copulation, thus suggesting coitus *a retro.*

7. The hijab is in fashion particularly during Ramadan and the festivals of the Korite (the end of Ramadan) and Tabaski, Abraham's sacrifice. Moreover, it constitutes a still-marginal reaction on the part of women intellectuals and/or women belonging to castes who are complaining about government policy.

WORKS CITED

Bayart, J.-F. 1989. *L'etat en Afrique: La politique du ventre.* Paris: Fayard.

———. 1993. *The State in Africa: The Politics of the Belly.* London: Longman.

Biaya, T. K. 1996. "La culture urbaine dans les arts populaires d'Afrique: L'analyse de l'ambiance zaïroise." *Canadian Journal of African Studies* 30: 345–70.

———. 1998. "Hair Statement in Urban Africa: The Beauty, the Mystic, and the Madman." In *The Art of African Fashion,* ed. E. van der Plas and M. Willemsen. The Hague, The Netherlands: Prince Claus Fund.

———. 1999. "Erotisme et sexualité en Afrique: Pistes et illusions." Paper presented at the seminar on Transformation of Sexuality in Africa, at CODESRIA—Robben Island Workshop on Contemporary Culture, 3–5 July.

Coppiert's Wallant, E. 1993. *Les jeunes et l'avenir de l'Afrique: Un juge d'enfants témoigne.* Paris: L'harmattan.

Delaunay, V. 1994. *L'entrée en vie féconde: Expression démographique des mutations socio-économiques d'un milieu rural sénégalais.* Paris: CEPED.

Dieng, S. 1998. *El-Hadj, la perle de l'Islam: Réalité historique, dimension mystique.* Dakar: Les Nouvelles Editions Africaines.

Diop, M.-C., ed. *Sénégal: Les trajectoires d'un état.* Dakar: CODESRIA.

Gerholm, T. 1997. "The Islamization of Contemporary Egypt." In *African Islam and Islam in Africa,* ed. D. Westerlund and E. E. Rosander. Athens: Ohio University Press.

La Fontaine, J. S. 1970. *City Politics: A Study of Leopoldville, 1962–63.* Cambridge: Cambridge University Press.

Ly, A. 1999. "L'oralité paillarde des Lawbés." *Bulletin du CODESRIA,* no. 3–4: 46–48.

Martin, P. 1996. *Leisure and Society in Colonial Brazzaville.* Cambridge: Cambridge University Press.

Mbembe, A. 1992. "Provisional Notes on the Postcolony." *Africa* 62, no. 1: 3–37. Also published as "The Banality of Power and the Aesthetics of Vulgarity in the Postcolony," trans. Janet Roitman. *Public Culture* 4 (1992): 1–30.

Ngaide, A. 1998. "Le royaume Peul du Fuladu de 1867 à 1936: L'esclave, le colon et le marabout." Thèse de doctorat de 3e cycle en histoire, Faculté des Lettres, Université Cheikh Anta Diop, Dakar.

Nicolas, B. 1985. "L'islam au Zaïre." Thèse de 3e cycle en Etudes africaines, Faculté des Lettres, Université de Paris.

Ommer, U. 1986. *Black Ladies.* Paris: Editions du Jaguar.

———. 1997. *Noumia.* Tournai: Éditions Vents d'Ouest.

Pivin, J.-L., and P. L. Saint Martin. 1995. *Ousmane Sow: Sculptures.* Paris: Éditions Revue Noire.

Thiobane, M., and B. D. Wade. 1999. "Une longue histoire: La photographie est présente au Sénégal depuis bientôt un siècle et demi." *Nouvel Horizon, L'Hebdo du Vendredi,* no. 193, 29 October.

The Many Faces of Cosmo-polis:

Border Thinking and Critical Cosmopolitanism

Walter D. Mignolo

How shall cosmopolitanism be conceived in relation to globalization, capitalism, and modernity? The geopolitical imaginary nourished by the term and processes of globalization lays claim to the homogeneity of the planet from above—economically, politically, and culturally. The term *cosmopolitanism* is, instead, used as a counter to globalization, although not necessarily in the sense of globalization from below. Globalization from below invokes, rather, the reactions to globalization from those populations and geohistorical areas of the planet that suffer the consequences of the global economy. There are, then, local histories that plan and project global designs and others that have to live with them. Cosmopolitanism is not easily aligned to either side of globalization, although the term implies a global project. How shall we understand cosmopolitanism in relation to these alternatives?

Let's assume then that globalization is a set of designs to manage the world while cosmopolitanism is a set of projects toward planetary conviviality. The first global design of the modern world was Christianity, a cause and a consequence of the incorporation of the Americas into the global vision of an orbis christianus. It preceded the civilizing mission, the intent to civilize the world under the model of the modern European nation-states. The global design of Christianity was part of the European Renaissance and was constitutive of modernity and of its darker side, coloniality. The global design of the civilizing mission was part of the European Enlightenment and of a new configuration of modernity/coloniality. The cosmopolitan project corresponding to Christianity's global design was mainly articulated by Francisco de Vitoria at the University of Salamanca while the civilizing global design was mainly articulated by Immanuel Kant at the University of Königsberg.

In other words, cosmopolitan projects, albeit with significant differences, have been at work during both moments of modernity. The first was a religious project; the second was secular. Both, however, were linked to coloniality and to the emergence of the modern/colonial world. Coloniality, in other words, is the hidden face of modernity and its very condition of possibility. The colonization of the Americas in the sixteenth and the seventeenth centuries, and of Africa and Asia in the nineteenth and the early twentieth centuries, consolidated an idea of the West: a geopolitical image that exhibits chronological movement. Three overlapping macronarratives emerge from this image. In the first narrative, the West originates temporally in Greece and moves northwest of the Mediterranean to the North Atlantic. In the second narrative, the West is defined by the modern world that originated with the Renaissance and with the expansion of capitalism through the Atlantic commercial circuit. In the third narrative, Western modernity is located in Northern Europe, where it bears the distinctive trademark of the Enlightenment and the French Revolution. While the first narrative emphasizes the geographical marker *West* as the keyword of its ideological formation, the second and third link the West more strongly with modernity. Coloniality as the constitutive side of modernity emerges from these latter two narratives, which, in consequence, link cosmopolitanism intrinsically to coloniality. By this I do not mean that it is improper to conceive and analyze cosmopolitan projects beyond these parameters, as Sheldon Pollock does in "Cosmopolitan and Vernacular in History" (in this volume). I am stating simply that I will look at cosmopolitan projects within the scope of the modern/colonial world — that is, located chronologically in the 1500s and spatially in the northwest Mediterranean and the North Atlantic. While it is possible to imagine a history that, like Hegel's, begins with the origin of humanity, it is also possible to tell stories with different beginnings, which is no less arbitrary than to proclaim the beginning with the origin of humanity or of Western civilization. The crucial point is not when the beginning is located but why and from where. That is: What are the geohistorical and ideological formations that shape the frame of such a macronarrative? Narratives of cosmopolitan orientation could be either managerial (what I call *global designs* — as in Christianity, nineteenth-century imperialism, or late-twentieth-century neoliberal globalization) or emancipatory (what I call *cosmopolitanism* — as in Vitoria, Kant, or Karl Marx, leaving aside the differences in each of these projects), even if they are oblivious to the saying of the people that are supposed to be emancipated. The need for a critical cosmopolitanism arises from the shortcomings of both.

My story begins, then, with the emergence of the modern/colonial world and of modernity/coloniality, as well as with the assumption that cosmopolitan narratives have been performed from the perspective of modernity. That coloniality remains difficult to understand as the darker side of modernity is due to the fact that most stories of modernity have been told from the perspective of modernity itself, including, of course, those told by its internal critics. In consequence, I see a need to reconceive cosmopolitanism from the perspective of coloniality (this is what I call *critical cosmopolitanism*) and within the frame of the modern/colonial world. It should be conceived historically as from the sixteenth century until today, and geographically in the interplay between a growing capitalism in the Mediterranean and the (North) Atlantic and a growing colonialism in other areas of the planet.

In this scenario I need to distinguish, on the one hand, cosmopolitanism from global designs and, on the other, cosmopolitan projects from critical cosmopolitanism. While global designs are driven by the will to control and homogenize (either from the right or from the left, as in the Christian and civilizing mission or in the planetary revolution of the proletariat), cosmopolitan projects can be complementary or dissenting with regard to global designs. This is the tension we find in Vitoria, Kant, and Marx, for example. In the sixteenth century, the Christian mission embraced both global designs of conversion and the justification of war, on the one hand, and a dissenting position that recognized the "rights of the people" that were being suppressed and erased by Christian global designs, on the other. A similar argument could be made with respect to the global design articulated by the civilizing mission as a colonial project and the "rights of man and of the citizen"—this argument opens up a critical perspective on global designs, although global designs were historically contradictory (for example, the Haitian revolution). The civilizing and Christian missions shared colonization as their final orientation, while cosmopolitan projects such as Vitoria's and Kant's were attentive to the dangers and the excesses of global designs. Today, the modernizing mission that displaced the Christian and civilizing missions after World War II (having the global market as its final destination) is witness to the revival of cosmopolitan projects that are attentive to the dangers and excesses of global designs. Rather than having fomented globalization from below, cosmopolitan projects — since the inception of the modern/colonial world — have provided a critical perspective on global designs, as well as on fundamentalist projects that originated and justified themselves in local histories, both national and religious.

The cosmopolitan projects I have identified arose from within modernity, however, and, as such, they have failed to escape the ideological frame imposed by global designs themselves. Thus, their critical dimensions must be distinguished from what I will here articulate as critical cosmopolitanism, which I conceive as the necessary project of an increasingly transnational (and postnational) world. In a subsequent section of this essay, I illustrate the distinction between cosmopolitan projects from the perspective of modernity and critical cosmopolitanism from the exteriority of modernity (that is, coloniality). By exteriority I do not mean something lying untouched beyond capitalism and modernity, but the outside that is needed by the inside. Thus, exteriority is indeed the borderland seen from the perspective of those "to be included," as they have no other option. Critical cosmopolitanism, in the last analysis, emerges precisely as the need to discover other options beyond both benevolent recognition (Taylor 1992) and humanitarian pleas for inclusion (Habermas 1998). Thus, while cosmopolitan projects are critical from inside modernity itself, critical cosmopolitanism comprises projects located in the exteriority and issuing forth from the colonial difference.

The distinctions I have drawn between global designs and cosmopolitan projects, and between cosmopolitan projects and critical cosmopolitanism, presuppose the complex geopolitical scenario that I am exploring in this essay. I examine three historical and complementary moments, and sketch a fourth, all of which define the profile of the modern/colonial world from the sixteenth century until today. The four moments shall be conceived not within a linear narrative of succession but, rather, in terms of their diachronic contradictions and geohistorical locations. The ideological configuration of one moment does not vanish when the second moment arrives but is reconfigured. The Renaissance did not disappear with the Enlightenment! Museums, tourism, media, scholarly centers, and journals bear witness to the fact. Neither did liberalism vanish with the emergence of Marxism, nor Christianity after its displacement by liberal and Marxist projects. Keeping in mind diachronic contradictions in the density of the imaginary of the modern/colonial world, we can conceive these three moments each as defined by a particular global design. The fourth moment—after the end of the Cold War—can be characterized as a new form of colonization in a postnational world.

The first of these designs corresponds to the sixteenth and seventeenth centuries, to Spanish and Portuguese colonialism, and to the Christian mission. The second corresponds to the eighteenth and nineteenth centuries, to French and English colonialism, and to the civilizing mission. The third corresponds to the second half of the twentieth century, to U.S. and transnational (global) colonialism, and to the modernizing mission. Today we witness a transition to a fourth moment, in which the ideologies of development and modernization anchored in leading national projects are being displaced by the transnational ideology of the market—that is, by neoliberalism as an emergent civilizational project. In each case examined—and this is the main argument of my essay—the question of rights (rights of the people, of men, of the citizen, or of human beings) erupts as, and still remains, a hindrance to cosmopolitan projects.

Given that in the sixteenth and the seventeenth centuries rights were discussed in relation to humans and (Christian) believers, that from the eighteenth century onward rights were discussed in terms of man and national citizenship, and that since World War II rights have been discussed in terms of humanity, critical cosmopolitanism today faces at least two critical issues: human rights and global citizenship to be defined across the colonial difference (see the last section of this essay). Critical cosmopolitanism must negotiate both human rights and global citizenship without losing the historical dimension in which each is reconceived today in the colonial horizon of modernity. Let's explore in more detail (the coexistence of) the three moments (religion, nation, ideology) in the constitution of the modern/colonial world in order to better understand the present scenario in which critical cosmopolitanism became thinkable.

In the imaginary of the modern world or, if you prefer, in the macronarrative of Western civilization, everything imaginable began in Greece. Since my own interests and personal investments are historically framed in the emergence and consolidation of the modern/colonial world during the sixteenth century, I do not look for antecedents of cosmo-polis among the Greeks. I posit a different beginning: the emergence of the Atlantic commercial circuit in the sixteenth century that linked the Spanish Crown with capitalist entrepreneurs from Genoa, with Christian missionaries, with Amerindian elites, and with African slaves. I argue that a new sense of international and intercultural relations emerged at that time, and it helped to consolidate the idea of European Christianity and to inscribe the colonial difference that became the historical foundation of modernity/coloniality. The final victory of Christianity over Islam in 1492, the conversion of Amerindians to Christianity after Hernán Cortés's victory over the Aztec "emperor" Mocthecuzoma, the arrival of Franciscan missionaries to dialogue with the Aztec wise men, the arrival of Vasco da Gama at India in 1498, the entry of the Jesuits into China around 1580, the massive contingent of African slaves in the Americas—these are the landmarks of macronarratives whose beginnings lie not in Greece but in the sixteenth century and in the making of planetary colonial differences. Let us call this the macronarrative of the modern/colonial world from the perspective of coloniality that has been suppressed by hegemonic stories of and from modernity.

In the sixteenth century, the emerging hegemonic imaginary of modernity was built around the figures of orbis and, more specifically, orbis universalis christianus. The idea of orbis universalis received support from Renaissance cartography. The sixteenth century was the first time in the history of humankind that a world map was drawn on which the continents of Africa, Asia, America, and Europe could be connected on the basis of empirical information. The diversity of local cosmographies in complex civilizations (of China, India, Islam, Europe, Tawantinsuyu, Anahuac) were unified and subsumed by a world map drawn by cartographers of Christian Europe. The map, rather than the Internet, was the first step of the imaginary of the modern/colonial world that we today call globalization (Mignolo 1998: 35–52). Orbis, not cosmos (as in the eighteenth century), was the preferred figure of speech, and it was a vital figure in the Christian imaginary. The emergence of this imaginary happened in tandem with that of the Atlantic commercial circuit, at a particular stage of historical capitalism/colonialism that was also the initial configuration of modernity/coloniality. I even suggest that it was with the emergence of the Atlantic commercial circuit, and at that particular historical moment of the Christian world, that the matrix for global designs in the modern/colonial world was produced — a matrix, as imaginary, in which we continue to live and in relation to which there is need to reflect on past cosmopolitan projects and on the future of critical cosmopolitanism.

There is a specific local history to which Christian global design responds that is quite complex. I summarize here a few of its aspects, most of which are related to the internal conflicts of Christianity during the second half of the sixteenth century. First, the religious war that concluded with the Peace of Westphalia (1648) created the conditions and the need to look for a rational society that would transcend and avoid previous horrors. Second, the law of nature provided an attractive alternative to the design of God with which to imagine a society that replicated the regularities of nature. Third, since this law of nature applied to the universe (or at least to the solar system), the regulation of society by its principles could be conceived as universal, or at least planetary. Fourth, the path toward a universal secularism or a secular universalism was laid open by competing interpretations within Christianity and continuing conflicts between the three religions of the book: Christianity, Judaism, and Islam — all of which worked to render dubious the universality of the Christian God. The law of nature could now be declared universal precisely when a Christian God no longer could. Thus, a "natural"-based idea of cosmopolitanism and universal history came together in one stroke.

Within this local history, I am interested in a particular aspect of the idea of cosmo-polis: its relation to the idea of nation-state. Once God became questionable, the pope and the emperor became questionable as well, and orbis christianus lost its power to unify communities. In the sixteenth century, the church and the state emerged as institutional replacements for the pope and the emperor. As the church continued to be questioned by an increasingly secular world and as the state became sovereign, the category of the infidel (gentiles, Jews, pagans) that comprised the population exterior to the orbis christianus (Höffner [1947] 1957: 289–335) was reconverted into that of the foreigner (Kristeva 1991: 127–68; Held 1995: 48–99). If Christians were those who inhabited the interior of a transnational orbis christianus, citizens were inhabitants of the new, emergent space of the nation-state; in consequence, the Renaissance idea of man was also reconverted and given center stage, thus transcending the division of citizen and foreigner (Gordon 1995).

Michel-Rolph Trouillot has recently underlined this point in an argument that explains the silence surrounding the Haitian revolution. Philosophers who during the Renaissance asked themselves "What is man?", Trouillot (1995: 75) writes, "could not escape the fact that colonization was going on as they spoke. Men (Europeans) were conquering, killing, dominating, and slaving other beings thought to be equally human, if only by some." The famous debates of Valladolid, between Juan Ginés de Sepúlveda and Bartolomé de Las Casas about the degree of humanity of the Amerindian, bears witness to this convergence of events (Ramos et al. 1984). However, the eighteenth century obscured the religious cosmpolitanism based on the rights of the people and supplanted it with a national cosmopolitanism based on the rights of man and of the citizen.

The sixteenth-century debates, which took place in Valladolid and were followed up in the University of Salamanca, are of extreme relevance in world history, and yet they were forgotten during the eighteenth century. However, they are becoming relevant today to discussions of group and individual rights, as well as of migration and multiculturalism (Pérez Luño 1992). The debates fostered the inquiries of philosopher-theologians in the Salamanca school, who examined the ethical and legal circumstances of Spaniards in the Indias Occidentales, or the New World. They remain crucial to world history not merely because they focused on the human nature of Amerindians and the right of Spaniards to declare war, enslave Amerindians, and take possession of their land and bodies, but their repercussions travel further.

The debates broke out several decades after the triumph of Christianity over the Moors and the Jews, which was followed by the expulsion of both groups from the Iberian Peninsula. The debates were indirectly but powerfully related to the initiation of massive contingents of slaves brought from Africa. Since Amerindians were considered vassals of the king and serfs of God, they were assigned a niche above Africans in the chain of being, which meant that, theoretically, they were not to be enslaved.

Several cities in sixteenth-century Europe (Salamanca [Spain], Coimbra [Portugal], Rome [Italy], Paris [France], Lovaina [the Netherlands], and Dilinga and Ingolstadt [Germany]) were busy with this legal and theological investigation and were concerned with the Valladolid debates. The "Indian doubt," as it developed, was defined around two issues: the right of Amerindians to the possession of their land, and the right of Spaniards to declare war against Indians. As is well known, the debates drew the attention of Vitoria and led him to a series of legal-theological inquiries, motivated by an interest in the behavior of Spaniards in the New World. These inquiries circulated in Europe first in manuscript form and later as the book entitled *Relectio de Indis* (Vitoria ([1539] 1967). In published form, the inquiries were organized into three major issues: (1) whether Amerindians were true "owners" of their lands and other properties and in control of their own social organization; (2) whether instead the emperor and the pope were "owners" and had the right to control both Amerindians and other non-Christian people (infidels); and (3) what the "legal entitlements" were that justified (from a Spanish point of view) Spanish domination of Amerindians.

In today's terminology, Vitoria's inquiry was principally concerned with the idea of "the inclusion of the other." The political aspects of society and international relations were examined with the assumption that there is a "natural right" that every human and rational being (under Greek/Christian parameters) has.[1] Vitoria extended the principle of natural right to the "rights of the people" to adjudicate new questions of international relations raised by developments in the New World. Theology in Vitoria (as opposed to philosophy in Kant) was the ultimate ground on which to examine all kinds of human relations among individuals and among nations (pueblos, people). But the inquiries included also a profound ethical concern: to be a Christian meant to be self-conscious and to act consciously on behalf of the common good. Of course, Christian ethical concerns were to Vitoria no less honest or earnest than philosophical concerns were to philosophers of the Enlightenment, and the law of nature is of course no better warranty with which to build arguments on behalf of the common good than are natural rights. There was not in Vitoria a fully developed notion of the state, as there would be in the eighteenth century, but neither was one necessary given historical conditions. While Vitoria's horizon was the planetary scope open to sixteenth-century Renaissance intellectuals, the Enlightenment operated with a different set of concerns—namely, European peace and the construction of the Europe of nations. A conception of the state, however, did begin to emerge in Vitoria, although it remained coupled with the church: Vitoria removed the emperor and pope as "owners" of the world and of all imaginable communities, and he conceived the religion-state as the civil and spiritual order of society. The cosmo-politan ideology of possession enjoyed by the pope and emperor was replaced by Vitoria's proposal in favor of international relations based on the "rights of the people" (community, nation). *Derecho de gentes,* which required the discussion and regulation of theology and jurisprudence, were then assigned to the religion-state instead of to the pope and emperor.

When in the third part of *Relectio de Indis,* Vitoria examined the "legal entitlements" that justified war against the Indians, he proceeded to enunciate a series of "fundamental rights" for people—nations of human communities—the violation of which was justification of war. Vitoria had a vision of a "natural society" grounded in communication, conviviality, and international collaboration. Vitoria's utopia was cosmo-polis, a planetary society or a world community of religion-states founded on the principle of natural right (instead of on the law of nature) and subject to the regulation of the religion-state. The fact that the "Indian doubt" was prompted at the same time as the emergence of the Atlantic commercial circuit—a crucial step in the formation of capitalism after Christianity obtained victory over the Moors and the Jews—justifies conceiving this moment as the historical foundation of modernity/coloniality, or, if you prefer, as the historical foundation of the modern/colonial world system to which Kant and the European Enlightenment contributed to transform and expand. I have the impression that if one stripped Vitoria of his religious principles, replaced theology with philosophy, and the concern to deal with difference in humanity with a straightforward classification of people by nations, color, and continents, what one would obtain indeed would be Kant. Is that much of a difference? In my view it is not. These are two different faces of the same imaginary—the imaginary of the modern/colonial world as an interstate system regulated by the coloniality of power. The reason the "Indian doubt," the "rights of the people," and the Christian idea of orbis were erased in the eighteenth century is another matter and one of the issues with which I deal below.

Relevant to my argument, however, was a change that Vitoria introduced into the principle established by Gaius, the Roman jurist who related *ius naturalis* (natural law) to *homines* (human beings). Vitoria replaced homines by *gentes* (people) — perhaps an almost imperceptible change, but one of enormous significance. Vitoria was facing a situation in which the gentes in question had been previously unknown to Christianity and obviously were not clearly homines. Certainly there was a difference between the Amerindians on the one hand and the Moors, Jews, or Chinese on the other. But this was precisely the difference that would become the historical foundation of colonial differences. Thus, it was no longer the question of thinking of men or human beings (homines) but of thinking of different people within a new structure of power and rights: the right to possess, the right to dispossess, the right to govern those outside the Christian realm. Vitoria began to rethink the international order (the cosmo-polis) from the perspective of the New World events and from the need to accommodate, in that international order, what he called "the barbarians," that is, the Amerindians. On the one hand, Vitoria had orbis christianus as the final horizon on which he would justify the rights of barbarians and pagans; on the other, he had a spectrum of Christian-European "nations" already established in the sixteenth-century imaginary (Castile, France, Italy). Interaction between the two levels was never made explicit by Vitoria; he treated them as equals in his thinking on international rights and international communication, although it was obvious at the time that barbarians or pagans were considered unequal to the French or Italians. More explicit in Vitoria, however, was the balance between the rights of commerce, peregrination, and settlement on the one hand and the rights Castilians have to preach and convert Amerindians on the other. This was the domain in which the religion-state became instrumental as a replacement for the emperor and the pope in international relations, and in which a Christian cosmopolitanism was advanced as a correction of the Castilian crown's global designs.

In the sixteenth century, "the rights of the people" had been formulated within a planetary consciousness — the planetary consciousness of the orbis christianus with the Occident as the frame of reference. In the eighteenth century, the "rights of man and of the citizen" was formulated instead within the planetary consciousness of a cosmo-polis analogous to the law of nature, with Europe — the Europe of nations, specifically — as the frame of reference. There was a change but within the system, or, better yet, within the imaginary of the modern/colonial world system.

Cosmo-polis recently has been linked to the hidden agenda of modernity and traced back to the seventeenth century in Western Europe, north of the Iberian Peninsula (Toulmin 1990). In the postnational historical context of the 1990s, the same issue was reformulated in terms of national diversity and cosmopolitanism (Cheah and Robbins 1998) and by refashioning Kant's cosmopolitan ideas (McCarthy 1999). In the same vein, but two decades earlier, cosmopolitanism was attached to the idea of the National State and located in Germany (Meinecke 1970). What is missing from all of these approaches to cosmopolitanism, however, is the link with the sixteenth century. This is not simply a historiographical claim, but a substantial one with significance for the present. Multiculturalism today has its roots in the sixteenth century, in the inception of the modern/colonial world, in the struggles of jurist/theologians like Vitoria or missionaries like Las Casas, which were at the time similar to the struggles of postliberal thinkers such as Jürgen Habermas. If Kant needs today to be amended to include multiculturalism in his cosmopolitan view as Thomas McCarthy (1999) suggests, we must return to the roots of the idea — that is, to the sixteenth century and the expulsion of the Moors and the Jews from the Iberian Peninsula, to the "Indian doubt" and the beginnings of the massive contingent of African slaves in the Americas.

There are two historical and two structural issues that I would like to retain from the previous section in order to understand cosmopolitan thinking in the eighteenth century and its oblivion of sixteenth-century legacies. The two historical issues are the Thirty Years' War that concluded with the Peace of Westphalia in 1648 and the French Revolution in the 1700s. The structural aspects are the connections made at that point between the law of nature (cosmos) and the ideal society (polis). One of the consequences of the structural aspect was to derive *ius cosmopoliticum* from the law of nature as a model for social organization. For eighteenth-century intellectuals in France, England, and Germany, theirs was the beginning.[2] And such a beginning (that is, the oblivion of Vitoria and the concern for the "inclusion of the other") was grounded in the making of the imperial difference — shifting the Iberian Peninsula to the past and casting it as the South of Europe (Cassano 1996; Dainotto 2000). By the same token, the colonial difference was rearticulated when French and German philosophy recast the Americas (its nature and its people) in the light of the "new" ideas of the Enlightenment instead of the "old" ideas of the Renaissance (Gerbi [1955] 1982; Mignolo 2000: 49–90). Their beginning is still reproduced today as far as the eighteenth century is accepted as the "origin" of modernity. From this perspective, the emergence of the Atlantic commercial circuit that created the conditions for capitalist expansion and French revolution remains relegated to a premodern world. The imperial difference was drawn in the eighteenth century even as a cosmopolitan society was being thought out. It was simultaneous to (and part of the same move as) the rearticulation of the colonial difference with respect to the Americas and to the emergence of Orientalism to locate Asia and Africa in the imaginary of the modern/colonial world. This "beginning" (that is, the South of Europe as the location of the imperial difference and the North as the heart of Europe) is still the beginning for contemporary thinkers such as Habermas and Charles Taylor, among others. The "other" beginning instead, that of the modern/colonial world, is more complex and planetary. It connects the commercial circuits before European hegemony (Abu-Lughod 1989) with the emergent Mediterranean capitalism of the period (Braudel 1979; Arrighi 1994) and with the displacement of capitalist expansion from the Mediterranean to the Atlantic (Dussel 1998: 3–31; Mignolo 2000: 3–48).

Why is this historical moment of the making of the imperial difference and the rearticulation of the colonial differences with the Americas and the emergence of Orientalism relevant to my discussion on cosmopolitanism? Not, of course, because of national pride or historical accuracy, but because of the impediment that the linear macronarrative constructed from the perspective of modernity (from the Greeks to the today) presents to the macronarratives told from the perspective of coloniality (the making and rearticulation of the colonial and imperial differences). Bearing this conceptual and historical frame in mind (that is, the modern/colonial world system), there are at least two ways to enter critically into Kant's signal contribution to cosmopolitanism and, simultaneously, his racial underpinning and Eurocentric bias. One would be to start with an analysis of his writings on history from a cosmopolitan point of view and on perpetual peace (Kant [1785] 1996, [1795] 1963; McCarthy 1999). The other would be to start from his lectures on anthropology, which he began in 1772 and published in 1797 (Van De Pitte 1996). In these lectures, Kant's Eurocentrism enters clearly into conflict with his cosmopolitan ideals (Eze 1997: 103–40; Serequeberhan 1997: 141–61; Dussel 1995: 65–76, 1998: 129–62). The first reading of Kant will take us to Habermas and Taylor. The second reading will return us to the sixteenth century, to Las Casas and Vitoria, to the relations between Europe, Africa, and America, and from there onward to Kant's racial classification of the planet by skin color and continental divides.

Let me explore these ideas by bringing into the picture the connections of cosmopolitanism with Eurocentrism. Enrique Dussel, an Argentinian philosopher resident in Mexico and one of the founders of the philosophy of liberation in Latin America, linked modernity with Eurocentrism and proposed the notion of "transmodernity" as a way out of the impasses of postliberal and postmodern critiques of modernity. Dussel argues that if modernity includes a rational concept of emancipation, it also should be pointed out that, at the same time, it developed an irrational myth, a justification for genocidal violence. While "postmodernists criticize modern reason as a reason of terror," Dussel (1995: 66) writes, "we criticize modern reason because of the irrational myth that it conceals." The pronoun *we* here precisely situates the enunciation in the colonial difference, in the irreducible difference of the exteriority of the modern/colonial world. Much like the slave who understands the logic of the master and of the slave while the master only understands the master's logic, Dussel's argument reveals the limits of modernity and makes visible the possibility and the need to speak from the perspective of coloniality. Thus, there is a need for Dussel (as there is for African philosophers—e.g., Eze 1997) to read Kant from the perspective of coloniality (that is, from the colonial difference), and not only critically but from within modernity itself (that is, from a universal perspective without colonial differences). Dussel observes that

> Kant's answer to the question posed by the title of his essay "What Is Enlightenment?" is now more than two centuries old. "Enlightenment is the exodus of humanity by its own effort from the state of guilty immaturity," he wrote. "Laziness and cowardice are the reasons why the greater part of humanity remains pleasurably in this state of immaturity." For Kant, immaturity, or adolescence, is a culpable state, laziness and cowardice is existential ethos: the *unmundig*. Today, we would ask him: an African in Africa or as a slave in the United States in the eighteenth century; an Indian in Mexico or a Latin American mestizo: should all of these subjects be considered to reside in a state of guilty immaturity? (Dussel 1995: 68)

In fact, Kant's judgment regarding the American or Amerindian was complemented by his view of the African and the Hindu, for to him they all shared an incapacity for moral maturity, owing to their common ineptitude and proximity to nature. African philosopher Emmanuel Eze (1997: 117–19) provides several examples in which Kant states that the race of the Americans cannot be educated since they lack any motivating force, they are devoid of affect and passion, and they hardly speak and do not caress each other. Kant introduces then the race of the Negroes, who are completely opposite of the Americans: the Negroes are full of affect and passion, very lively but vain; as such, they can be educated, but only as servants or slaves. Kant continues, in tune with the naturalist and philosophic discourses of his time, by noting that inhabitants of the hottest zones are, in general, idle and lazy—qualities that are only correctable by government and force (Gerbi [1955] 1982: 414–18).

In part 2 of *Anthropology from a Pragmatic Point of View*, devoted to "Classification," Kant's argument ([1797] 1996) comes into full force. It begins with a consideration of the character of the person, moves next to the character of the sexes and then to the character of nations, and concludes with speculation on the characters of races and species. The fact that the "person" is Kant's beginning and reference point is already indicative of the presuppositions implied in the universal neutral imaginary that for him constitutes the person. Kant obviously was not thinking about the Amerindians, the Africans, or the Hindus as paradigmatic examples of his characterization. "Person" was for Kant an empty signifier around which all differences may be accommodated and classified. Also, "person" is the unit upon which sexes and nations are built (Gregor 1993: 50–75). But let us pause for a while over Kant's discourse on the character of nations, since it more strictly relates to cosmopolitanism. Cosmo-polis implies the possibilities and the capabilities of people (*populus*) to live together, and the unity of the people is organized around the concept of nation. A nation, for Kant, "is not (like the ground on which it is located) a possession patrimonium. It is a society of men whom no one other than the nation itself can command or dispose of. Since, like a tree, each nation has its own roots, to incorporate it into another nation as a graft, denies its existence as a moral person, turns into a thing, and thus contradicts the concept of the original contract, without which a people (Volk) has no right" (Kant [1795] 1963: para. no. 344).

A nation has roots, and a state has laws, and people have rights. But, of course, the character of each nation varies, and a successful cosmopolitanism and a perpetual peace would very much depend on the characters of (peoples in) nations and on the state they constitute together. Thus, England and France (and Germany, by implication of the enunciating agency) are "the two most civilized nations on earth" ([1797] 1996: 226). The fact that they constantly feud because of their different characters does not diminish their standing as paragons of civilization. Thus, the French and the English are the first national characters Kant describes in the section entitled "The Characters of the Nations." The third national character is the Spanish. And this makes sense, since Kant's order of things is not alphabetical but imperial: Spain, the empire in decay, follows England and France, the new and emerging imperial nations. The first feature that Kant observes in the Spaniards is that they "evolved from the mixture of European blood with Arabian (Moorish) blood." And (or perhaps) because of this the Spaniard "displays in his public and private behavior a certain solemnity; even the peasant expresses a consciousness of his own dignity toward his master, to whom he is lawfully obedient" (Kant [1797] 1996: 231). Kant further adds: "The Spaniard's bad side is that he does not learn from foreigners; that he does not travel in order to get acquainted with other nations; that he is centuries behind in the sciences. He resists any reform; he is proud of not having to work; he is of a romantic quality of spirit, as the bullfight shows; he is cruel, as the former auto-da-fé shows; and he displays in his taste an origin that is partly non-European" ([1797] 1996: 231–32).

The entire philosophical debates of the sixteenth century, the contributions of Las Casas and Vitoria, are here abandoned in the name of the negative features of national characters. The mixture of Spaniard with Moorish blood sets the character of the nation in racial terms; this time not in relation to Africa, Asia, or the Americas, but to Europe itself—the South of Europe. In this regard, Kant contributed to drawing the imperial difference between the modern/North (England, France, Germany) and the traditional/South (Spain, Portugal, Italy). Russians, Turks, Greeks, and Armenians belong to a third division of national character. While still within Europe, these nations do not belong to the core, as Kant paved the way for Hegel's tripartite division of Europe: the core (England, France, and Germany), the south, and the northeast (Hegel [1822] 1956: 102). Thus, according to Kant's geopolitical distribution of national characters that anticipates Hegel's geopolitical distribution of Europe, Kant's cosmopolitanism presupposes that it could only be thought out from one particular geopolitical location: that of the heart of Europe, of the most civilized nations. Indeed, we owe much to Kant's cosmopolitanism, although we must not forget that it plagued the inception of national ideology with racial prejudgment. It is not difficult to agree with both Vitoria and Kant on their ideas of justice, equality, rights, and planetary peace. But it remains difficult to carry these ideas further without clearing up the Renaissance and Enlightenment prejudices that surrounded concepts of race and manhood. One of the tasks of critical cosmopolitanism is precisely clearing up the encumbrances of the past. The other is to point toward the future.

For instance, when Kant thinks in terms of "all nations of the earth" ([1795] 1963: 121; para. no. 62) he assumes that the entire planet eventually will be organized by the terms he has envisioned for Western Europe and will be defined by his description of national characters. With this scenario in mind, our options today are several. One would be to update Kant, as McCarthy does (1999: 191–92) and to account for the multiculturalism of the postnational world in which we live and which was less foreseeable to Kant (Habermas 1998). Another would be to start from Vitoria and to learn how multiculturalism was handled in the sixteenth century, in a Christian (prenational) world faced for the first time with a planetary horizon—a globo-polis perhaps. However, Vitoria in the sixteenth century and Kant in the eighteenth century belong to the same "world" — the modern/colonial world. They are divided by the imperial difference of the eighteenth-century European imaginary. It is necessary, then, to reestablish the commonality between both cosmopolitan projects that was obscured by the convergence of industrial capitalism, cosmopolitanism, and the civilizing mission.

Today, in a postnational moment of the same modern/colonial world, the problems of rights, justice, equality, and so on are thought out by way of inclusion, as Vitoria and the Salamanca school did in the sixteenth century. But inclusion doesn't seem to be the solution to cosmopolitanism any longer, insofar as it presupposes that the agency that establishes the inclusion is itself beyond inclusion: "he" being already within the frame from which it is possible to think "inclusion."[3] Today, silenced and marginalized voices are bringing themselves into the conversation of cosmopolitan projects, rather than waiting to be included. Inclusion is always a reformative project. Bringing themselves into the conversation is a transformative project that takes the form of border thinking or border epistemology — that is, the alternative to separatism is border thinking, the recognition and transformation of the hegemonic imaginary from the perspectives of people in subaltern positions. Border thinking then becomes a "tool" of the project of critical cosmopolitanism.

HUMAN RIGHTS: THE CHANGING FACE OF THE MODERN/COLONIAL WORLD IMAGINARY

Vitoria and Kant anchored cosmopolitan projects and conceptualizations of rights that responded to specific needs: for Vitoria, the inclusion of the Amerindians; for Kant, the redefinitions of person and citizen in the consolidation of the Europe of nations and the emergence of new forms of colonialism. The "United Nations Declaration of Human Rights" ([1948] 1997) that followed World War II also responded to the changing faces of the coloniality of power in the modern/colonial world (Koshy 1999: 1–32). During the Cold War, human rights were connected to the defense of the Western world against the danger of communism, as if communism was not an outcome of the Western world. At the conclusion of the Cold War, human rights became linked to world trade and to the diversity of capitalism (Raghavan 1990; Koshy 1999: 20–30).

Neither Vitoria nor Kant had to deal with a world in which the state took a leading role in a conflicting discussion over human rights (Tolley 1987).

The conclusion of World War II reconfigured the scenario of a narrative of which the first chapter was written by the Salamanca school, and the second by Kant's conception of a universal history from a cosmopolitan point of view—of perpetual peace and cosmopolitan rights. This chapter of Western history could be read today as a prolegomenon to a model for planetary liberal democracy. It ended, however, with the postwar realization that such dreams were no longer viable (Friedman 1962). Decolonization in Africa and Asia brought to the foreground an experience that Kant could not have foreseen when British and French colonization were not yet fully in place. The nation-state alone and Europe were on Kant's horizon, and less so colonization. Curiously enough, the scenario that presented itself after World War II brought us back to Vitoria and the Salamanca school. Not curiously enough, the Cold War and the intensification of the conflict between the two previous phases of the modern/colonial world system left the exteriority of the system in the shade, as an expectant Third World contemplated the struggle between the First and the Second. Coloniality remained hidden behind the struggle of modernity. The horrors of National Socialism that contributed to the transformation of the "rights of man and of the citizen" into "human rights" were horrors whose traces stretch back to the sixteenth century (the expulsion of Jews from Spain) and to the eighteenth century (the imaginary of national characters). During the Cold War, human rights as a strategy to control communism was similar to the control of pagans, infidels, and barbarians by the model of international relations devised by the Salamanca school, or of foreigners by the model of relations urged by Kant. Thus, while for Vitoria and the Salamanca school the master discourse was theology, and for Kant and the Enlightenment it was philosophy, after World War II the master discourse was political economy (Hayek [1944] 1994; Friedman 1962; Brzezinski 1970; Cooper 1973).

The "United Nations Declaration of Human Rights" ([1948] 1997), which followed by a few years the constitution of the United Nations, announced, paradoxically, the closure of the nation-state and international laws as conceived since Kant. A couple of decades later, dependency theory in Latin America voiced the concern that international relations were indeed relations of dependency. Theoreticians who supported transnational corporations did not agree with that view. In one stroke, they put a closure to Kant's trust in the nation and transformed dependency into interdependency (that is, with the 1973 Trilateral Commission between the United States, Europe, and Japan).[4] They ended the sovereignty of the nation-state and revamped the language of developing underdeveloped nations as an alternative to communism. Thus, as communists (and no longer pagans, infidels, or foreigners) represented the danger to the system, parallel to decolonization in Asia and Africa, dictatorial regimes were ascending in Latin America (Brazil, Uruguay, Chile, and Argentina). Human rights commissions, no doubt, played a fundamental role in abating the atrocities of dictatorial regimes, at the same time that human rights served as an instrument to promote liberal democracy against communism. During the Cold War, the world was divided into three geopolitical areas, and human rights were caught in the middle of the transformation of liberal into neoliberal democratic projects. In this battle within the new imperial borders of the modern world, the problem was no longer the racial South, as in Kant's time, but the communist East. Decolonized countries were striving for a nation-state, at the same time that the ideologues of the new world order no longer believed in them. Zbigniew Brzezinski in 1970 was promoting interdependence — apparently a good ground for cosmopolitanism — while despising the nation-state. He believed, or at least said, that "on the formal plane, politics as a global process operates much as they [nation-states] did in the past, but the inner reality of that process is increasingly shaped by forces whose influence or scope transcend national lines" (1970: 8).

Interdependence redraws the lines of the imperial difference (now between the First and the Second Worlds) and the colonial difference (now between the First and the Third Worlds) either by the process of decolonization through nation-building (Asia and Africa) or military dictatorship (Latin America). But, from Vitoria to Brzezinski, through Kant, the modern/colonial world kept on growing and transforming itself, while simultaneously maintaining the colonial space as derivative, rather than as constitutive, of modernity. Alternatives to human rights have been removed from the question, and one of the consequences has been to elicit suspicious responses (China's position on human rights) to suspicious proposals (Western ambiguities on human rights).

The difficulties I am trying to convey here have been cast in different words by Abdullahi A. An-Na'im, a lawyer and Muslim advocate for human rights. He points out that the universality of human rights is undermined by both Western and non-Western cultural relativism.

> Similar to the claims of some elites in non-Western societies that their own cultural norms should prevail over international human rights standards, Western elites are claiming an exclusive right to prescribe the essential concept and normative content of human rights for all societies to implement.[5] Both types of relativism not only take a variety of conceptual and practical forms, but also play an insidious role in inhibiting even the possibilities of imagining supplementary or alternative conceptions and implementation strategies. (An-Na'im 1994: 8)

This dilemma calls for a radical reconceptualization of the human rights paradigm as the next step toward cosmopolitan values (ethics) and regulations (politics). And this will be the topic of my next and last section.

BORDER THINKING:
A NEXT STEP TOWARD A COSMO-POLITAN ORDER

I have shown three stages of cosmopolitan projects of the modern/colonial world system or, if you prefer, of modernity/coloniality. In the first, cosmopolitanism faced the difficulties of dealing with pagans, infidels, and barbarians. It was a religious and racial configuration. In the second, cosmopolitanism faced the difficulties of communities without states and the dangers of the foreigners that, at that point in time, were the foreigners at the edge of the Europe of nations. In the third stage, communists replaced pagans and infidels, barbarians and foreigners, as the difficulties of cosmopolitan society were reassessed. Today the scenario Kant was observing has changed again with the "dangers" presented by recent African immigration to Europe and Latin Americans to the United States. Religious exclusion, national exclusion, ideological exclusion, and ethnic exclusion have several elements in common: first, the identification of frontiers and exteriority; second, the racial component in the making of the frontier as colonial difference (linked to religion in the first instance and to nationalism in the second); and third, the ideological component in the remaking of the imperial differ-ence during the third historical stage (liberalism versus socialism within the modern/colonial world). Ethnicity became a crucial trademark after the end of the Cold War, although its roots had already been established in connection with religion and nationalism. While there is a temporal succession that links the three stages and projects them onto the current post–Cold War globalization, they are each constitutive of the mod-ern/colonial world and cohabit today, as Kosovo clearly bears witness to. Furthermore, the three stages that I am reconstituting historically but that are the "ground" of the present, are successive and complementary moments in the struggle for the survival and hegemony of the North Atlantic or, if you wish, the reconstituted face of the Western world.

I suspect that it is possible now to talk more specifically about a fourth stage, perhaps a postmodern/postcolonial moment, of the mod-ern/colonial world, which I have been announcing in the previous para-graph and in which current discussions on cosmopolitanism are taking place—a stage that Immanuel Wallerstein (1999) described as the "end of the world as we know it." It also may be possible now to have a "cos-mopolitan manifesto" to deal with the "world risk society" (Beck 1999).[6] The erasure of the imperial difference that sustained the Cold War and the current process of its relocation in China brings us back to a situa-tion closer to the one faced by Vitoria: imagining conviviality across religious and racial divides. Global coloniality is drawing a new sce-nario. Capitalism is no longer concentrating in the Mediterranean (as in Vitoria's time) or in the Europe of nations and the North Atlantic (as in Kant's time) when liberalism went together with Christian Protestant-ism and skin color began to replace blood and religion in the recon-figuration of the colonial difference. At that time, capital, labor control, and whiteness became the new paradigm under which the colonial dif-ference was redefined. In the second half of the twentieth century but more so after the end of the Cold War, capitalism is crossing the former colonial difference with the Orient and relocating it as imperial differ-ence with China—thereby entering territories in which Christianity, lib-eralism, and whiteness are alien categories. Perhaps Samuel Hunting-ton (1996) had a similar scenario in mind when he proposed that in the future, wars would be motivated by the clash of civilizations rather than by economic reasons. Which means that when capitalism crosses the colonial difference, it brings civilizations into conflicts of a different order. In any event, relevant to my argument is the fact that while capitalism expands, and the rage for accumulation daily escapes further beyond control (for instance, the weakening of nation-states or the irrational exuberance of the market), racial and religious conflicts emerge as new impediments to the possibility of cosmopolitan societies.

The new situation we are facing in the fourth stage is that cosmopolitanism (and democracy) can no longer be articulated from one point of view, within a single logic, a mono-logic (if benevolent) discourse from the political right or left. Vitoria, Kant, the ideologues of interdependence, the champions of development, and the neoliberal managers believing, or saying, that technology will lift poverty left little room for those on the other side of the colonial difference. And, obviously, managed cosmopolitanism could (and more likely will) remain as a benevolent form of control. In the New World order, how can critical and dialogic cosmopolitanism be thought out without falling into the traps of cultural relativism (and the reproduction of the colonial difference) as pointed out by An-Na'im? I have been suggesting, and now will move to justify, that cultural relativism should be dissolved into colonial difference and that the colonial difference should be identified as the location for the critical and dialogic cosmopolitanism that confronts managerial global designs of ideologues and executives of the network society. Instead of cosmopolitanism managed from above (that is, global designs), I am proposing cosmopolitanism, critical and dialogic, emerging from the various spatial and historical locations of the colonial difference (Mignolo 2000). In this vein, I interpret the claim made by An-Na'im.

Replacing cultural differences with the colonial difference helps change the terms, and not only the content, of the conversation: *Culture* is the term that in the eighteenth century and in the Western secular world replaced *religion* in a new discourse of colonial expansion (Dirks 1992). The notion of cultural relativism transformed coloniality of power into a semantic problem. If we accept that actions, objects, beliefs, and so on are culture-relative, we hide the coloniality of power from which different cultures came into being in the first place. The problem, then, is not to accommodate cosmopolitanism to cultural relativism, but to dissolve cultural relativism and to focus on the coloniality of power and the colonial difference produced, reproduced, and maintained by global designs. Critical cosmopolitanism and new democratic projects imply negotiating the coloniality of power and the colonial difference in a world controlled by global capitalism (Redrado 2000). Rights of man or human rights, of course, would have to be negotiated across gender lines (Wollstonecraft [1792] 1997; Beijing Declaration [1995] 1997), but also across the coloniality of power that structured and still structures the modern/colonial world around the racially grounded colonial difference. Human rights can no longer be accepted as having a content that Vitoria, Kant, and the United Nations discovered and possessed. Such expressions, as well as democracy and cosmopolitanism, shall be conceived as connectors in the struggle to overcome coloniality of power from the perspective of the colonial difference, rather than as full-fledged words with specific Western content. By *connectors* I do not mean empty signifiers that preserve the terms as the property of European Enlightenment while they promote benevolent inclusion of the Other or making room for the multicultural.

The Zapatistas have used the word *democracy,* although it has different meaning for them than it has for the Mexican government. Democracy for the Zapatistas is not conceptualized in terms of European political philosophy but in terms of Maya social organization based on reciprocity, communal (instead of individual) values, the value of wisdom rather than epistemology, and so forth. The Mexican government doesn't possess the correct interpretation of democracy, under which the Other will be included. But, for that matter, neither do the Zapatistas have the right interpretation. However, the Zapatistas have no choice but to use the word that political hegemony imposed, although using the word doesn't mean bending to its mono-logic interpretation. Once democracy is singled out by the Zapatistas, it becomes a connector through which liberal concepts of democracy and indigenous concepts of reciprocity and community social organization for the common good must come to terms. Border thinking is what I am naming the political and ethical move from the Zapatistas' perspective, by displacing the concept of democracy. Border thinking is not a possibility, at this point, from the perspective of the Mexican government, although it is a need from subaltern positions. In this line of argument, a new abstract universal (such as Vitoria's, or Kant's, which replaced Vitoria's, or the ideologies of transnationalism, which replaced Kant's abstract universal) is no longer either possible or desirable.

The abstract universal is what hegemonic perspectives provide, be they neoliberal or neo-Marxist. The perspective from the colonial difference (illustrated in the dilemma formulated by An-Na'im and further developed with the example of the Zapatistas) instead opens the possibility of imagining border thinking as the necessary condition for a future critical and dialogic cosmopolitanism. Such a critical and dialogic cosmopolitanism itself leads toward "diversality," instead of toward a new universality grounded (again) "on the potential of democratic politicization as the true European legacy from ancient Greece onward" (Žižek 1998: 1009). A new universalism recasting the democratic potential of the European legacy is not necessarily a solution to the vicious circle between (neo)liberal globalization and "regressive forms of fundamentalist hatred" (Žižek 1998: 1009). It is hard to imagine that the entire planet would endorse the democratic potential of "the European legacy from ancient Greece onward." The entire planet could, in fact, endorse a democratic, just, and cosmopolitan project as far as democracy and justice are detached from their "fundamental" European heritage, from Greece onward, and they are taken as connectors around which critical cosmopolitanism would be articulated. Epistemic diversality shall be the ground for political and ethical cosmopolitan projects. In other words, diversity as a universal project (that is, diversality) shall be the aim instead of longing for a new abstract universal and rehearsing a new universality grounded in the "true" Greek or Enlightenment legacy. Diversality as the horizon of critical and dialogic cosmopolitanism presupposes border thinking or border epistemology grounded on the critique of all possible fundamentalism (Western and non-Western, national and religious, neoliberal and neosocialist) and on the faith in accumulation at any cost that sustains capitalist organizations of the economy (Mignolo 2000). Since diversality (or diversity as a universal project) emerges from the experience of coloniality of power and the colonial difference, it cannot be reduced to a new form of cultural relativism but should be thought out as new forms of projecting and imagining, ethically and politically, from subaltern perspectives. As Manuel Castells (1997: 109) puts it, the Zapatistas, American militia, and Aum Shinrikyo are all social movements that act politically against globalization and against the state. My preference for the Zapatistas and not for the other two is an ethical rather than a political choice. Diversality as a universal project, then, shall be simultaneously ethical, political, and philosophical. It cannot be identified, either, with oppositional violence beyond the European Union and the United States. And of course, by definition, it cannot be located in the hegemonic global designs that have been the target of critical reflections in this essay. As John Rawls would word it in his explorations on the "law (instead of the right) of peoples," diversity as a universal project shall be identified with "the honest non-liberal people" (Rawls 1999: 90, see also 89–128). But also with "the honest non-Western people or people of color" that Rawls, following Kant, doesn't have in his horizon.

Critical and dialogic cosmopolitanism as a regulative principle demands yielding generously ("convivially" said Vitoria; "friendly" said Kant) toward diversity as a universal and cosmopolitan project in which everyone participates instead of "being participated." Such a regulative principle shall replace and displace the abstract universal cosmopolitan ideals (Christian, liberal, socialist, neoliberal) that had helped (and continue to help) to hold together the modern/colonial world system and to preserve the managerial role of the North Atlantic. And here is when the local histories and global designs come into the picture. While cosmopolitanism was thought out and projected from particular local histories (that became the local history of the modern world system) positioned to devise and enact global designs, other local histories in the planet had to deal with those global designs that were, at the same time, abstract universals (Christian, liberal, or socialist). For that reason, cosmopolitanism today has to become border thinking, critical and dialogic, from the perspective of those local histories that had to deal all along with global designs. Diversality should be the relentless practice of critical and dialogical cosmopolitanism rather than a blueprint of a future and ideal society projected from a single point of view (that of the abstract universal) that will return us (again!) to the Greek paradigm and to European legacies (Žižek 1998).

*

I suggested, at the beginning, that cosmopolitanism is linked to human rights and, indirectly, to democracy. I suggested further that these expressions would be taken as connectors for critical and dialogic cosmopolitan conversations, rather than as blueprints or master plans to be imposed worldwide. Thus, critical and dialogical cosmopolitanism demands a different conceptualization of human rights and democracy; and, of course, of citizenship, a notion that belongs to the ideology of the nation-state. If all human beings are rational, as had been recognized by Vitoria and Kant and the United Nations, then let it be. But then "natural rights" or the "law of nature" can hardly be the only principles upon which rationality and the rationality of society shall be defended. To "let it be" means to take seriously "human rationality" as another connector that will contribute to erase the coloniality of power ingrained in the very conceptualization of "natural rights" and the "law of nature" as models for human cosmo-polis. At this point in history, a critical and dialogic cosmopolitanism leading to diversity as a universal project can only be devised and enacted from the colonial difference.

I have also assumed a framework in which the three cosmopolitan designs with human rights implications were also linked to three different stages of the modern/colonial world system: the Spanish empire and Portuguese colonialism (Vitoria); the British empire and French and German colonialism (Kant), and U.S. imperialism (human rights). All three cosmopolitan designs shall be seen not only as a chronological order but also as the synchronic coexistence of an enduring concern articulated first through Christianity as a planetary ideology, second around the nation-state and the law as grounds for the second phase of colonialism, and third as the need to regulate the planetary conflict between democracy and socialism during the Cold War. I concluded by arguing for diversality as a universal project and for border thinking as a necessary epistemology upon which critical cosmopolitanism shall be articulated in a postnational world order governed by global capitalism and new forms of coloniality.

Finally, my argument intended to be from a subaltern perspective (which implies not inferiority but awareness of a subaltern position in a current geopolitical distribution of epistemic power). In a sense, it is an argument for globalization from below; at the same time, it is an argument for the geopolitically diversal — that is, one that conceives diversity as a (cosmopolitan) universal project. If you can imagine Western civilization as a large circle with a series of satellite circles intersecting the larger one but disconnected from each other, diversality will be the project that connects the diverse subaltern satellites appropriating and transforming Western global designs. Diversality can be imagined as a new medievalism, a pluricentric world built on the ruins of ancient, non-Western cultures and civilizations with the debris of Western civilization. A cosmopolitanism that only connects from the center of the large circle outward, and leaves the outer places disconnected from each other, would be a cosmopolitanism from above, like Vitoria's and Kant's cosmopolitanism in the past and Rawls's and Habermas's cosmopolitanism today, and like the implications of human rights discourse, according to which only one philosophy has it "right."

NOTES

For their insightful critical observations, I am indebted and thankful to the *Public Culture* editorial committee; to anonymous reviewers; and to Homi Bhabha, Carol A. Breckenridge, and Sheldon Pollock. I have also received helpful critical comments from Paul Eiss, Tim Watson, and Pramod Mishra.

1. Vitoria's notion of a "natural right" is not quite like Kant's "natural law," which indirectly obscured the question of "the other" that recently became Jürgen Habermas's (1998) concern.

2. I am here repeating a well-known story (Cassirer [1932] 1951) and displacing it with a reading that takes the perspective of "Man of Colors," rather than the perspective of the "White Man's Burden" (Gordon 1995).

3. Dussel (1998: 411–20) has confronted Habermas, Taylor, and Rawls from the perspective of the philosophy of liberation. Dussel's argument is grounded in the relevance of the sixteenth-century debates on the humanity of Amerindians and their relevance to current debates on multiculturalism, recognition, and "people rights" (as Vitoria and now Rawls call it).

4. In 1973, David Rockefeller, then-CEO of Chase Manhattan Bank, initiated the Trilateral Commission. President Jimmy Carter's national security adviser Zbigniew Brzezinski was its main ideologue.

5. An-Na'im's observation at this point could be applied to Vitoria, Kant, and the "United Nations Declaration of Human Rights."

6. "Cosmopolitan desires" can no longer emanate from the same epistemic location of global designs, unless "cosmopolitanism" is conceived as a new global design from the left and converted into a "cosmopolitan manifesto" (Beck 1999: 1–18). Among the many issues cosmopolitan (postnational) projects will have to deal with is what is often called "intercultural critique" and "cultural differences" (Beck 1998: 99–116; Fornet-Betancourt 1994). The main problem here is to change the terms of the conversation from cultural to colonial difference. A world risk society has coloniality of power imbedded into it and the reproduction of colonial differences in a planetary and postnational scale.

WORKS CITED

Abu-Lughod, Janet L. 1989. *Before European Hegemony: The World System A.D. 1250–1350.* New York: Oxford University Press.

An-Na'im, Abdullahi A. 1994. "What Do We Mean by Universal?" *Index of Censorship* 4/5: 120–27.

Arrighi, Giovanni. 1994. *The Long Twentieth Century.* London: Verso.

Beck, Ulrich. 1998. *Què es la globalización? Falacias del globalismo, repuestas a la globalización*, trans. Bernardo Moreno and María Rosa Borrás. Buenos Aires: Paidos.

———. 1999. *World Risk Society*. Cambridge, U.K.: Polity Press.

"Beijing Declaration." [1995] 1997. In *The Human Rights Reader*, ed. Micheline R. Ishay. New York: Routledge.

Braudel, Fernand. 1979. *Afterthoughts on Material Civilization and Capitalism*. Baltimore, Md.: Johns Hopkins University Press.

Brzezinski, Zbigniew. 1970. *Between Two Ages: America's Role in the Technetronic Era*. New York: Viking.

Cassano, Franco. 1996. *Il pensiero meridiano*. Bari: Sagittari Laterza.

Cassirer, Ernst. [1932] 1951. *The Philosophy of the Enlightenment*, trans. F. C. A. Koelln and J. P. Pettegrove. Princeton, N.J.: Princeton University Press.

Castells, Manuel. 1997. *The Power of Identity*. New York: Blackwell.

Cheah, Pheng, and Bruce Robbins, eds. 1998. *Cosmopolitics: Thinking and Feeling Beyond the Nation*. Minneapolis: University of Minnesota Press.

Cooper, Richard, ed. 1973. *Towards a Renovated International System: A Report of the Trilateral Integrators Task Force to the Trilateral Commission*. New York: Trilateral Commission.

Dainotto, Roberto. 2000. "A South with a View: Europe and Its Other." In *Nepantla: Views from South* 1, no. 2: 375–90.

Dirks, Nicholas. 1992. "Introduction: Colonialism and Culture." In *Colonialism and Culture*, ed. Nicholas B. Dirks. Ann Arbor: University of Michigan Press.

Dussel, Enrique. 1995. "Eurocentrism and Modernity (Introduction to the Frankfurt lectures)." In *Postmodernism in Latin America*, ed. J. Beverley, J. Oviedo, and M. Arona. Durham, N.C.: Duke University Press.

———. 1998. *Ética de la liberación en la edad de la globalización y de la exclusión*. Mexico City: Universidad Autónoma Nacional de México.

Eze, Emmanuel Chukwudi. 1997. "The Color of Reason: The Idea of 'Race' in Kant's Anthropology. In *Postcolonial African Philosophy: A Critical Reader*, ed. E. C. Eze. Cambridge, Mass.: Blackwell.

Fornet-Betancourt, Raúl. 1994. *La filosofía intercultural*. Mexico City: Universidad Pontificia de México.

Friedman, Milton (with the assistance of Rose Friedman). 1962. *Capitalism and Freedom*. Chicago: University of Chicago Press.

Gerbi, Antonello. [1955] 1982. *La disputa del Nuevo Mundo: Historia de una polémica, 1750–1900*, trans. Antonio Alatorre. Mexico City: Fondo de Cultura Económica.

Gordon, Lewis R. 1995. *Fanon and the Crisis of European Man: An Essay on Philosophy and the Human Sciences*. New York: Routledge.

Gregor, Mary. 1993. "Kant on 'Natural Rights.'" In *Kant and Political Philosophy*, ed. R. Beiner and W. J. Booth. New Haven, Conn.: Yale University Press.

Habermas, Jürgen. 1998. *The Inclusion of the Other*, trans. C. Cronin and P. De Greiff. Cambridge, Mass.: MIT Press.

Hayek, F. A. [1944] 1994. *The Road to Serfdom*. Chicago: University of Chicago Press.

Hegel, G. W. F. [1822] 1956. *The Philosophy of History,* trans. J. Sibree. New York: Dover.

Held, David. 1995. *Democracy and the Global Order.* Stanford, Calif.: Stanford University Press.

Höffner, Joseph. [1947] 1957. *La ética colonial española del siglo de oro: Cristianismo y dignidad humana.* Versión española de Franscisco de Asis Caballero. Madrid: Ediciones de Cultura Hispánica.

Huntington, Samuel P. 1996. *The Clash of Civilizations and the Remaking of World Order.* New York: Simon and Schuster.

Kant, Immanuel. [1785] 1996. *The Metaphysics of Morals,* ed. and trans. Mary Gregor. Cambridge: Cambridge University Press.

———. [1795] 1963. "Perpetual Peace." In *Kant on History,* ed. Lewis White Beck, and trans. Lewis White Beck, Robert E. Anchor, and Emil L. Fackenheim. Englewood Cliffs, N.J.: Macmillan.

———. [1797] 1996. *Anthropology from a Pragmatic Point of View,* trans. Victor Lyle Dowdell. Carbondale: Southern Illinois University.

Koshy, Susan. 1999. "From Cold War to Trade War: Neocolonialism and Human Rights. *Social Text* 58, 1–32.

Kristeva, Julia. 1991. *Strangers to Ourselves,* trans. L. S. Roudiez. New York: Columbia University Press.

McCarthy, Thomas. 1999. "On reconciling Cosmopolitan Unity and National Diversity." *Public Culture* 11: 175–208.

Meinecke, Friedich. 1970. *Cosmopolitanism and the National State,* trans. F. Gilbert. Princeton, N.J.: Princeton University Press.

Mignolo, Walter D. 1998. "Globalization and the Relocation of Languages and Cultures." In *The Cultures of Globalization,* ed. F. Jameson and M. Miyoshi. Durham, N.C.: Duke University Press.

———. 2000. *Local Histories/Global Designs: Coloniality, Subaltern Knowledges, and Border Thinking.* Princeton, N.J.: Princeton University Press.

Pérez Luño, Antonio-Enrique. 1992. *La polémica sobre el nuevo mundo: Los clásicos españoles de la filosofía del derecho.* Madrid: Editiorial Trotta.

Raghavan, Chakravarthu. 1990. *Recolonization: GATT, the Uruguayan Round, and the Third World.* London: Zed.

Ramos, D., A. García, I. Pérez, M. Lucena, J. González, V. Abril, L. Pereña, R. Hernández, J. Brufau, C. Bacieron, J. Barrientos, A. Rodríguez, P. Cerezo, P. Borges, and G. Lohmann. 1984. *La ética en la conquista de América.* Madrid: Consejo Superior de Investigaciones Científicas y Técnicas.

Rawls, John. 1999. *The Law of Peoples.* Cambridge: Harvard University Press.

Redrado, Martín. 2000. *Cómo sobrevivir a la globalización: Una guía para protegerse de la economía global.* Buenos Aires: Prentice Hall.

Serequeberhan, Tsenay. 1997. "The Critique of Eurocentrism and the Practice of African Philosophy. In *Postcolonial African Philosophy: A Critical Reader,* ed. E. C. Eze. Cambridge, Mass.: Blackwell.

Taylor, Charles. 1992. "The Politics of Recognition." In *Multiculturalism and "The Politics of Recognition": An Essay.* Princeton, N.J.: Princeton University Press.

Tolley, Howard, Jr. 1987. *The U.N. Commission on Human Rights.* Boulder, Colo.: Westview Press.

Toulmin, Stephen. 1990. *Cosmopolis: The Hidden Agenda of Modernity.* New York: Free Press.

Trouillot, Michel-Rolph. 1995. *Silencing the Past: Power and the Production of History.* Boston: Beacon Press.

"United Nations Declaration of Human Rights." [1948] 1997. In *The Human Rights Reader,* ed. Micheline R. Ishay. New York: Routledge.

Van De Pitte, Frederick P. 1996. "Introduction." In *Anthropology from a Pragmatic Point of View,* by Immanuel Kant, and trans. Victor Lyle Dowdell. Carbondale: Southern Illinois University Press.

Vitoria, Francisco de. [1539] 1967. *Relectio de Indis o libertad de los Indios.* Bilingual (Latin and Spanish) and critical edition by L. Pereña and J. M. Perez Prendes. Introductory studies by V. Belgran de Heredia, R. Agostino Iannarone, T. Urdanoz, A. Truyol, and L. Pereña. Madrid: Consejo Superior de Investigaciones Científicas.

Wallerstein, Immanuel. 1999. "Social Science and the Communist Interlude, or Interpretations of Contemporary History." In *The End of the World as We Know It: Social Science for the Twenty-First Century.* Minneapolis: University of Minnesota Press.

Wollstonecraft, Mary. [1792] 1997. "The Rights of Women." In *The Human Rights Reader,* ed. Micheline R. Ishay. New York: Routledge.

Žižek, Slavoj. 1998. "A Leftist Plea for 'Eurocentrism.'" *Critical Inquiry* 24: 989–1009.

Zhang Dali's *Dialogue:* Conversation with a City

Wu Hung

A public controversy surfaced in Beijing's newspapers in early 1998. At its center was an image that had become familiar to the city's many urban residents: a spray-painted profile of a large bald head, sometimes two meters tall. The graffiti head seemed to have been duplicating itself, and its appearances gradually spread from the inner city to beyond the Third Ring Road. Alone or in groups, the head was found within the confines of small neighborhoods and along major avenues. Who was the man behind these images? What did he want to say or do? Should he be punished when identified? What kind of penalty should he receive? Was the image a sort of public art and therefore legitimate? What is public art anyway? To a city of 10 million that had not been exposed to the graffiti art of the West, these questions were new. None of them had straightforward answers.

Neither did Zhang Dali who created these images. Shortly after the debate started, he came forward as the anonymous painter; by March 1998, he began to give interviews to reporters and art critics. It turned out that, far from a "punk" or "gang member" as some local people had guessed, he was a professional artist trained in Beijing's prestigious Central Academy of Art and Design. Moreover, he was not a typical Chinese professional artist because he had emigrated to Italy in 1989 and first forged the image of the bald head in Bologna, where he had lived for six years. He continued to paint the same head after returning to China in 1995, and by 1998 he had sprayed more than 2,000 such images throughout Beijing. It also turned out that he had developed a theory to rationalize his seemingly mindless act. In published interviews, Zhang explained that the image was a self-portrait through which he hoped to engage the city in a "dialogue" with himself: "This image is a condensation of my own likeness as an individual. It stands in my place to communicate with this city. I want to know everything about this city—its state of being, its transformation, its structure. I call this project *Dialogue*. Of course there are many ways for an artist to communicate with a city. I use this method because, for one thing, it allows me to place my work at every corner of this city in a short period."[1]

Instructive as it is, there is a disturbing deviation between the artist's sure voice and the uncertainty involved in the images themselves. Looking through hundreds of Zhang's photographs of his graffiti portraits from different places and circumstances, one gains less knowledge of Beijing than of the artist's contested relationship with the city. It is true that these photos show Beijing's changing cityscape—vanishing old lanes, dilapidated demolition sites, scaffold-embraced high-rises, and protected traditional monuments. But as the title of Zhang's project indicates, what these photographs mean to record is not a city as an object of sociological observation or aesthetic appreciation, but a "dialogue" initiated by an artist's subjective intervention, which in this case is his self-image forced on the community at large. In fact, the question these photographs evoke is not so much about the content or purpose of dialogue, but whether the artist's desire to communicate with the city can actually be realized—whether the city is willing or ready to be engaged in a forced interaction. Thus, while each photograph is invariably animated by a yearning for dialogue, the response by Beijing's residents ranges from indifference to suspicion, fear, misunderstanding, and rejection. Searching for a solution, the artist is forced to change the meaning of his project, to the point that he has to retreat, however unconsciously, to the position of an observer or accomplice, letting the city speak to itself.

What interests me most about Zhang's project, therefore, is not its theoretical consistency or its impressive scale and durability, but the paradox between the premeditated insistence of a signifier and the unpremeditated permutation of signification: although each of the graffiti portraits is a deliberate repetition, its meaning and effect as the locus of an intended dialogue with the city is generally beyond the artist's control. Only because of such impossibility to precondition a dialogue, and to predict its result, can the dialogue itself—successful or not—gain a genuine sense of spatiality and temporality. Guided by this interest, my purpose in compiling this photo essay is not to provide an illustrated explication of the stated agendas of the artist (which have been detailed in several interviews and reports, combined with the writers' own social critiques or art analyses) or to interpret Zhang's project as a remote echo of the "international graffiti art" that had been enshrined in Western museums by the early 1980s. Rather, the seven images reproduced here, selected from some four hundred photographs made available to me by Zhang, document an intense negotiation between a public-minded artist and a rapidly changing city over a period of five years, from 1995 to 1999. Since such negotiation has also become a central issue in contemporary Chinese art, this photo essay addresses a broad phenomenon through a specific case.

Zhang was one of a considerable number of Chinese artists who left China after the student demonstrations in 1989 ended in bloodshed. This sudden dislocation and the difficulty of fitting into alien cultures exasperated the trauma of Tiananmen Square, with the result that emigration was experienced as self-exile. In an interview with me in September 1999, Zhang described his first job in Italy of making exotic "oriental paintings" for a commercial gallery as nothing but a base means for survival. He finally gave it up, but then he found himself surrounded by a cultural void and deeply depressed. A turning point was his discovery of graffiti—not in museums but in Bologna's back alleys. Suddenly, there was a possibility for him to divorce the past and join the present. He began to spray his self-image of a bald head on the walls of Bologna, and it was immediately responded to by other graffiti. The sense of spontaneous communication was uplifting, and he titled his graffiti *Dialogue.* But was there a real dialogue? In a way, he was reliving the prehistory of graffiti—before it was admitted into the art history canon—and his origin in another time/place enabled him to make this fantastic return. His graffiti were a veiled fantasy also because he still considered himself an artist, even though he had abandoned his academic training and the painting studio. Therefore, his self-image on the street both exhibited his new self and masked his old self, and his "dialogue" with other street painters was equally about communication and miscommunication. This photo records when one of his two graffiti heads was superimposed overnight by other graffiti: first a Communist hammer and sickle sign and then the insignia of a right-wing party. Later he learned that this "graffiti war" was triggered by a mistake: his "skinhead" was taken as a neo-Nazi symbol. Thus while he continued to be excited by making images in public, the interactions they provoked were rarely substantiated by real exchanges of lived experiences. Graffiti had created an illusion of a shared language and culture, but, in fact, they concealed linguistic and cultural differences. Most tellingly, when Zhang traveled to Slovenia in 1993 and made street graffiti to express his antiwar sentiment, on walls already adorned with signs and signatures incomprehensible to him, he sprayed a slogan in Chinese that was likewise incomprehensible to the local graffiti artists.

Zhang is also one of a considerable number of Chinese artists who have ended their self-exile and returned to China during recent years. The reasons for their homecoming are complex, and each case varies, but, in many instances, an enormous attraction was to liberate oneself from the ambiguous status of being an "overseas Chinese"; there would be no more need to go through a painful and often unrewarding cultural conversion. These artists can be both "avant-garde" and "Chinese" only in China. Besides, as the 1989 tragedy had gradually subsided into people's subconscious, Deng Xiaoping's new economic policy began to transform China from a socialist monolith into a huge contradiction that was full of opportunities. In the 1990s, Beijing was an oversized construction site embellished with a cacophony of commercial ads. Dust, mud, and torn papers were everywhere, and gleaming high-rises soared above the remnants of demolished houses. Foreign investors, domestic businessmen, and 3.5 million illegal immigrants from the countryside poured into this city, and the bewildering transformations promised hope to visionaries and gold diggers.

Zhang contributed to this chaos with his sprayed profiles. Following his Italian experience, he started with Beijing's "underground" and first painted in shadowy alleyways and under freeway bridges. He continued to call these images *Dialogue* and looked for interaction; but the graffiti met only with silence. In an interview, I asked him whether the 2,000 heads he had been spraying in Beijing since 1995 had ever provoked any responding graffiti. His answer came quick and firm: "No."

This photograph shows a traditional Beijing house's outer wall, which had been used as a local billboard before Zhang sprayed his graffiti head on it. To the left of the head is the character for "vehicle" inside a used tire—the sign of a bicycle repair stand. To the right is a printed sheet promising instant cure for all sorts of venereal diseases. The shop sign and the advertisement lie side by side with Zhang's head but have nothing to do with it. In fact, even though the head seems to thrust forward in an aggressive manner, it does not generate any interaction or dialogue, neither with the words/images next to it nor with the man napping underneath it. A more appropriate title for the photograph may be *No Dialogue*. Back in Beijing, Zhang could now speak in his native tongue, but the Beijingers had to learn the language of graffiti art.

Without concrete images responding to his graffiti, Zhang turned his attention beyond the images to capture people's reactions: it was perhaps in their eyes, on their faces, or from their casual remarks that he could find their responses to his work. He began to hang around the places where he had sprayed the graffiti head, secretly watching the passersby and catching their every word. He had become an invisible man made double—an anonymous painter combined with a voyeur/eavesdropper. To avoid being caught, he only painted in a guerrilla fashion, roaming on his bicycle through Beijing's deep night, finishing a head here and there in a few seconds when no one was around. His sustained anonymity during the day allowed him to complete the significance of his graffiti as *dialogue.* Later he told the art critic Leng Lin that by talking about a sprayed head on a wall as if it had been done by someone else he could detect unguarded "the cultural background and state of mind" of his conversation partner. A taxi driver told him that the head was a Mafia symbol like those in Hong Kong kung fu movies. A neighbor worried that the head was an official mark for houses slated to be demolished and whose current occupants would soon be kicked out. As Zhang said to Leng, "I have been collecting such reactions—reactions that turn my work from a monologue into a dialogue."[2]

A dialogue it may have been. But it was only a one-sided dialogue, as it merely consisted of a reaction, not an interaction. From 1995 to 1997, Zhang's interest lay in what people thought and said about his work, but not in developing an ongoing conversation with an audience. We can thus understand why the graffiti artist soon took up the camera after he returned to China: photography helped him capture people's instantaneous reactions and make such reactions eternal. This photograph, one of the earliest such snapshots Zhang took in Beijing, never fails to chill me with a feeling of inability to communicate. On a bare wall of a back alley there is again the lonely graffiti head. Still leaning forward, it seems to be following two local boys to appeal for their attention. Ignoring the head, one of the boys turns around to stare into the camera lens with a cool, dispassionate gaze. The artist's second self beyond the picture frame is acknowledged but not sympathized with.

FIGURE 4: DIALOGUE THROUGH MEDIA

A full year after Zhang sprayed his first graffiti head in Beijing, a printed response finally appeared in a popular magazine. This 1996 article starts with a vivid but bitter account of the two authors' reactions (or what they believed to be people's common reactions) to Zhang's images: "On Beijing's streets you can inadvertently come across a bizarre image, or a row of them. More than a meter tall, it is a huge face in profile outlined in black spray paint. Encountering it for the first time you wouldn't take it seriously, or you'd think it was only a naughty kid's scribble. But this is far from the truth, because when you go out again the same day or a few days later, the same monstrosity boldly greets you in another location, and you repeat this disturbing experience over and over. This ghost-like face seems omnipresent and to be chasing you around, and you feel powerless to avoid it."[3]

With such intuitive negativity and a subsequent "analysis" to justify it, this article introduced a group of reports with a shared attitude and tactic. Zhang's images were characterized as philistine imitations of Western "graffiti art" that, in turn, epitomized the "decadent aesthetics" of the West. Another common strategy of these writings was to cite "public opinion" that ridiculed the "ugly, monstrous head." Still, these writings are interesting for subtly distancing themselves from the official position. Speaking for "a general public," their authors rarely, if at all, evoked the government's authority to condemn the graffiti, and they quoted from people of divergent professions, backgrounds, and age groups to give their reports a sense of authenticity. The ten interviewees cited in the article, for example, included (in the original order) a middle-aged university professor, a local restaurateur, a passerby, a farmer-turned-construction worker, a college freshman, an American art student, an architect, an "old Beijing guy," a member of the local residential committee, and a policeman "who happened to be at the spot." The harshest opinion, coming predictably from the policeman and the committee member, demanded that "the troublemaker be found and arrested at once." The others voiced uncertainties and hesitations, but none supported the graffiti. The two authors could thus reach this conclusion: "We can say therefore that the public's basic attitude toward such graffiti in the capital is: incomprehension, repugnance, and rejection." Since no alternative views were offered in the media, this conclu-

sion became the unchallenged public opinion in 1996 and 1997. But since this opinion was not yet an official verdict, Zhang continued his project, and his images continued to receive responses from a constructed "public" in the media.

The tide was changing, however. In early 1998, several of Beijing's "cultural" newspapers and magazines featured a debate centered on Zhang's graffiti.[4] An increasing number of authors took a sympathetic stand. But what was more important, through this debate Zhang's art provided a focus for discussions about larger issues — cultural diversity and social mobility, urban violence and racial tolerance, public art and performance, artistic freedom and artists' responsibilities, city planning and environmental policies — that were gradually entering the media as Beijing was becoming a global metropolis. Finally, the artist abandoned his anonymity and joined this discussion: Zhang gave his first interview in March 1998 to directly address his audience through the newspaper. This form of communication between experimental artists and the public inspired Leng Lin to stage a special "exhibition." As figure 4 shows, Leng printed Zhang's graffiti (and works of three other experimental artists) in a newspaper format and distributed the material throughout the city. The purpose was, in his words, "to use the popular media of the newspaper as a form of artistic expression and exchange, a form that brings art and society into close contact at any time and in any place."[5]

FIGURE 5: PICTURING DIALOGUE (1) — DESTRUCTION/CONSTRUCTION

Although Zhang eventually did get reactions to his art on the street and through the media, these were verbal responses, not visual communication. His insistence on displaying thousands of his graffiti heads in public over several years was extraordinary; in the end, however, he still failed to engage other images into a spontaneous *visual* dialogue. Partly because of the city's irresponsiveness on this level of interaction, Zhang the artist (not Zhang the social critic) had to explore other possibilities to realize the theme of his project—dialogue. The result was a subtle but crucial change in the meaning of this theme: he was increasingly preoccupied with an ongoing "visual dialogue" internal to the city (rather than expecting an interaction with the city that could never materialize). In addition, photography gradually took over to become his means to represent such visual dialogue, often dramatic confrontations of architectural images with his sprayed self-images.

A major visual drama in Beijing during the 1990s was never-ending destruction and construction. Although large-scale demolition is a regular feature of any metropolis, the enormity and duration of the demolition in Beijing was unusual. Following China's "economic miracle," investment poured into the country from Hong Kong, Taiwan, and the West. Thousands of old houses were destroyed to make room for glimmering hotels, shopping malls, and business centers. Everywhere were cranes and scaffolding, the roaring sound of bulldozers, broken walls, and mountainlike waste. To some residents, demolition meant forced relocation; to others, it promised a larger apartment, albeit in a remote suburban area. In theory, demolition and relocation were conditions for the capital's modernization. In actuality, these conditions brought about a growing alienation between the city and its residents: they no longer belonged to one another.

A major subject of Chinese experimental art in the 1990s, demolition and relocation also dominated Zhang's work in 1998 and 1999.[6] He differed from other artists in two major ways, however. First, he was the only graffiti artist in Beijing who filled in half-destroyed, empty houses with his sprayed images, thus "reclaiming" an abandoned site, however temporarily. Second, he always contrasted destruction with construction, thus forming a visual dialogue between the two. Both

features are forcefully demonstrated in this 1998 photograph. In the foreground of the picture, still standing amid scattered garbage, are broken walls, remnants of a demolished traditional house on which Zhang has sprayed a row of his by now famous heads. Two huge modern buildings rise behind this wasteland. Still surrounded by scaffolding, one of them already advertises itself as the future "Prime Tower" and offers the telephone number of its sales department. This and many other photographs made by Zhang during this period serve a double purpose. On the one hand, they record site-specific environmental art projects that have been carried out by the artist. On the other hand, these projects were designed largely to be photographed, resulting in two-dimensional images as independent works of art. Consequently, the role of Zhang's graffiti head has also changed: no longer a stimulus for an expected interaction on the street, it now serves as a pictorial sign that points to and heightens an urban visual drama.

A second kind of architectural dialogue in Zhang's photographs takes place between demolished old houses and preserved ancient monuments; their sharply contrasting images allude to two radically different attitudes toward tradition. In this photograph, for example, the picture plane is filled almost entirely with the remaining wall of a destroyed house, on which Zhang has sprayed the bald head and hollowed it out with a hammer and chisel. The rough opening on the wall is analogous to a fresh wound, through which one sees in the distance a glorious, mirage-like image: the golden roof of one of the four corner pavilions of the Forbidden City.

In a succinct but quite literal way, this picture relates a twofold process of destruction and preservation that Beijing has been enduring throughout the modern period, especially over the past decade. Built during the Ming (1368–1644) and the Qing (1644–1911) dynasties, traditional Beijing consisted of a number of nested subcities — the Outer City, the Inner City, the Imperial City, and the Forbidden City. A series of magnificent tower gates punctuated the north-south axis to link these broken spaces into a rhythmic continuum. Until the early twentieth century, Beijing was, in the eyes of the noted architectural historian Liang Sicheng, incomparable for its supreme architectural precision and harmony.[7]

Now this city has been thoroughly destroyed, and its destruction can be simply summarized by reference to three historical moments. The Imperial City first vanished in the first half of the twentieth century when major modern avenues were constructed running east-west, burying the old north-south Imperial Way underneath. The walls of the Inner and Outer Cities were then destroyed in the 1950s and 1960s through a Herculean effort mobilized by the state; also gone were most of the tower gates and all the archways and brick landmarks across the city's traditional streets. Finally, the recent construction fervor ruined a large number of traditional courtyard houses. One of Beijing's major architectural projects from 1997 to 1999, for example, was to open up a thirty-meter-wide avenue across the most densely populated section of downtown Beijing. No published statistics inform us how many house-

holds were relocated. They just disappeared; their streets and lanes vanished from the city's map.

From this giant obliteration emerged modern Beijing, while traditional Beijing is being "preserved" as a prized collection of architectural fragments: a few old gardens, houses, temples, theaters, and mainly the isolated rectangle of the Forbidden City. These fragments are praised as masterpieces of Chinese architecture and are protected by law; the attention they receive contrasts alarmingly to the brutality that has been imposed on "other" traditional structures. Such brutality was most acutely felt during the recent demolition campaign when numerous private houses had been reduced to rubble. As Zhang's photograph shows, a house could be turned inside out without hesitation; any attempt at intimacy is silenced by an organized violence of forced demolition and relocation.

Zhang's decision to gouge out his graffiti image—to tear the wall open for a second time—can thus be understood as a response to this organized violence. The method was to amplify this violence through an art project. As he said in an interview: "Many things are happening in this city: demolition, construction, car accidents, sex, drunkenness, and violence infiltrates every hole. . . . I choose these walls. They are the screen onto which the show of the city is projected. . . . Only one and a half hours. The sound of hammer and chisels. Bricks fall, stirring up clouds of dust."[8] Such simulated violence is given a visual expression in this photograph: a broken wall frames one of the nation's most admired architectural jewels.

The images in this photograph resemble those in the last one: a dilapidated wall bearing Zhang's graffiti is again juxtaposed with a palace-style building in the background. But to every Chinese artist, the message delivered here is specific and transparent because the building in the distance, rather than an ancient structure, is immediately recognizable as the National Art Gallery, the headquarters of official art in China. It is the place where every state-sponsored National Art Exhibition is held, and it also houses the all-powerful Association of Chinese Artists, through whose vast network the government controls the art world. The building defines the center in the official map of Chinese art. For the same reason, it is also a heavily contested space; its authority has been challenged by a growing unofficial art during the past twenty years.

The two most important events in the short history of this unofficial art took place at the National Art Gallery. The first, the *Star* exhibition in 1979, marked the emergence of this unofficial art after the Cultural Revolution. Members of the group staged their show on the street outside the National Art Gallery, but as soon as a large crowd gathered, the police interfered and canceled the exhibition. The second event, the much larger *China/Avant-garde* exhibition, took place exactly ten years later. This time, unofficial artists occupied the National Art Gallery and turned it into a solemn site that resembled a tomb: long black carpets, extending from the street to the exhibition hall, bore the emblem of the show — a "No U-turn" traffic sign signaling "There is no turning back." The show itself was a rebellion against the established order in Chinese art. Three months later, many organizers and artists in this exhibition participated in the prodemocracy demonstrations in Tiananmen Square, which ended in the bloody massacre on 4 June 1989.

This history explains Zhang's 1999 photograph: the struggle continues, as here is another artist who takes a position "outside" the National Art Gallery's "center." But what is this outside position in Zhang's case? In retrospect, we realize that he has always identified himself with an outlying region circling a conventional center of gravity, be it a commercial high-rise, a protected ancient monument, or an official institution. It is clear that this self-positioning defines a space around which he has formed his self-identity as an individual artist opposed to any kind of hegemony. By inscribing his self-image on ruined walls,

however, he also problematizes his position and identity because this image is meant to be destroyed with the walls, not to be expanded into a new territory. Zhang said to me: "Walking alone inside a destroyed house I hear tiles breaking under my feet. The sound seems to come from inside of me. I am part of this vanishing scene." There is no desire to cross this wasteland; instead, he prefers to view himself from a future-past perspective as a memory in the making: "With the development of Beijing, my graffiti images will eventually disappear on their own. But they will leave a trace of memory—a dialogue between an artist and this city."[9]

Graffiti are universal: there is no culture in the ancient or modern world that has failed to invent its own local custom of writing on rocks, trees, or walls. Today what we call "graffiti art" is not universal but global: it is an artistic, cultural, political, and economic practice extending beyond the local. Many articles and books have been written to trace the spread of this art from the far-flung boroughs of New York to Europe, Australia, and Asia. Looking back, the Manhattan graffiti artist Phase 2 (M. L. Marrow) was proud of the vast network his art had helped forge: "This thing has reached all the way around the world from Harlem to Japan. When has something else had an impact like that on every ethnic group in the entire world? . . . You don't even have to be able to talk English. All you gotta do is get a spraycan and paint something."[10]

Here Phase 2 was speaking about the networking of international graffiti artists, an early 1980s phenomenon that was coupled with the explosion of films, videos, and books, all of which promoted rap music, break dancing, and spraycan writing around the world. This grassroots movement was intertwined with another kind of globalization of graffiti art, which had less to do with the geographical spread of this art than with its changing materiality and social status. Graffiti images were transcribed from walls to canvases and dislocated from dilapidated inner-city neighborhoods into glittering galleries and museums. Graffiti-inspired works, now featured in major art exhibitions and lavish catalogs, were appreciated as a distinct art style—a style that alluded to the surface images of graffiti but negated their original bearers, contexts, and messages. For this reason, these works have never been able to replace their lowly prototypes (which have continued to be associated with local communities and outlaws), and they have continued to travel from one neighborhood to another across urban and national boundaries.

With this two-tier globalization at work, graffiti art presents us with a unique case to reflect on the cosmopolitanism of a contemporary metropolis. It becomes clear that such cosmopolitanism — exemplified here by the coexistence and interaction of various graffiti cultures in a shared urban space—is far from a harmonious state of being produced by a desire for all-inclusiveness. Rather, it is fundamentally a reality forced on the city; it encompasses contesting spaces, intentions, and attitudes that the city cannot escape. Graffiti art exists both in the museum and on the street; to decide which part of it is "inside" or "outside" means precisely to come to terms with one's own positioning in relation to a city at large. Do we hang a poster of Keith Haring's pop figures in the living room while demanding a stop to graffiti vandalism? Do we share graffitist Bando's feeling when he says, "Graffiti is . . . a very beautiful crime"?[11] Do we support Philadelphia's Anti-Graffiti Network or similar projects to confine street graffiti to designated areas? Can we define graffiti as an art by separating "good" graffiti from "bad"? Clear-cut answers to these questions tend to be self-serving and depart from the ideal of cosmopolitanism; but the situation that forces these questions upon us is cosmopolitan.

With Zhang's homecoming in 1995, this international graffiti art finally reached Beijing fifteen years after its formation. A major reason for its belated arrival, of course, is that only at this moment did China's capital begin to surface as a cosmopolitan city that could tolerate, however unwillingly, this art form. Zhang's graffiti signal Beijing's emerging cosmopolitanism not simply through their existence but by renewing the internal conflicts of graffiti art in a particular setting. In fact, as the city's only known graffiti artist, Zhang internalizes these conflicts in himself. His street graffiti were motivated by a genuine desire to bypass the established art system and to develop a dialogue with the city. But now his photographs of his graffiti are sold in a foreign-owned commercial gallery in Beijing; one of these pictures even appeared on the cover of *Newsweek*. The plot of this success story is not unfamiliar, but the logic is new: having failed to engage Beijing in a direct conversation, Zhang and his art have nevertheless come to symbolize a new image of this city.

NOTES

1. Leng Lin, *Shi wo* [It's me] (Beijing: Zhongguo Wenlian Chubanshe, 2000), 168 (my translation).
2. Leng, *Shi wo*, 171.
3. Yang Fudong and Jiang Zhi, "Kan! Beijing jietou de tuya" [Look! Graffiti on Beijing's streets], *Jiedao* [Streets] 6 (1996): 42 (my translation).
4. These articles include the following: Yu Zhong, "Ping'an Dadao youren tuya" [Someone's graffiti on Ping'an Avenue], *Beijing Qingnian Bao* [Beijing youth daily], 24 February 1998, 1; Hang Cheng, "Benbao dujia fangdao jietou tuyaren" [Exclusive

interview with the street graffiti artist], *Shenghuo Shibao* [Life times], 18 March 1998, 16; Zhao Guoming, "Weihe qiangshang hua renxiang" [Why draw a portrait on the wall?], *Beijing Qingnian Bao* [Beijing youth daily], 18 March 1998, 2; Hang Cheng, "Jietou renxiang: shibushi yishu" [Street portraits: Are they art?], *Shenghuo Shibao* [Life times], 21 March 1998, 8; Jiang Tao, "Jujiao Beijing rentouxiang" [Focus on Beijing street portraits], *Lantian Zhoumo* [Bluesky weekend], no. 1471, 27 March 1988, 1; Bo Maxiu, "Qiangshang de biaoji" [Marks on walls], *Yinyue Shenghuo Bao* [Musical life], 16 April 1998, B1; Dao Zi, "Shengtai yishu de wenhua luoji" [Cultural logic of outdoor art], *Zhonghua Tushu Bao* [China readers], 6 May 1998, 14.

5. Leng, *Shi wo,* 69–70. Calling the "newspaper" *Yibiao Rencai* [Talents], Leng organized this project in July 1999. The paper featured four experimental artists, including Zhang, Wang Jin, Zhu Fadong, and Wu Xiaojun.

6. Some of these works are discussed in Wu Hung, *Transience: Chinese Experimental Art at the End of the Twentieth Century* (Chicago: Smart Museum of Art, 1999), 108–26.

7. See Lin Zhu, *Jianzhushi Liang Sicheng* [Liang Sicheng the architect] (Tianjin: Kexue Jishu Chubanshe, 1996), 110.

8. Cited in Mathieu Borysevicz, "Zhang Dali's Conversation with Beijing," in *Zhang Dali: Demolition and Dialoque* (Beijing: Courtyard Gallery, 1999), 13. This excellent article was first published in *ART AsiaPacific* 22 (1999): 52–58.

9. Hang, "Banbao dujia fangdao jietou tuyaren," 16.

10. Henry Chalfant and James Prigoff, *Spraycan Art* (London: Thames and Hudson, 1987), 91.

11. Chalfant and Prigoff, *Spraycan Art,* 72.

Cosmopolitan De-scriptions: Shanghai and Hong Kong

Ackbar Abbas

I like all big cities. More than Japanese, I feel I'm from Tokyo, where I was born. . . . Tokyo has no nationality.— Yohji Yamamoto, in Wim Wenders's 1989 film *Notebook on Cities and Clothes*

One of the most moving, and revealing, texts of the Argentinian writer Jorge Luis Borges is his short 1954 preface to *A Universal History of Infamy,* a collection of stories first published in 1935. During the two decades between the original publication and the 1954 preface, Borges had established himself as a cosmopolitan writer who belonged not just to Argentina but to the world. However, it is possible to see Borges's cosmopolitanism both as the great cultural achievement that it unquestionably is and as a response to a quasi-colonial situation that inevitably leaves its traces, however indirectly. In Borges, we find these traces in the excessive and exhaustive erudition that he is famous for and that he calls the baroque: "I would define as baroque the style that deliberately exhausts (or tries to exhaust) its own possibilities, and that borders on self-caricature."[1] That there is some relation between style and situation, between the baroque and the colonial, becomes clear when we learn a little later in the same preface that Borges's baroque originated as "the sport of a shy sort of man who could not bring himself to write short stories, and so amused himself by changing and distorting (sometimes without aesthetic justification) the stories of other men." In a colonial or quasi-colonial situation, even our "own" stories have to begin as "stories of other men." No wonder that it was some time before Borges could turn from "these ambiguous exercises" to "the arduous composition of a straightforward short story—'Man on Pink Corner.'"

Besides being a mask for shyness, there is another, less attractive, side to Borges's erudition: it can be related to a tendency toward displays of knowledge or knowingness that comes from the colonial's anxiety to be recognized. This is perhaps what the Spanish director Luis Buñuel intuited in the Argentinian writer, without quite understanding its provenance. Buñuel mentions Borges in some cutting remarks in his autobiography *My Last Sigh:* "Just because someone writes well doesn't mean you have to like him . . . he struck me as very pretentious and self-absorbed. There's something too academic (or as we say in Spanish, *sienta cátedra*) about everything he says, something exhibitionistic. Like many blind people, he's an eloquent speaker, albeit the subject of the Nobel Prize tends to crop up excessively each time he talks to reporters."[2] (This is a tendency, we might add, to which many Chinese aspirants to the prize are also prone.) Buñuel's cruel way of snubbing Borges is simply to remark in parentheses "as we say in Spanish," a *we* that shoulders Borges back onto the margins; as if the metropolitan and the colonial were clearly divided by a common language. For all Borges's aloofness or air of detachment (as when he writes in his essay "The Argentine Writer and Tradition": "I believe our tradition is all of Western culture. . . . our patrimony is the universe; we should essay all themes, and we cannot limit ourselves to purely Argentine subjects in order to be Argentine") a certain shrillness is discernable—at least to a European like Buñuel—in his advocacy of a cosmopolitan stance.[3]

*

I begin with this encounter between Borges and Buñuel because it illustrates some of the ambiguities of the cosmopolitan. In Borges's case, cosmopolitanism was, first, a modernist argument against the tyranny of "tradition" as narrow parochialisms and ethnocentrism: this was the critical aspect of his cultural universalism ("our patrimony is the universe")—in much the same way that the universalism of "structure" was to Claude Lévi-Strauss a critical safeguard against ethnocentric bias.[4] The problem begins when this universalism is identified with Western culture ("I believe our tradition is all of Western culture"). This identification did not happen by chance. In the modern era, which corresponded to the economic and political dominance of Western nations, cosmopolitanism by and large meant being versed in Western ways, and the vision of "one world" culture was only a sometimes unconscious, sometimes unconscionable, euphemism for "First World" culture.

This relationship of cosmopolitanism to power suggests that it cannot be thought of simply as an honorific or a universalist term, connoting either an ability to transcend narrow loyalties and ethnocentric prejudices or a sympathetic disposition to "the other." The ideal of cosmopolitanism, to quote a much-discussed essay of Ulf Hannerz's, as "an orientation, a willingness to engage with the Other . . . an intellectual and aesthetic stance of openness toward divergent cultural experiences" may be an admirable one, but it is sustainable only in metropolitan centers where movement and travel are undertaken with ease and where the encounter with other cultures is a matter of free choice, negotiated on favorable terms.[5] But what about a situation where these conditions are not available—a situation where "divergent cultural experiences" are not freely chosen but forced on us, as they are under colonialism? What form of "openness" should we cultivate then, and would this constitute a cosmopolitan stance or a compradorist one? Could cosmopolitanism be one version of "cultural imperialism"? Is there a chapter missing in Borges's *A Universal History of Infamy,* a chapter on colonialism as infamy?

These questions need to be asked, but to answer them by equating cosmopolitanism with cultural imperialism is ultimately as simplistic as it is to see it in purely celebratory terms. If we take the position I have been pursuing—that to understand cosmopolitanism and its valences, we will have to take account of the historical conditions under which it arises—then we will need to turn from Borges's time to our own and to consider the question of globalism. Globalism is the historical condition of our time, but it also raises new questions and threatens to make old ones redundant. Thus, the information technologies often associated with globalism promise to make parochialism, and hence the urgency of its critique, a thing of the past. At the same time, these technologies have been accompanied by such radical mutations in economic and political space (variously theorized as "post-Fordism," "disorganized capitalism," "the risk society," and "the network society") that "imperialism" in the classical sense as the clear-cut exploitation of one nation-state by another is becoming almost unrecognizable.[6] How can we describe cosmopolitanism under these changed conditions?

Instead of approaching such a question theoretically, I look again at the cosmopolitan through the history of two Asian cities, Shanghai and Hong Kong, and the urban cultures they developed. Cities have historically been the privileged, if not necessarily exclusive, sites for the emergence of the form of life that we call the cosmopolitan. In Shanghai and Hong Kong, in particular, some form of the cosmopolitan did indeed emerge under colonial conditions, and some other form of cosmopolitanism may be developing today. Nevertheless, the description of Shanghai and Hong Kong I give here is not intended to be a straightforward empirical account of what kind of cosmopolitan city each became under colonial rule or what crucial changes each is undergoing as communist China today reasserts itself as a global power. Rather, I direct attention to a certain elusive quality of both cities and to the fact that the most familiar images of these cities do not necessarily describe them best. To put this another way: cosmopolitanism must take place somewhere, in specific sites and situations—even if these places are more and more beginning to resemble those "non-places" that French anthropologist Marc Augé has argued characterize the contemporary city. In a non-place, "one is neither *chez soi* nor *chez les autres.*"[7] Like the city, Augé's non-place must be understood not literally, but as paradox: a non-place is far from being nonexistent. Rather, it is a result of excess and overcomplexity, of a limit having been exceeded. Beyond a certain point, there is a blurring and scrambling of signs and an overlapping of spatial and temporal grids, all of which make urban signs and images difficult to read. The overcomplex space of non-places means, among other things, that even the anomalous detail may no longer be recognizable as such because it coexists with a swarm of other such details. This means the anomalous is in danger of turning nondescript, in much the same way that the more complex the city today, the more it becomes a city without qualities. The cosmopolitan as urban phenomenon is inevitably inscribed in such non-places and paradoxes, raising the question we will have to address at some later point of how it might survive there.

To grapple with the anomalous/nondescript nature of overcomplex spaces, I draw on what Ludwig Wittgenstein called "description" and appropriate it for the analysis of cities.[8] On the one hand, when Wittgenstein writes that "we must do away with all *explanation,* and description alone must take its place," description can be understood as a kind of *de-scription.* This means that it is concerned not with knitting together explanations that make smooth connections between disparate series; rather, it welcomes friction—that is, disjuncture—and the mobile, fugitive, fragmentary detail. Wittgenstein writes: "We want to walk: so we need *friction.* Back to the rough ground!" On the other hand, Wittgenstein also insists that what concerns description is "of course, not empirical problems": "And this description gets its light, that is to say its purpose, from the philosophical problems. These are, of course, not empirical problems; they are solved, rather, by looking into the workings of our language, and that in such a way as to make us recognize those workings: in despite of an urge to misunderstand them." For our purposes, what might correspond to "language" is space. As philosophical issues are resolved by looking into the workings of language, so urban issues like cosmopolitanism might be clarified through a critique of space. Like language, space produces "an urge to misunderstand" its workings, an urge that needs to be resisted through de-scription.

What follows, then, is neither a theoretical nor an empirical account, but a de-scription of the cosmopolitan in relation to the spatial history of Shanghai and Hong Kong.

*

Shanghai and Hong Kong have always had a special relation to each other, if only through their relationship to the rest of the world. The historical facts about them are well known. Both cities were essentially created by Western colonialism in the aftermath of the Opium Wars: Shanghai as a lucrative treaty port and Hong Kong as a British colony and staging post for trade with China. For better or for worse, the two cities seemed to have been linked at birth, which makes it possible sometimes to read what is tacit in the history of one city in the history of the other. Each developed a form of cosmopolitanism under colonialism. From the outset, Shanghai generated a set of images about itself that contributed to its mystique but that we sometimes think of as merely outlandish or bizarre. Nevertheless, it is these often conflicting and contradictory images that we will need to interrogate. It may be that every city gives itself away in the self-images that it produces; somewhat like dream images that lead us to another history, or like cinema where, as Gilles Deleuze has argued, it is the filmic image that underlies the film narrative and not the other way around.[9]

We can begin with Shanghai, which was historically the senior city. Consider the political anomaly of extraterritoriality. In Shanghai, within the space of a hundred years, the extraterritorial presence of foreigners — British, American, and French, and, after 1895, Japanese (to name only the most obvious) — turned the city into the Shanghai of legend, into what J. G. Ballard called "this electric and lurid city more exciting than any other in the world."[10] The existence of the different concessions, each with its own set of extraterritorial laws, meant that internal control of the city always had to be negotiated, often with the triad underworld operating as unofficial arbiters. However, this created less an anarchic city than a polycentric, decentered city controlled by many different hands. For example, the French Settlement used a 110-volt electric system, while the International Settlement used 220 volts! But far from being lawless, the space of Shanghai was subject to constant negotiations, and every initiative was observed from multiple perspectives. It was the existence of such a negotiated space that helped Shanghai in the 1920s and 1930s develop its own special brand of cosmopolitan urban culture: what we might call a cosmopolitanism of extraterritoriality.

The most visible signature of extraterritoriality was in the city's built space, with its proliferation of different styles of architecture, by turns elegant and kitschy. There were Tudor-style villas, Spanish-style townhouses, Russian-style churches, and German-style mansions, along with the internationalism of the buildings on the Bund and, of course, the Shanghainese lanehouses or Li Long housing complexes, these last also built by foreign architects with their preconceptions of what vernacular housing should look like. It was all a question of style imported from elsewhere—a shallow kind of cosmopolitanism, a dream image of Europe more glamorous even than Europe itself at the time; the whole testifying, it seems, to the domination of the foreign, especially if we remember the decrepitude of the Chinese section of the city. But, at least in part, this was a deceptive testimony because within this setting something contrary was also happening. It could be argued, as Leo Ou-fan Lee has done in "Shanghai Modern," that the foreign presence produced not only new kinds of public and social spaces (such as cinemas, department stores, coffeehouses, dance halls, parks, and racecourses), but also spaces that could be appropriated by the Chinese themselves and used to construct a Chinese version of modern cosmopolitan culture. From this point of view, cosmopolitanism in Shanghai could be understood not as the cultural domination by the foreign but as the appropriation by the local of "elements of foreign culture to enrich a new national culture."[11] Lee's persuasive account, rich in fascinating details, is interesting, too, for its attempt to steer the argument away from too facile "political critiques" of the cosmopolitan as cultural imperialism, toward a more nuanced reading of cultural history.

Still, foreign domination and local appropriation are not necessarily mutually exclusive. For example, it should not be forgotten that Shanghai's strength as a cosmopolitan city was always based on China's weakness as a nation. As such, there was always an underlying tension between national culture on the one hand, which could only be constructed as anticolonial resistance, and Shanghai cosmopolitanism on the other. Shanghai was always a subtly nonviable city, where splendor and squalor existed side by side. It was precisely the city's characteristic multivalence—its capacity to be all at once a space of negotiation, domination, and appropriation—that generated yet another image, perhaps the most telling of all: the grotesque. This grotesque nature of the city is captured best in a scene in Ballard's semiautobiographical novel, *Empire of the Sun,* documenting the last days of old Shanghai. The scene is set outside the Cathay Theater, at the time the largest cinema in the world. For its showing of *The Hunchback of Notre Dame,* the management recruited two hundred real-life hunchbacks from the back streets of Shanghai to form an "honour guard" for the glitterati attending the show! A *grand guignol* quality was never far behind the cosmopolitanism of Shanghai.

This grotesque element hints at something quite significant about Shanghai's cosmopolitanism, which could be extended even to the cosmopolitanism of other cities. It suggests that the cosmopolitan "attitude" in this case consists not in the toleration of difference but in the necessary cultivation of indifference: the hunchbacks were hired not in the spirit of equal opportunity employment but to create a gross sensation. Furthermore, to some extent the colonial experience had shattered the innocence of difference. The end result of having to negotiate a multivalent space that makes so many contrary demands on the individual was the cultivation of indifference and insensitivity to others. Even scandal and outrage could be openly accepted. Indeed, in its time old Shanghai had the reputation of being the most "open" city in the world. It was the one place in China that was free from the control of a debilitated and bureaucratic state apparatus, giving it an air of freedom that drew in both political reformers and intellectuals, both prostitutes and adventurers. The other side of this freedom and openness, however, was a certain isolation—a linkage to the world that went together with a delinkage from the rest of China. There was always something very fragile about Shanghai cosmopolitanism. After 1949, Chinese communism, born in Shanghai, quickly made Shanghai's urban culture no more than a memory.

It took Mao Zedong's genius to see, against the grain of orthodox Marxism, that even rural spaces, at least in the historical situation of China, had a crucial role to play in modern and national life. This was the insight that allowed Mao to displace cities in general from their role as the sole exclusive site of modernity — and Shanghai in particular from its claim to be China's preeminent city. After 1949, the city could no longer enjoy the privilege of being a law unto itself: it was clearly the nation that now held sway over the city. During these years, Shanghai did tacit penance for its past Babylonian ways. It remained a center of industrial production, but only to help finance the modernization of the rest of the country; however, it was forced to discard its cosmopolitan cultural life that Maoist puritanism regarded as bourgeois and decadent. And as China moved into the phase of national rebuilding under communism, the conditions for the emergence of a different kind of cosmopolitan space moved elsewhere — to the British crown colony of Hong Kong.

*

The story is often told that it was an act of emigration, the flight of twenty-one Shanghai industrialist families to Hong Kong with their capital and business expertise, that formed the basis of Hong Kong's industrial development from the 1950s onward. In chronological terms, the rise of Hong Kong indeed succeeded the fall of Shanghai. The injection of capital and human resources to the colony that followed was certainly one factor in its growth as an international city, but it was not the only or even necessarily the most important factor. What was equally decisive, paradoxical as this may sound, was Hong Kong's dependent position and the way it made a career of dependency.[12] In Shanghai even at its most corrupt, there was always some vestigial interest in issues of nationalism as a means of liberation and independence. For example, it is well known that even notorious triad societies like the Green Gang, when not engaged in nefarious activity, had nationalist concerns — and both Sun Yatsen and Chiang Kaishek drew on them for help. In Hong Kong, by contrast, there was no possibility of — and hence little interest in—nationalism. Hong Kong could never have been a city nation like Singapore, only a hyphenation. It therefore accepted its colonial status as a priori and turned toward the international, fully exploiting its position as a port city or, in Mao's picturesque phraseology, as a pimple on the backside of China. Hong Kong was less a site than a para-site. If colonialism in Hong Kong had a certain benign-looking aspect to it, it was because it was a mutant political entity and a living demonstration of how the relative autonomy that comes from economic success could be based on dependency. While Shanghai was multiple and polyvalent, Hong Kong was single and paradoxical.

For a long time, Hong Kong did not develop the kind of cosmopolitan culture that Shanghai exhibited in the 1920s and 1930s, a cosmopolitanism that emerged from the anomalous space of extraterritoriality. Dependency meant that for most of its history, Hong Kong, culturally speaking, was caught in the double bind of divided loyalties. It was politically ambivalent about both Britain and China; ambivalent about what language, English or Chinese, it should master; and confident only about capital. The one moment when it began to rival the cultural vibrancy of Shanghai in the 1930s was during the 1980s and 1990s, after the Joint Declaration announcing the return of Hong Kong to China in 1997: that is, at precisely the moment when Hong Kong felt most vulnerable and dependent. This was the period when more and more people discovered, invented, and rallied behind what they called "Hong Kong culture." This Hong Kong culture was a hothouse plant that appeared at the moment when something was disappearing: a case of love at last sight, a culture of disappearance. In contrast to Shanghai in the 1930s, nationalism was a negative stimulus: one major anxiety was that the internationalism of the port city would be submerged and smothered by its reinscription into the nation. But the anxiety was tempered by a tacit hope that Hong Kong might indeed be a special case. This was what redirected attention back to the city's local peculiarities, in an attempt to reinvent it one last time even as it disappeared. This sense of disappearance as the experience of living through the best and the worst of times was the seminal theme of the New Hong Kong Cinema. If filmmakers like Wong Kar-wai, Stanley Kwan, Ann Hui, and Tsui Hark managed to convey in their films a cosmopolitan sensibility, it was partly by focusing on local issues and settings, but in such a way that the local was dislocated: through the construction of innovative film images and narratives and, above all, through the introduction of the disappearing city as a major protagonist in their films.[13] Hong Kong cosmopolitanism was stimulated then not so much by a space of multivalence—which was the case in 1930s Shanghai—as by a space of disappearance, one effect of which was the transformation of the local into the translocal as a result of historical exigencies.

*

To recapitulate: in Shanghai in the 1920s and 1930s we found a cosmopolitanism of extraterritoriality, and in Hong Kong from the 1980s onward, a cosmopolitanism of dependency, with its thematic of the disappearing city. But what of today and tomorrow? Two events in the 1990s can be considered symptoms that the cultural space these two cities seem destined to cohabit is once again changing. The 1990s saw not only the return of Hong Kong to China as an SAR (Special Administrative Region) but also the economic and cultural reappearance of Shanghai after more than four decades in the political cold. To consider if a new kind of cosmopolitanism is emerging today in Shanghai and Hong Kong, we will first have to consider the changing historical space of these two cities.

Now that Hong Kong is part of China again, there is a lot of speculation about whether Shanghai will replace it as the country's main economic and financial center once the Chinese yuan becomes fully convertible. The mayor of Shanghai, Xu Kuangdi, in a Hong Kong newspaper interview, addressed the issue of Shanghai and Hong Kong as follows: "You don't have to worry about Shanghai replacing Hong Kong; or that because of Hong Kong, Shanghai is not going to become a financial centre. They play different roles. . . . In the future, their relationship will be like two good forwards on a football team. They will pass the ball to each other and both will do their best to score more goals. But they are on the same team—China's national team." In the same interview, he conceded that Hong Kong "is more international than Shanghai. It is a financial centre for Southeast Asia. Not only does it link China with the world, it also serves as a trading market for Southeast Asian countries. Shanghai primarily serves as a link between the mainland and the rest of the world."[14]

Xu's homely image of Shanghai and Hong Kong as two good forwards on the national team is reassuring because as a public statement it understandably minimizes whatever tensions might exist between the city, the nation, and the transnational or global. But such tensions do exist. In Hong Kong, for example, these tensions produced a skewing of cultural and political space that could be read in the city's cultural forms, such as its architecture and new cinema. The return of Hong Kong to China threatened to make the former disappear in the sense that the transnational status it had established for itself might be merged and submerged into the national. In Shanghai, because of the different relation of the city to the nation, it is not a question of the city's disappearance but of its reappearance, a reappearance coinciding with China's reinscription, after decades of closure, into the global economy. But Shanghai's "reappearance" is as complexly situated as Hong Kong's culture of disappearance in a space of tensions and skewed images. For example, since the early 1990s Shanghai has been obsessed with a mania for building and urban development, but accompanying it like a shadow is something that at first sight seems rather puzzling: the state's interest in preservation projects. It is within the problematic of tensions between the city, the nation, and the transnational that comparisons between "reappearance" in Shanghai and "disappearance" in Hong Kong can be made and the question of cosmopolitanism can be posed.

Let's take the Shanghai case. Before the early 1990s, there was very little interest among the Shanghainese in the buildings they lived and worked in. If a large part of old Shanghai was preserved, it was by default, because the city had too few resources to embark on major programs of urban restructuring. As late as the early 1990s, visitors to Shanghai often remarked how little Shanghai had changed visually from its pre-1949 days, except to note that a large part of the glitter had gone. However, after Deng Xiaoping's 1992 visit, and within the space of a few years, the Pudong area of Shanghai across the Huangpu River from the Bund has developed into a mini-Manhattan, following Deng's agenda for it: "A new look each year, a transformation in three years." Today, even Hong Kong visitors, blasé about new buildings, are amazed by Shanghai. In a few short years, Shanghai saw the construction of over a thousand skyscrapers, a subway line, a highway overpass ringing the city, another bridge and tunnel across the Huangpu to Pudong, and the urbanization of Pudong itself, now coming into being before our eyes like the speeded-up image of time-lapse film. Interestingly enough, together with this frenzy of building and development — subsidized by the sale of land leases and joint venture capital—the city has shown an interest in preservation, something not specifically recommended by Deng. So far, around 250 buildings have been registered as municipal listed buildings, with another 200 more being considered. This is remarkable enough for us to ask, What, in fact, is happening?

Let me offer the following hypothesis: Preservation in Shanghai is motivated by something quite different from the usual pieties about "cultural heritage," which, given the city's colonial past, can only be ambiguous. It is motivated more by anticipations of a new Shanghai to rival the old than simply by nostalgia for the past. In other words, preservation is something more complex than just a question of the past remembered: in Shanghai, the past allows the present to pursue the future; hence "memory" itself is select and fissured, sometimes indistinguishable from amnesia. This paradox of the past as the future's future also throws a particular light on Shanghai's urban development, which, like preservation, takes on a special quality: Shanghai today is not just a city on the make with the new and brash everywhere—as might be said more aptly of Shenzhen, for example. It is also something more subtle and historically elusive: *the city as remake,* a shot-by-shot reworking of a classic, with the latest technology, a different cast, and a new audience. Not "Back to the Future" but "Forward to the Past." The minor story of preservation in Shanghai gives an important *gloss*—in both senses of the word—to the major story of urban development.

In rapidly developing cities, urban preservation as a rule is either ignored or merely paid lip service. Take the case of Hong Kong, in many ways a role model for Shanghai and other Chinese cities. Yet Hong Kong offers a comparatively straightforward example of the relationship between development and preservation. Though it is true that there are some preserved buildings in this former British colony—the best known being the clock tower of the demolished Hong Kong–Canton Railway Station, now a part of the Hong Kong Cultural Centre Complex; the old Supreme Court building; Western Market; and Flagstaff House, formerly British military headquarters and now a tea museum—on the whole, preservation happens ad hoc, with no systematic plan for municipal preservation comparable to Shanghai's. An interest in Hong Kong and its history, moreover, and hence in preservation, is only a recent phenomenon with origins tied to 1997 and an anxiety that Hong Kong as we knew it might come to an end with the handover. However,

such an interest in preservation never proved strong enough to pre-
vent hard-nosed development decisions from being made in the market
economy of a so-called noninterventionist state, and this circumstance
has changed little since Hong Kong became an SAR. By contrast, the
twist that Shanghai provides is in opting to develop and, at the same
time, preserve at least part of the city, as if deliberately giving the lie to
the notion that development and preservation are incompatible. This
presents us with enough of an anomaly to prompt the question: Precisely what role is preservation meant to play in Shanghai's impending
transformation?

To begin with the obvious, the economic importance of preservation cannot be underestimated. Invoking a continuity with a legendary
past—no matter how ambiguous that past may have been—enhances
the city's attractiveness, gives it historical cachet, and hence equips it
to compete for foreign investment and the tourist trade on more favorable terms. The past is a kind of symbolic capital. At the same time,
preservation often accompanies the revitalization and gentrification of
decaying areas of the city and contributes to urban renewal. But preservation has a third feature peculiar to Shanghai itself: namely, the way
the economic role of preservation maps onto the tensions inherent in
China's "socialist market economy." Since late 1978, this economy has
created a private sector within a socialist state; that is, it has allowed
the global into the national. Moreover, the new private sector has con-
sistently outperformed the state in the marketplace, raising questions
of to what degree the state is in touch with the new market conditions.
Mao had succeeded in curtailing capitalism by establishing the socialist state, just as Europe had ameliorated capitalism's effects through the
welfare-democratic state. But that was a bygone capitalism. The new
capitalism, global capital, is freshly able to act, constantly outpacing the
interventions of the nation-state and making it look heavy-footed.[15]

In this context, the state's interest in preservation, via municipal
policy, makes a lot of sense. Not only is preservation well within the
competence of the state; it is also a way by which the state can enter
the global market through promoting the city's past—that is, through
the heritage industry. It is an implicit assertion of the state's involvement
in and contribution to the future development of Shanghai—a way of
mediating the need of the state for legitimacy and the demand of the
private sector for profitability. By a strange twist, the state's interest in

preservation is an assertion that it is still a player in the new global game. Hence, the entirely different relation to preservation in Hong Kong and Shanghai: in the one, ad hoc and linked to anxieties about the city's disappearance; in the other, state-planned and related to the city's reappearance as a soi-disant "city of culture."

*

The working together of development and preservation in Shanghai suggests that a new problematic is emerging. Something peculiar must be happening if preservation produces not a sense of history but the virtuality of a present that has erased the distinction between old and new—or where local history is another gambit in the game of global capital. Perhaps virtual cities can only look like what Shanghai today looks like, with old and new compressed together in an apocalyptic now. The listed buildings on the Bund and the chaos of skyscrapers in Pudong do not so much confront as complement each other on either side of the Huangpu River; in a sense, both old and new are simply steps in the remake of Shanghai as a City of Culture in the new global space. In such a space, heritage issues can be fused and confused with political and economic interests. And precisely because of this, urban preservation in the global era cannot be seen in isolation from other urban and social phenomena. Links begin to emerge between what at first sight seem to be unrelated social spaces—between, for example, the municipal preservational projects such as the old buildings around Yu Yuen Garden, in the old "Chinese city," now turned into a kind of vernacular mall, and the city's much more publicized developmental projects of cultural modernization, such as the new Shanghai Museum and the Grand Theater, both in an already modernized Renmin Square. We can see hints of a similar logic of globalism operative in each.

Take the new Shanghai Museum, which was opened in 1996. It is designed to resemble a giant *ting*, an antique Chinese bronze vessel. The obvious visual message here is that in the city's pursuit of modernity, Chinese tradition is not forgotten. But there is also something else. Consider the experience of entering the museum. In the exhibition halls, we find the rare artworks that the museum is famous for expertly displayed: the ancient bronzes, the Sung and Yuan paintings. But what also catches the attention is how ostentatiously clean the museum is, not a common experience in Shanghai. There always seem to be some workers polishing the brass on the railings or the marble on the floor. Even the toilets are kept meticulously clean. The dirtier the streets around it, the cleaner the museum. And suddenly you realize that the museum does not think of itself as being part of a local space at all, but as part of a virtual global cultural network. The Shanghai Museum is not just where artworks are being shown in Shanghai; it is also where Shanghai shows itself off in its museum, with its image cleaned up and in hopes that the world is looking.

But "globalism" is not without its own aporias and anomalies. For example, something of the tensions in Shanghai's new social space can be felt in one admittedly minor but symptomatic example: the etiquette of mobile phones. For the newly affluent entrepreneurial class, these phones are as much functional tools as symbols of the culture of globalism. It is also this class that, along with foreign visitors, can patronize the expensive and elegant restaurants that are reappearing in Shanghai. One of the most expensive of these is the Continental Room at the Garden Hotel, whose standards of elegance require guests to switch off their mobile phones out of consideration for fellow diners. What seems an unobjectionable policy from one point of view has produced many a contretemps. For these new entrepreneurs, dining at the Garden Hotel and using mobile phones go together. There is no conception that these electronic devices can be in certain social situations sources of irritation for oneself or others. What we find here is an example of transnationalism without a corresponding transnational subject. These new kinds of social embarrassment may not be insignificant in that they are symptoms of how the speeded-up nature of social and cultural life inevitably results in the production of multiple, sometimes conflicting, paradigms confusing for the person who needs to negotiate them.

Of course, it is true that social life since the modern era has always been marked by change and confusion. Cosmopolitanism has been seen as an ability to acquit oneself, to behave well, under difficult cultural situations by juggling with multiple perspectives — even when these perspectives were forced upon us or adopted in indifference. The question is: Are the kinds of changes taking place in Asian cities and elsewhere today forcing upon us situations in which we cannot behave well, because these changes are threatening to destroy the space of cities as we know them and creating cities we do not know? From this point of view, the apparently slight example of the use of mobile phones in "inappropriate" situations now takes on greater weight. Their indiscriminate use in the present case is neither an example of boorishness nor a lack of consideration for others, nor even a transgression of the boundaries of social etiquette. It is, rather, a genuine confusion about where the boundaries are, making both "transgression" and "behaving well" equally problematic.

*

If the speed of change is creating spaces we do not understand, then one strategy might be to slow things down — to preserve some almost erased concept of civility and respect for otherness in the midst of chaos. This was what the older cosmopolitanisms had strived for. But, it seems to me, such a conservative strategy has little space for maneuver. One of the most interesting things we can learn from the example of urban preservation in Shanghai today is how it, too, is infused with the spirit of globalism. "Preservation" and "heritage" do not act as brakes against development; in some strange way, they further a developmental agenda. The problem of cosmopolitanism today still remains how we are to negotiate the transnational space that global capital produces.

   In the corporate sphere, strategies are already in place for negotiating such a space. The key strategy is quite clearly summarized by the notion of arbitrage. In its restricted economic sense, arbitrage refers to the way profits are obtained by capitalizing, through the use of electronic technologies, on price differentials in markets situated in different time zones and parts of the world. That is: arbitrage maximizes profits by setting up operations in a world of speed and virtuality, and thereby breaking down the traditional boundaries of time and space. The term also refers in a more general sense to the business practices of transnational corporations, including, for example, the export of jobs to countries with the lowest labor costs and fewest labor laws, or spreading the manufacturing process over different parts of the world so that it becomes difficult to assign to manufactured goods a national provenance. These "business practices," it has been well pointed out, constitute a novel kind of politics: "Without a revolution, without even any change in laws or constitutions, an attack has been launched 'in the normal course of business', as it were, upon the material lifeline of modern national societies. . . . We are thus dealing with *politicization through a depoliticization of states.*"[16]

Arbitrage can also be related to the posture now known as *glocalization,* a portmanteau word blending the "global" and the "local."[17] The term was first used by Japanese businessmen to describe the need to *adapt* a global outlook to local conditions, a kind of "micromarketing." Glocalization, encapsulated now in the corporate slogan "think globally, act locally," is a top-down approach to society, however: a hybrid term, it concludes by homogenizing the hybrid and local. We can read the contemporary value placed by cultural and social critics on hybridity precisely as a protest against homogenization. Sympathetic though such a position is, it seems to be losing political leverage against approaches like glocalization, which can be seen as a kind of micromanagement of hybridity. Benetton, McDonald's, and Walt Disney all seem to understand this.

Arbitrage may consist of a powerful set of strategies for dealing with the nature of transnational space, but the forms that arbitrage has taken so far give as much cause for concern as for celebration. It is possible to micromanage ourselves to death, as Paul Virilio's work on urbanism and technologies of speed warns. Virilio shows how these technologies — transport, circulation, information — promise or threaten to change in an unprecedented way our experience of space and the city by introducing a new dimension (namely, the global/virtual) that indeed breaks down the limitations of space and time but that also has the potential, if we are not careful, to produce a global accident as catastrophic in its own way as Chernobyl:

> Beyond the old *cosmopolis* modelled on ancient Rome, the world-city will surge forth, an *omnipolis* whose major clinical symptom is the stock exchange system, today computerized and globalized, generating as it does, at more or less constant intervals, *a virtual financial bubble* which is nothing less than the early-warning signal of the dire emergence of a new kind of accident, an accident no longer local and precisely located in space and time as before, but *a general global accident* which could well have radio-activity as its emblem.[18]

Is the omnipolis the ominous end of cities as we know them, of space and time as we know them, and of the cosmopolitan?

This specter invoked by Virilio of an unprecedented kind of global accident that implosions in the global system could produce is not apocalyptic prophecy but a provocation to thought. It makes us see that globalism has quietly upped the ante, making a redefinition of cosmopolitanism a matter of great historical urgency. Clearly, cosmopolitanism can no longer be simply a matter of behaving well or even of an openness to otherness. Otherness lost its innocence as a result of the colonial experience. Even less attractive is the alternative of a brutal embrace of ethnocentric vision, an anticosmopolitanism made more extreme because it exists in the new and charged situation of information and speed. Information does not only dispel bigotry but also disseminates it. Can there be a cosmopolitanism for the global age, and what would it be like?

We might look for an answer in the analysis of the nature of cities today, particularly an analysis of their linkage to the transnational more so than to the national. As the fashion designer Yohji Yamamoto said in Wim Wenders's 1989 film *Notebook on Cities and Clothes*, "I like all big cities. More than Japanese, I feel I'm from Tokyo. . . . Tokyo has no nationality." Large nation-states like the previous Soviet Union have been breaking up, but this is not because some kind of transnational state is coming into being, only a transnational or global space where nation-states are still located. And cities are the locales or nodal points of this transnational space, which exists not in some abstract dimension but in the very specific sites and problem areas of the city. It exists, for example, in the problematic details of heritage and preservation in present-day Shanghai, in the non-places that Augé has pointed to, or in new kinds of social embarrassment that are the result of quickly shifting cultural paradigms. Whether a cosmopolitanism for the global age will emerge depends on our ability to grasp a space, that of the global city, that is always concrete even in its elusiveness. And this involves not so much imagining a transnational state as reimagining the city.

In a similar vein, the cosmopolitan today will include not only the privileged transnational, at home in different places and cultures, as an Olympian arbiter of value. Such a figure, it could be argued, has too many imperialistic associations. The cosmopolitan today will have to include at least some of the less privileged men and women placed or displaced in the transnational space of the city and who are trying to make sense of its spatial and temporal contradictions: the cosmopolitan not as a universalist arbiter of value, but as an arbitrageur/arbitrageuse.

This is arbitrage with a difference. It does not mean the use of technologies to maximize profits in a global world but refers to everyday strategies for negotiating the disequilibria and dislocations that global-ism has created. Arbitrage in this sense does not allude to the exploita-tion of small temporal differences but refers to the larger historical les-sons that can be drawn from our experiences of the city. This is where the de-scriptions of Shanghai and Hong Kong, to return to these cities one last time, can contribute to a rethinking of the cosmopolitan today. In Shanghai, negotiating the anomalies of extraterritoriality so that a kind of grace comes out of the grotesque; and in Hong Kong, the develop-ment of a culture of disappearance under conditions of dependency — these were already examples of cultural arbitrage. As for Borges, a more ambiguous relationship exists between him and the figure of the arbi-trageur. To embrace "universal values" in Buenos Aires as Borges did was to be trapped to some extent in the imperialist game. Where Borges showed himself to be a supreme arbitrageur was in the other games he chose to play: the games with time and infinity, with language, and with the space of the labyrinthine city.

Whether arbitrage reworked as cultural strategy can counter Virilio's dire warnings remains an open question. But it is cosmopolitanism's best chance. Cosmopolitanism has always been a way of being in the world, however confusing the world is, and nothing so far is as con-fusing as globalism. Cultural arbitrage may be a way of creating a global culture worthy of the name.

NOTES

I wish to thank Mario Gandelsonas, Benjamin Lee, Jeremy Tambling, and the editors of *Public Culture* for their helpful comments during various stages of completion of this essay.

1. All quotations are from the preface in Jorge Luis Borges, *Collected Fictions*, trans. Andrew Hurley (New York: Viking, 1998), 4–5.

2. Luis Buñuel, *My Last Sigh*, trans. Abigail Israel (New York: Vintage, 1984), 221.

3. Borges, *Labyrinths*, ed. Donald A. Yates and James E. Irby (New York: New Di-rections, 1964), 184.

4. See, for example, the final chapters of Claude Lévi-Strauss, *Tristes Tropiques*, trans. John and Doreen Weightman (New York: Atheneum, 1974).

5. Ulf Hannerz, "Cosmopolitans and Locals in World Culture," in *Global Culture*, ed. Mike Featherstone (London: Sage, 1990), 239.

6. See, for example, David Harvey, *The Condition of Postmodernity* (Oxford: Black-well, 1989); Scott Lash and John Urry, *The End of Organized Capitalism* (Cambridge: Polity Press, 1987); Ulrich Beck, *Risk Society* (London: Sage, 1992); and Manuel Cas-tells, *The Rise of the Network Society* (Oxford: Blackwell, 1996).

7. Marc Augé, *A Sense for the Other,* trans. Amy Jacobs (Stanford, Calif.: Stanford University Press, 1998), 106.

8. All quotations are from paragraphs 107 and 109 of Ludwig Wittgenstein, *Philosophical Investigations,* trans. G. E. M. Anscombe (Oxford: Basil Blackwell, 1974), 46–47.

9. See Gilles Deleuze, *Cinema,* 2 vols., trans. Hugh Tomlinson and Barbara Habberjam (Minneapolis: University of Minnesota Press, 1986–89).

10. J. G. Ballard, *Empire of the Sun* (London: Grafton Books, 1985), 17.

11. Leo Ou-fan Lee, "Shanghai Modern: Reflections on Urban Culture in China in the 1930s," *Public Culture* 11 (1999): 104.

12. I have written at greater length on Hong Kong and the paradoxical meaning of dependency elsewhere. See, for example, Ackbar Abbas, *Hong Kong: Culture and the Politics of Disappearance* (Minneapolis: University of Minnesota Press, 1997).

13. See Abbas, "The Erotics of Disappointment," in *Wong Kar-wai,* ed. Jean-Marc Lalanne, David Martinez, Ackbar Abbas, and Jimmy Ngai (Paris: Editions Dis Voir, 1997), 39–81.

14. Xu Kuangdi, interview by Matthew Miller and Foo Choy Peng, *South China Morning Post* (Hong Kong), China Business Review section, 9 July 1998, 8.

15. On these issues, see Ulrich Beck, *What Is Globalization?* (Cambridge: Polity Press, 2000).

16. Beck, *What Is Globalization?,* 3–4, 103 (Beck's emphasis).

17. See Roland Robertson, *Globalization* (London: Sage, 1992), 173–74. See also Robertson, "Glocalizations: Time-Space and Homogeneity-Heterogeneity," in *Global Modernities,* ed. Mike Featherstone, Scott Lash, and Roland Robertson (London: Sage, 1995), 25–44.

18. Paul Virilio, *Open Sky,* trans. Julie Rose (London: Verso, 1997), 83 (Virilio's emphasis).

Contributors

Ackbar Abbas is Chair of the Department of Comparative Literature and Codirector of the Center for the Study of Globalisation and Cultures at the University of Hong Kong. His recent publications include *Hong Kong: Culture and the Politics of Disappearance* (1997) and "Dialectic of Deception" (*Public Culture,* spring 1999).

Arjun Appadurai is Samuel N. Harper Distinguished Service Professor of Anthropology and South Asian Languages and Civilizations at the University of Chicago. His recent publications include "Deep Democracy: Urban Governmentality and the Horizon of Politics" (*Public Culture,* winter 2002); the edited volume *Globalization* (Duke University Press, 2001); and "The Grounds of the Nation-State: Identity, Violence, and Territory" in *Nationalism and Internationalism in the Post-Cold War Era* (2000), edited by K. Goldmann, U. Hannerz, and C. Westin.

Homi K. Bhabha is Professor of English and African-American Studies at Harvard University. His publications include *The Location of Culture* (1994) and the edited volume *Nation and Narration* (1990).

T. K. Biaya a research Associate at the Council for the Development of Social Science Research in Africa (CODESRIA) in Dakar, Senegal, currently lives in Addis Abba, Ethiopia. He is the author of *Acteurs et mediations dans la resolution et la prevention des conflits en Afrique de l'Ouest* (1999) and the coeditor (with G. Bibeau) of *L'Afrique revisitee,* a special issue of *Anthropologie et Societes* (1998).

Carol A. Breckenridge teaches at the University of Chicago in the department of South Asian languages and civilizations. She is the founding editor of *Public Culture.* She recently edited (with Candace Vogler) a special issue of *Public Culture* entitled "The Limits of Embodiment: Disability Criticism." She is currently at work on a project called "Mumbai Modern."

Dipesh Chakrabarty teaches in the departments of history and South Asian languages and civilizations at the University of Chicago. His recent publications include *Provincializing Europe* (2000) and "*Adda,* Calcutta: Dwelling in Modernity" (*Public Culture,* winter 1999).

Ousmane Ndiaye Dago is a photographer from Senegal who was educated at the Royal Fine Arts Academy in Belgium. His work has been exhibited in France, Italy, and Spain and can also be viewed in his book *Odes Nues* (1998) (with text and poems by Amadou Lamine Sall). He lives in Senegal where he is well-known for his graphic design and his research on women's issues.

Mamadou Diouf teaches history at the University of Michigan, Ann Arbor. His publications include the edited volumes *L'historiographie indienne ed débat: Colonialisme, nationalisme et sociétés postcoloniales* (1999) and (with Momar Coumba Diop) *Les figures du politique en Afrique: Des pouvoirs hérités aux pouvoirs élus* (1999).

Wu Hung is Harrie H. Vandersteppen Distinguished Service Professor in the departments of Art History and East Asian Languages and Civilizations at the University of Chicago. His recent publications include "Photographing Deformity: Liu Zheng and His Photo Series 'My Countrymen'" (*Public Culture,* fall 2002); "A Chinese Dream by Wang Jin" (*Public Culture,* winter 2000); *Exhibiting Experimental Art in China* (2000); *Transience: Chinese Experimental Art at the End of the Twentieth Century* (1999); and *Double Screen: Medium and Representation in Chinese Painting* (1996).

Walter D. Mignolo is William H. Wannamaker Professor of Romance Studies and Professor of Literature and Cultural Anthropology at Duke University. He is the author of *Local Histories/Global Designs: Coloniality, Subaltern Knowledges, and Border Thinking* (2000) and *The Darker Side of the Renaissance: Literacy, Territoriality, and Colonization* (1995).

Sheldon Pollock is George V. Bobrinskoy Professor of Sanskrit and Indic Studies at the University of Chicago. He is the editor of *Literary Cultures in History: Reconstructions from South Asia* (Berkeley: University of California Press, 2002).

Steven Rendall is a freelance translator currently living in France. He formerly taught romance languages at the University of Oregon and was the editor of *Comparative Literature*.

Index

Abu-Lughod, Janet, 169

Amerindians: Christianity and, 162, 167; Kant on, 171; personhood of, 162, 164–67, 174, 184 n.3; slavery, 164–65, 168

Anderson, Benedict, 28, 50 n.27

An-Na'im, Abdullahi, 177, 179, 181, 184 n.5

Appadurai, Arjun, 111–12, 132 n.2

Arbitrage, 224–27

Architecture, urban: and Beijing reconstruction, 194, 200–203; and Hong Kong preservation, 220–22; and Shanghai development, 219–20; in Touba, 118, 128, 136 n.51

Aristotle, 84–85, 89

Art: avante-garde art in Beijing, 204; demolition and reconstruction themes in, 200–203; glass painting, 120, 125, 135 n.29; graffiti in Beijing, 189–200, 201–7, 207 n.4, 208 n.5; museums, 60, 204, 222–23; nudity, 138–40, 153. *See also* Photography

Assimilation: and Murid community, 116–17, 119, 120, 124–29, 136 n.60; national identity and, 25–26, 49 n.20; of Sanskrit idioms in southern Asia, 31

Atlantic commercial circuit (sixteenth century), 162, 166, 169

Augé, Marc, 212, 226

Babri Masjid (India), 73–74, 77

Bakhtin, Mikhail, 31, 33, 50 n.29

Ballard, J. G., 214, 215

Beck, Ulrich, 47, 53 n.57, 178, 184 n.6

Beijing: avant-garde art in, 204–7; graffiti in, 189–200, 201–7, 207 n.4, 208 n.5; National Art Gallery, 204; reconstruction of, 194, 200

Benda, Julien, 42–43, 52 n.46

Bernal, Victoria, 129, 136 n.60

Bhakhti (religious movement), 35

Bharatiya Janata Party (BJP), 40–41, 52 n.44, 74

Biaya, T. K., 146, 151

Black market, 60–62, 67–68

Body image: African versus European concepts of beauty, 142–44, 148, 150, 152–53; erotic clothing and adornment, 145–47, 149, 150, 154; nudity, 138–40, 153

Bombay: anti-Muslim violence in, 76–79, 80 n.1; cash commerce in, 58–62; civic activism in, 79–80; Hindutva (Hindu fundamentalism) in, 56, 72–78; homelessness in, 63–66, 75–76; life insurance in, 59–60; as Mumbai, 56, 73; poverty in, 55, 64–65; racketeering in, 58–59, 67–68; real estate speculation in, 63, 67–68, 75; street vendors in, 70–72, 77; textile industry in, 68–69; trade unionism in, 69; transportation, public in, 55

Borges, Jorge Luis, 209–11, 227

Brzezinski, Zbigniew, 175, 176, 184 n.4

Buñuel, Luis, 210

Capitalism: abstract labor, 86–87, 91; Atlantic commercial circuit (sixteenth century), 162, 166, 169; citizenship and, 106; coloniality and, 178–79; commodity and, 84–87, 98–101, 108 n.13; and factory worker discipline, 88–93, 101–2, 104–5, 107 n.5, 108 n.8; history of capital, 82–84, 97–101, 106–7, 108 nn.11, 12; human rights and, 174–75; and the idea of the "West," 158, 162–63; industrialization, 92–93; vernacular nationalism, 44–45;

Capitalism (*continued*)
worker-capitalist relations, 90–91, 95, 108 n.9. *See also* Cosmopolitanism; Economics; Globalization; Labor

Carter, D. M., 122, 123

Castells, Manuel, 181

Castes: Lawbé griots, 138, 145, 146, 154 n.5; Murid brotherhood and, 115–16

Castoriadis, Cornelius, 85, 86, 107 n.4

Censorship, 138, 145

Chatterjee, Partha, 46, 53 nn.54, 55

China: Hong Kong, relations with, 217–18, 221; human rights in, 176; Shanghai, relations with, 215–16

Christianity: Amerindians and, 162, 167; Church authority, 163–64, 167; citizenship and the nation-state, 167; eroticism and, 140–41; expulsion of Jews and Moors, 164–65, 166, 168; globalization and, 157, 158–59; human rights and, 159, 161, 167; Islam and, 162; modernity and, 157, 158–59; multiculturalism and, 173–74; *orbis universalis christianus*, 162–64, 167, 168

Citizenship: capital and, 106; cosmopolitanism and, 8, 161, 182–83; Kant on, 174; and migration, 54–55; Murid brotherhood and French citizenship, 113, 133 n.11; Muslims in Bombay, 57, 74–75, 76–79, 80 n.1; in the nation-state, 161–64, 167; poverty and, 57, 74, 76–78

Class, 26, 53 n.55, 117

Clothing: erotic and adornment, 139, 142–44, 145–47, 149, 150; *hijab,* 149–50, 155 n.7; Islam and, 146–47; of Murid brotherhood, 114, 125–26

Cold War, 161, 174, 175, 176, 178, 183

Coloniality: borders of, 177–81; capitalism and, 178–79; cosmopolitanism and, 158–61, 180; cultural relativism, 179–80, 184 n.6; democracy and, 180; human rights and, 174–75; and the

idea of the "West," 158, 162–63; Kant on, 170–71; multiculturalism, 168. *See also* Globalization; Modernity

Commerce: Atlantic commercial circuit (sixteenth century), 162, 166, 169; banking in Bombay, 59–60; cash commerce, 58–62, 67–68, 70–72, 75–77, 84–87, 98–101; human rights and, 167; and interdependence, 176, 179; life insurance in Bombay, 59–60; Murid brotherhood and, 113, 119–20, 122–27, 133 nn.8, 9; street vendors, 70–72, 77; transnational corporations, 176, 224; vernacular transformation, 34, 51 n.34

Commodity, 84–87, 98–101, 108 n.13

Communism, 174, 176

Community: Aristotle on, 84; of Murid brotherhood, 114–15, 116; Murid ritual community, 124, 126, 127, 130–32; Zapatista reciprocity, 180–81

Copans, Jean, 115, 132 n.6, 134 n.17

Cosmo-polis, 167–69, 172

Cosmopolitanism: borders and, 177–82, 184 n.6; citizenship, 8, 164, 182–83; compared to vernacularism in history, 20–22, 39–40; critical cosmopolitanism, 159–62; cultural relativism, 179–80; culture, 37–39, 42; democracy, 182–83; diversity and diversality, 168, 183–84, 211; ettiquette, 223–24, 226; Eurocentrism and, 170; gender and, 7–9, 151; globalism, 211–12, 224–27; in history, 1–6, 10–11, 21–22, 39–40; and human rights, 5, 162–66, 174, 177, 182–83, 184 nn.3, 5; inclusion and, 174, 184 n.2; interdependence, 176, 179; Islam, 115, 129; Latin and, 23–25, 28–29, 42, 49 nn.12, 15; literary culture, development of, 17–20, 26–28, 39–40, 51 nn.34, 38, 39, 41; of Murid brotherhood, 119–23, 131–32; Sanskrit and, 23–24, 26–32, 50 n.24. *See also* Glob-

alization; Migration and mobility;
Modernity

Cultural relativism, 179–80, 184 n.6

Culture: cosmopolitanism, 37–39, 42;
cultural relativism and cosmopolitanism, 179–80, 184 n.6; ettiquette, 223–
27; in Hong Kong, 217–19; human
rights and, 5–6; languages and, 15,
25–27; literary culture, development
of, 17–18, 24, 29–39, 49 n.15, 50 n.31,
51 nn.34, 38, 39, 41; Sanskrit culture,
23–24, 27–32, 50 nn.24, 26; in Shanghai, 214–15, 221–22; societal culture
(Kymlicka), 44–45, 52 n.52

Dago, Ousmane Ndiaye, 139–40, 142–52,
151–54

Dance, 146, 147, 155 n.6

Deleuze, Gilles, 213

Democracy: and coloniality, 180; cosmopolitanism and, 182–83; human
rights and, 176; Zapatistas' definition
of, 180–81

Deng Xiaoping, 194, 219

Dependency theory (Latin America),
176–77

Derrida, Jacques, 18

Dialogue (Zhang Dali's urban art
project), 189–96, 198–200, 204–7, 207
n.4, 208 n.5

Diaspora: Murid community in, 123–25,
128, 131–32

Diawara, Manthia, 114

Dièye, Cheikh Abdoulaye, 117, 119

Dimé, M., 138, 141 n.1

Discipline: of factory workers, 88–
93, 101–5, 107 n.5, 108 n.8; in Murid
community, 116–19, 120, 124, 125, 145

Diversity and diversality: cosmopolitanism, 168, 183–84, 211; cultural
diversity, 82; fundamentalism, 40–
41, 51 n.43, 52 n.44, 56, 72–78, 111, 181;
universalism, 181–84

Dussel, Enrique, 169, 170–71, 184 n.3

Ebin, Victoria, 123

Economics: arbitrage, 224–27; Beijing
reconstruction and, 194, 200–203;
cash commerce, 58–62, 67–68, 70–
72, 75–77, 84–87, 98–101; migration,
54–55; Murid brotherhood and commerce, 122–27, 136 n.56; risk and,
60–61

Education, 116, 134 n.17, 146, 154

Elias, Norbert, 19, 48 n.5

Eroticism: body posture, 154; Christianity, 140; dance, 146, 147, 155 n.6;
diskette, 147, 148; *drianké*, 147, 153;
erotic clothing and adornment,
139, 142–44, 145–47, 149, 150; Islam,
140–41, 146–47, 149–51, 154 n.4, 155
n.7; partnerships between women
(goor-djigen), 144, 151; perfumes, 146,
152; photography, 139–40, 151–54;
thiuraye, 147, 152, 154

Ettiquette: cosmopolitanism and, 223–
24; and mobile phones, 223–24; and
social space, 223–24, 226

Europe: cosmo-polis in, 167–69, 172;
cosmopolitanism versus vernacularism in, 39–40; Enlightenment in,
83, 106, 158, 166; Eurocentrism, 170;
European influence on Shanghai's
architecture, 214; Kant on, 175; and
languages, 35–39, 51 n.38; Latin in,
23–25, 28–29, 32–33, 42, 49 nn.12,
15; literary communication, 19–20;
Renaissance in, 157, 158, 160–61;
vernacularization in, 32–33

Exile, 128–29, 192, 194

Expulsion, of Jews and Moors, 164–65,
166, 168

Eze, Emmanuel, 170–71

Factories, 88–93, 101–2, 104–5, 107 n.5,
108 n.8

Feminism, 7–9

Film industry, 58, 60, 217–18, 219

Fordism, 54, 69, 211

Foucault, Michel, 89, 108 n.8

France: four communes in Senegal, 113–15, 120, 133 n.11; French Revolution, 158, 168–69; Murid brotherhood and French citizenship, 113, 133 n.11; Murid comunity in, 123, 130

Fundamentalism, 181; Hindutva (Hindu fundamentalism), 40–41, 51 n.43, 52 n.44, 56, 72–78; Islamic fundamentalism, 111

Gellner, Ernest, 34, 44, 50 n.33, 52 n.46

Gender, 7–9, 151, 180

Gide, André, 42

Globalization: Africa and, 113–14, 133 n.11, 134 n.13, 138–40; Christianity and, 157, 158–59; European Renaissance and, 157, 158, 160–61; four communes and, 113–15, 120, 133 n.11; glocalization, 225; Latin transformation of cultural systems, 25, 28–29; maps, 162–63; modernity and, 157–58, 162–63; Murid brotherhood and, 122–23, 130–31, 136 n.60

Glocalization, 225

Graffiti: *Dialogue* (Zhang Dali's urban art project), 189–96, 198–203, 204–7, 207 n.4, 208 n.5; global nature of, 206; and the media, 196–200, 207 n.4, 208 n.5

Gramsci, Antonio, 22, 33, 42–44, 50 n.32, 52 n.46

Gueye, Cheikh, 118, 128, 134 n.24

Habermas, Jürgen, 160, 168, 169, 170, 173, 184 nn.1, 3

Hall, Stuart, 112, 113, 132 n.3

Hannerz, Ulf, 211

Haring, Keith, 207

Hegel, G. W. F., 94–95, 173

Heidegger, Martin, 103–4, 108 n.16

Hijab, 149–50, 155 n.7

Hindutva (Hindu fundamentalism), 40–41, 51 n.43, 52 n.44, 56, 72–78

History: capital, 82–84, 97–101, 106–7, 108 nn.11, 12; commodity as antecedent of capital, 84–87, 98–101; cosmopolitanism in, 1–6, 10–11, 21–22, 39–40; historiography, 21–22, 34; literary culture, development of, 17–18, 24, 29–39, 49 n.15, 51 nn.34, 38, 39, 41; money as antecedent of of capital, 84–87, 98–101; and Murid collective memory, 120, 128–29; origins of people and languages, 35–37, 51 nn.34, 39; secularism, 46–47; urban preservation and, 220–22, 224; vernacularization process in, 45–47

Homelessness, 63–66, 75–76

Hong Kong: architecture, 219; colonialism, 213, 217; culture, 217, 219; relations with China, 217–18, 221; urban preservation in, 220–22

Horkheimer, Max, 102

Housing: Beijing reconstruction, 194, 200–203; homelessness, 63–66, 75–76; Murid diaspora communities, 123; neighborhood activism (mohulla committees), 79–80; poverty and, 55, 64–65; public space as, 64–65, 70; speculation in Bombay, 63, 66–67

Human rights: of Amerindians, 162, 164–66, 174, 184 n.3; capitalism and, 174–75; in China, 176; Christianity and, 159, 161, 166–67; coloniality and, 174–75; commerce and, 167; communism, 174, 175, 176; cosmopolitanism and, 5, 162–66, 174, 177, 182–83, 184 nn.3, 5; democracy, 176; gender, 180; *homines* (human beings) versus *gentes* (people), 167–68; United Nations Declaration of Human Rights, 175–76, 180, 184 n.5

Huntington, Samuel, 178–79

Iberia, 32, 50 n.31; Moors' expulsion from, 164–65, 166, 168

Identity, national: assimilation, 25–26,

49 n.20; Bombay becomes Mumbai, 73; defining, 177–78; Hindutva (Hindu fundamentalism), 40–41, 51 n.43, 52 n.44, 56, 72–78; homeland, 2–3; language and, 25, 27–33, 35–39, 51 n.41, 73; literature and, 17–18, 43, 48 n.2; and Murid brotherhood, 114, 133 n.11, 136 n.60; and national character, 170–73; vernacularization and, 33–34, 44–45, 51 n.34

India, 16, 31, 35, 40–41, 56, 106

Islam: Christianity and, 162; cosmopolitanism, 115–16, 129; eroticism, 140–41, 146–47, 149–51, 154, 154 nn.3, 4, 5; fundamentalism in, 111; *hijab*, 149–50, 155 n.7; Muslims in Bombay, 57, 74–75, 76–78, 80 n.1; orthodoxy in, 145; Sufism, 129, 145, 149; *thierno* (Koranic master), 147–48; universalism in, 115–16, 136 n.60. *See also* Murid brotherhood

Italy, 42, 43–44, 123

Jameson, Fredric, 62

Jews' expulsion from Iberia, 164–65, 166, 168

Kane, Cheikh Hamidou, 114, 134 n.13

Kant, Immanuel: on Amerindians, 171; citizenship, 174; on coloniality, 170–71; on cosmopolitanism, 158, 168; on globalization, 157, 158–59; on modernity and coloniality, 166, 170, 176; on national character, 170–73; on personhood, 174, 184 n.3; on states and human rights, 175

Kymlicka, Will, 44–45, 52 n.52

Labor: abstract labor (Marx), 83–88, 91; biological metaphors for, 91–92, 93, 94–96, 102, 108 n.9; capital, 103, 108 n.15; and factory worker discipline, 88–93, 101–2, 104–5, 107 n.5, 108 n.8; labor mobilization in Murid community, 116; machinery, 90–91, 102, 108 n.7; motivation of, 105, 108 n.17; productive labor, 103, 108 n.15; transnational corporations, 176, 224; worker-capitalist relations, 89–91, 95, 108 n.9

Languages: Asia, 36–39; class and, 26, 53 n.55; community, 35–36; culture and, 30–32, 35–39; culture and, 15, 25–27; Europe, 35–39, 51 n.38; fundamentalism, 40–41; geography, 35–37, 51 n.39; graffiti in Beijing as, 189–200, 201–7, 207 n.4, 208 n.5; history, 30–32, 35–37; Latin, 18, 23–25, 28–29, 32–34, 42, 49 nn.12, 15; national identity and, 25, 27–33, 35–39, 51 n.41, 73; origins of people and, 35–37; Sanskrit, 10, 11, 18, 23–24, 27–32, 50 nn.24, 26; vernacularization of, 29–39. *See also* Latin; Literature; Sanskrit

Latin: circulation of texts, 32–33; dissemination of, 23–25, 28–29, 42, 49 nn.12, 15; elites and vernacularization, 33–34, 42; literary culture, 18; script of, 28

Lawbé griots (musicians), 138, 145, 146, 154 n.5

Leadership, 116, 124, 145, 147–48

Lee, Leo Oufan, 214

Leng Lin, 196, 199

Lévi-Strauss, Claude, 210

Liang Sicheng, 202

Liberalism, 5, 7, 82, 161, 176

Literature: literary communication, 19, 29–32, 48 n.6; literary culture, development of, 17–18, 24, 29–39, 49 n.15, 51 nn.34, 38, 39, 41; literary culure and political power (Gramsci), 42–43; religious movements and, 35

Machinery, 90–91, 102, 108 n.7

Maharashtra, 56, 73–74

Mao Zedong, 216, 217, 221

Maps, 162–63

Markets, 70–72, 77, 122–27, 136 n.56

Marx, Karl: on abstract labor, 83–88, 91; on Aristotle, 84, 85, 89; on bourgeois society, 99–100, 108 n.12; on factory worker discipline, 88–93, 101–2, 104–5, 107 n.5, 108 n.8; on history of capital, 82–84, 97–101, 108 nn.11, 12; on liberalism, 161; on postcolonialism, 82; on productive labor, 103–4; on use value, 103, 108 n.14

Mbacké, Abdou Lahat, 121, 128, 129

Mbacké, Amadou Bamba, 112, 115, 117–20, 125, 129, 130–31, 145

McCarthy, Thomas, 168, 170, 173

Media, 145, 198–200, 207 n.4, 208 n.5

Memory: erotica and, 146; glass painting and, 120, 125, 135 n.29; Murid brotherhood and, 118–20, 128–30, 136 nn.51, 60; prayer and, 134 n.25

Mexico, 180–81

Mignolo, Walter, 168, 169, 179

Migration and mobility: citizenship and, 54–55; *Dialogue* (Zhang Dali's urban art project) and, 198–99; multiculturalism, 2, 6, 168, 173–74, 180, 184 n.3; of Murid brotherhood, 121–28, 131–32, 135 n.32; urban relocation, 202–3; vernacular transformation, 34, 51 n.34

Mobile phones, 223–24

Modernity: in Africa, 114, 134 n.13, 138–40; Christianity and, 157, 158–59; cosmo-polis and, 167–69, 172; cosmopolitanism (critical cosmopolitanism), 159–62; Eurocentrism and, 170; globalization and, 157–58, 162–63; Murid intellectuals, 128, 130–31, 137 n.62; *orbis universalis christianus,* 162–64, 167, 168; rural areas and, 216; tradition and, 114, 119, 134 n.13. *See also* Vernacularization

Money, 84–87, 98–101

Mosques, 118, 127, 128, 134 n.25

Multiculturalism, 2, 168, 173–74, 180, 184 n.3

Mumbai. *See* Bombay

Murid brotherhood: Amadou Bamba's writings, 120, 129, 130, 136 n.60; assimilation and, 114–17, 119, 120, 124, 125–27, 136 n.60; baye fall, 118, 134 n.23; cemeteries, 118, 127, 134 n.25, 136 n.51; clothing, 114, 125–26; commerce and, 113, 119–20, 122–27, 133 nn.8, 9; cosmopolitanism of, 119–23, 131–32; diaspora community, 123–25, 128, 131–32; discipline in, 116–19, 120, 124, 125, 145; glass painting, 120, 125, 135 n.29; intellectuals (Hizbut Tarkya), 128, 130–31, 137 n.62; literacy, 116–17, 129; markets of, 122–27, 136 n.56; modumodu, 125, 126, 127, 128–29, 136 n.50; Murid schools (dahras), 116, 134 n.17; peanut cultivation, 113–17, 119; Touba as spiritual focus, 117–19, 122–25, 128, 134 n.25, 136 n.51; Wolofs, 112–13, 116, 119

Museums, 60, 204, 222–23

Nagaraj, D. R., 46, 53 n.54

Nairn, Tom, 45, 52 n.53

Nation-states: authority of, 163, 167–68; citizenship in, 163–64, 167; dependency theory (Latin America), 176–77; interdependency of, 176, 179; national character in, 170–73; religion-states, 165–67; Senegal as, 114, 121, 135 n.31, 145; sovereignty of, 176; Trilateral Commission (1973), 176, 184 n.4; United Nations Declaration of Human Rights, 175–76, 180, 184 n.5

New Hong Kong Cinema, 217–18, 219

Nicolet, Claude, 24, 49 n.16

Orbis universalis christianus, 162–64, 167, 168

Peanut cultivation, 113–17, 119
Personhood, 171–72, 184 n.3
Phase 2 (M. L. Morrow), 206
Photography: demolition and reconstruction in Zhang Dali's art, 200–203; as dialogue, 196, 204; *Dialogue* (Zhang Dali's urban art project), 189–94, 207; the nude in, 138–40, 153; of Ousmane Ndiaye Dago, 139–40, 151–54; of Zhang Dali, 196–204, 207
Politics: elites and vernacularization, 33–34; Hindutva (Hindu fundamentalism), 40–41, 51 n.43, 52 n.44, 56, 72–78; languages and, 36–39; Latin culture, 25–26, 28–29; literary culture and political power (Gramsci), 42–43; Sanskrit culture and, 27–32, 50 nn.24, 26
Poverty, 64–65, 70, 75–78, 179

Race, 7, 115–16, 119, 173, 178–80
Racketeering, 58–59, 67–68
Rashtriya Swayamsevak Sangh (RSS), 41, 51 n.43
Rawls, John, 182, 184 n.3
Real estate speculation, 63, 67–68, 75, 220
Religion-states, 165–67
Riots: anti-Muslim violence in Bombay, 76–79, 80 n.1; Babri Masjid destruction, 56–57, 73–74; Tiananmen Square, 192, 194, 204
Ross, Eric, 128, 134 n.25, 136 nn.51, 56

Sandaga market, 122–23, 124, 127
Sangh Parivar (Family of Organizations), 41, 56
Sanskrit: culture, 27–32, 50 nn.24, 26; dissemination of, 23–32, 50 n.24; politics and, 27–29, 30–32; Rashtriya Swayamsevak Sangh (RSS), 41, 51 n.43; script of, 28, 50 n.27; vernacularization of, 28–31

Secularism, 46, 73–74, 145, 163–64
Senegal: Christianity in, 140–41; eroticism in, 138, 146–48, 149–54, 154 nn.3, 4, 5; four communes in, 113–15, 120, 133 n.11; *hijab,* 149–50, 155 n.7; as nation-state, 114, 121, 135 n.31, 145; peanut cultivation in, 113–17, 119; Sufism in, 145, 149. *See also* Murid brotherhood
Sexuality, 138, 139, 144, 151, 154 nn.4, 5
Shaiva (Virshaiva), 35
Shanghai: architecture, 214; as city of culture, 221–22; climate of indifference in, 215–16; colonialism and, 213–14; development of, 219–20; nationalism in, 216–17; preservation of, 220–24; relations with China, 215–16, 218
Shiva Sena, 56–57, 73, 75–76, 79, 80 n.1
Slavery, 119, 162, 164–65, 168
Smith, Adam, 103, 108 n.15
Spaces: arbitrage and transnational spaces, 224–27; Baol (Murid homeland) as sacred space, 121, 128; cemeteries, 118, 127, 134 n.25, 136 n.51; eroticism in public space, 140, 146, 149; ettiquette and social space, 223–24, 226; graffiti as dialogue in urban space, 189–96, 201, 204–7; *hijab* wearing in public, 149–50, 155 n.7; Hindutva (Hindu fundamentalism) and public space, 72–78; homelessness in Bombay, 63–66, 70, 75–76, 78; local space versus global network, 223; mosques, 118, 127, 128, 134 n.25; Murid communities in cities, 120–24; Murid markets, 122–27, 136 n.56; museums, 60, 204, 222–23; negotiated space in Shanghai, 214–15; public space as sacred space, 72–74, 80 n.1; regional vernacularization, 33–34, 38–40, 51 n.34; rural areas and modernity, 216; of Sanskrit culture, 24, 27–32, 50

Spaces (*continued*)
nn.24, 26; Touba as holy city, 117–19, 122–25, 128, 136 nn.51, 56
Spain, 32, 50 n.31, 164–65, 166, 168
Spivak, Gayatri (strategic essentialism), 82, 90, 108 nn.6, 14
Stoicism, 25–26, 50 n.21
Street vendors, 70–72, 77
Sufism, 129, 145, 149

Taylor, Charles, 95, 160, 169, 170, 184 n.3
Technology, 90–91, 96, 102, 108 n.7, 179
Third World, 175
Thompson, E. P., 90, 104–5
Touba sanctuary, 117–19, 122–25, 128, 136 nn.51, 56
Toulmin, Stephen, 168
Tradition: assimilation and, 114, 116–17, 119, 120, 124, 125–27; modernity and, 114, 119, 131–32, 134 n.13; Touba sanctuary as spiritual focus, 117–19, 122–25, 128, 134 n.25, 136 n.51
Transnational corporations, 176, 224
Transportation, public, 55, 63
Trilateral Commission (1973), 176, 184 n.4
Trouillot, Michel-Rolph, 164

United Nations Declaration of Human Rights, 175–76, 180, 184 n.5
Universalism: and Christianity, 162–64, 167, 168; cultural universalism of Borges, 210; diversity and diversality, 7–8, 82, 181–84; feminism and, 7–9; Hindutva (Hindu fundamentalism) and, 40–41, 56; in Islam, 115–16, 136 n.60; vernacular nationalism and, 42–45

Vernacularization: in Asia, 16, 31, 35–37; cosmopolitanism and, 20–22, 39–40, 43–47, 53 n.55; in Europe, 16; in India, 40–41; Latin and, 23–25, 28–29, 33–34, 42; literary culture, development of, 17–24, 28–39, 49 n.15, 51 nn.34, 38, 39, 41; multiculturalism and, 2, 168, 173–74, 180, 184 n.3; nationalism and, 44–45; regional vernacularization, 33–34, 38–39, 51 n.34; Sanskrit and, 28–31
Violence: Muslims in Bombay and, 57, 74, 76–78, 80 n.1; riots, 56–57, 72, 74–75, 76, 192, 194, 204; war, 158, 163, 168–69, 175, 178–79
Virilio, Paul, 225–26
Vishwa Hindu Parishad (VHP), 41
Vitoria, Francisco de: on Amerindians, 165, 174, 184 n.3; on cosmopolitanism, 157, 158; on globalization, 157, 158–59; modernity and coloniality, 176; multiculturalism, 168, 173; on natural rights, 165–66, 184 n.1; religious and racial conviviality, 178, 182; states and human rights, 175

Wallerstein, Immanuel, 178
Wittgenstein, Ludwig, 212
Wollstonecraft, Mary, 180
Wolofs, 113, 116, 119
Women: African versus European concepts of beauty, 142–44, 148, 150, 152–54; dance, 146, 147, 155 n.6; *diskette*, 147, 148; *drianké*, 147, 153; erotic clothing and adornment, 139, 142–44, 145–47, 149, 150; feminism, 7–9; *hijab*, 149–50, 155 n.7; partnerships between (*goor-djigen*), 144, 151; perfumes, 146, 152; sexual education in Senegal, 154; *thiuraye*, 147, 152, 154
Workers: discipline of, 88–93, 101–2, 104–5, 107 n.5, 108 n.8; labor and, 89–91; machinery and, 90–91, 102, 108 n.7; motivation of, 105, 108 n.17; worker-capitalist relations, 90–91, 95, 108 n.9

Xu Kuangdi, 218

Yacouba (painter), 139
Yamamoto, Yohji, 226

Zapatistas, 180–81
Zhang Dali: critical responses to his
    grafitti, 198–200, 207 n.4, 208 n.5;
    demolition and reconstruction in his

art, 200–203; *Dialogue* (Zhang Dali's
    urban art project), 189–96, 204–
    7; expatriotism of, 189–90, 192–94;
    graffiti as dialogue in urban space,
    189–96, 201, 204–7; photography,
    196–204, 207
Žižek, Slavoj, 181

Library of Congress Cataloging-in-Publication Data

Cosmopolitanism / edited by Carol A. Breckenridge ... [et al.].

p. cm. — (Millenial quartet book)

"Public culture books."

Originally presented as vol. 12, no. 3 of *Public Culture*.

Includes index.

ISBN 0-8223-2884-4 (cloth : alk. paper)

ISBN 0-8223-2899-2 (pbk. : alk. paper)

1. Internationalism.   I. Breckenridge, Carol Appadurai

II. Public culture (Durham, N.C.)   III. Millennial quartet.

JZ1308 .C67 2002   303.48′2 — dc21   2001056859